REAL POWER

STAGES OF PERSONAL POWER IN ORGANIZATIONS

Third Edition

JANET O. HAGBERG

Sheffield Publishing Company

Salem, Wisconsin 53168

For information about this book, write or call:
Sheffield Publishing Company
P.O. Box 359
Salem, Wisconsin 53168
(262) 843-2281
Fax: (262) 843-3683
E-mail: info@spcbooks.com

ISBN 1-879215-46-2

Printed in the United States of America

7 6 5 4 3 2 1

I dedicate this book to all those involved with the Silent Witness National Initiative and to the women I have worked with at the Shakopee Correctional Facility. I have learned life-transforming lessons about real power from these two groups and I am grateful.

Where love rules, there is no will to power;
and where power predominates,
there love is lacking.
Carl Jung

Other books by Janet O. Hagberg:

The Inventurers: Excursions in Life and Career Renewal, with Richard Leider, New York, NY, Perseus Publishing, Revised Edition, 1986.

The Critical Journey: Stages in the Life of Faith, with Rev. Dr. Robert A. Guelich, Salem, WI, Sheffield Publishing Company, 1989.

The Silent Witness Story: Speaking Out against Domestic Violence, with Carrie Bardwell, St. Paul, MN, Minnesota Women's Consortium, 1993.

Wrestling with Your Angels: A Spiritual Journey to Great Writing, Holbrook, MA, Adams Publishing Company, 1995.

Results 2000: Silent Witness National Initiative Report on Domestic Homicide Reduction in the United States, 1976-1997, Minneapolis, MN, Silent Witness National Initiative, 2000.

Contents

Preface to the Third Edition

I am grateful to embark on the third edition of a book that captured much of my soul in the first writing. As I approached this edition I felt a monumental task ahead of me because I have learned so much from my readers, from observing people at various stages of power, and from my own research and life experience. The result is a deepening of the descriptions of each stage, especially Stages Four, Five and Six; a new way to think about the dark side of each stage; new stories of each stage derived from my readers; a connection to the spirituality expressed at each stage; a description of the "wall" between Stages Four and Five; more of my personal story as well as others' stories throughout the book; and a link to a web site for further information on research regarding the stages as well as access to the tools we have developed for a more in-depth understanding of the power model.

I believe that events of the last several years; nuclear threats, the development of countries in the Pacific Rim, terrorism, and astounding technological advances, in cloning for example, make our country and our world more receptive than ever before to the ideas in *Real Power*, especially soul leadership. The stakes for leaders are higher now and a deeper inner life is a necessity, not just a nice addition. We have all changed. This is a time of transformation in our world. The doors of our collective psyche do not open this wide very often. My hope is that we will take time to invest in soul transforming experiences so we can allow clarity and courage to move us more fully into our calling as individuals, as a country, and as a world. One example of moving into a transforming experience is to look at fear as an opportunity for change and growth and therefore not avoid things that frighten us.

Profound changes have occurred in my life since the last edition of this book. As I journeyed through my own transformation, I learned even more about inner power. I have experienced the Wall, my own core, that paradoxical place, that dark, painful place of intense light, where compassion and courage reveal themselves. Reflecting on these experiences has given me the courage to take more risks with this book and to reveal more of myself than I did in previous versions. I am willing to be more vulnerable, to let go and to entrust my life to the Holy, a part of the power journey that I elaborate on in this book. As a result, I find my life more of an adventure, less predictable, more full of humor, and more satisfying. I have found my passion, my deepest heart's desire, and I will challenge you to take the risk to find your heart's deepest desire as well.

Our deepest heart's desires are usually not difficult to state but they are sometimes difficult to acknowledge and form our lives around—mostly because of pressures within and around us. For example, a mother's deepest desire may be to create beauty in the form of a large garden, yet the culture suggests that this activity could never be as important as attending to her children. For a middle-aged man, focusing a law career on the practice of mediation and healing work with divorcing couples—which his soul longs to do—is not deemed profitable enough for a lawyer with a family to support. The challenge is to move towards our heart's desire one step at a time and deal with the issues that unfold, since this may be the journey that will heal and transform us. When we move forward, even one step towards our deepest heart's desire, the universe takes notice.

My soul is in this book. I hope it reaches out and touches your soul as you read it. I hope you are ready to experience your own inner power and the journey that will transform your life. Tilden Edwards frequently quotes one of the great spiritual mystics who once said that in the deeper spiritual life, our lives are consumed by the fire of the Holy Spirit, just as fire consumes a log, transforming us into the fire itself. He adds, "How close are you willing to come to the fire?" Ask yourself that question as you read this book. Is this a time to move closer to the "fire" and to allow yourself to be transformed by it?

Now as you begin this journey, sit quietly, close your eyes, go to a safe place within, and ask to be changed as a result of reading this book. Ask that you will be moved beyond your present stage of power once you've begun this journey. I can guarantee that it will not be an easy journey but it will change you forever and make your life into one grand adventure.

Janet O. Hagberg, April 2002

Preface to the First Edition, 1984

Let me tell you a story. Several years ago I had a friend who, I am quite convinced, was powerful and successful. She was almost totally in control of her life and able to plan systematically for her future. As far as I was concerned, she had it made. She traveled the world over with her clients and friends, always priding herself on doing things first class. She was making money and writing a book, was professionally respected, and could afford to be confident—even a little cocky. Her consulting clients were of the Fortune 500 and her friends were some of the movers and shakers of the community. She also had the knack of turning every experience into a plus for herself and spoke of her future as a series of new challenges to be met. She was a successful woman in a man's world, loving it and relishing her achievements. Her dreams had come true. I admit to being greatly intimidated by her at times because she seemed to be so clear in her direction, so sure of herself, so strong and not easily bemused. Her run of successes seemed to be endless.

Then her dreams turned into nightmares. The bottom dropped out of this carefully designed life. Her husband, the love of her life and her symbol of emotional stability, left her for another life. She was set adrift on a sea of anger, confusion, and self-doubt. She was crushed. Never before had she failed at anything. And this situation seemed to be out of her control. But she also felt a strange sense of exhilaration at times. She wanted to leap out of her emotional cocoon and start a new life. That was on the good days. Most of the time confusion reigned. Illness and death in her family added to the shock; more doubts and questions surfaced; and the confusion left her feeling totally alone in her tumultuous sea. I almost lost her there for a while, as she dove deep inside to sort out her sense of life, hope, and meaning. It was a long, slow process she experienced in starting to redefine herself, in struggling with the questions of what life means, what success is, and what it is all worth.

Gradually, oh so slowly, she started to return from the depths. But she was re-emerging with some different features—ones that were not so sharp at the edges but more rounded and smooth. She was warmer than before, not so cold to the touch. She was deeper and wiser, calmer and sadder, not as devoted to the goals she had previously held so dear but feeling success in a different way. It took us a long time to sort out what was happening to our friendship, too, because the rules and roles seemed to be changing. A part of me mourned the old friend because she was so familiar. But another part of me was curious and a little fearful of the new friend. Our experience was uncharted territory to us both. It was an uncertain time.

Eventually, I stopped thinking of this "friend" as someone outside of me, separate and distinct. I began to understand the deep changing and reshaping that was occurring in us both. Gradually, I came to admit that both of us were actually me. This acceptance was perhaps the most painful and healing step in my life's journey. I came to know this person as complex yet terribly simple, wise and at the same time childlike, strong at the center and wobbly at the edges, always curious, sometimes afraid, eager to experience life yet overly sensitive to it, wanting peace and needing love. This turning point in my life led me on a long, meandering path to a deeper understanding of personal power. This is the impetus and the story behind this book.

Now, why would you want to read this book? Well, I wrote it for a variety of special groups: for individuals who aspire to power, who long to understand what power really is; for leaders, to provoke their thinking about what true leadership is; for organizations, as a practical tool for developing people and vision for the future. I see power occurring in stages. And in the following chapters I describe seven distinct stages of power. They are arranged in this developmental order: Stage One: Powerlessness; Stage Two: Power by Association; Stage Three: Power by Symbols (renamed Power by Achievement for the third edition); Stage Four: Power by Reflection; The Wall (added to the third edition); Stage Five: Power by Purpose; and Stage Six: Power by Gestalt (renamed Power by Wisdom for the third edition).

In my experience in speaking about the stages of power, I find that the concept appeals to a wide variety of audiences because the idea can be applied to almost any work or life situation. Let's examine some specific motivations that may appeal to you as a reader of *Real Power*.

For Leaders:

As a leader or potential leader, you will see a vision of organizational leadership for the future. As the world becomes more of a global village, we will have to expand our concept of what power and leadership mean and how they are acted out. We will learn to go beyond our own egos.

In organizations many people see power as finite. In their view, power can be represented by a box of individually wrapped gold coins. Let's say I have twelve coins in a box, and they are mine. If you take two from me, I now have only ten, and therefore, you have taken power from me. There is only so much, and in order to pass it around it must be taken from one and given to another.

Now suppose power can be imagined differently: I have a bed containing eight lily bulbs and I give you half of each bulb. Because I believe power multiplies when I give it away, now instead of eight lilies my bed has grown to sixteen.

I am suggesting that true leadership does not begin until the later stages, in which power can be seen as infinite and valuable insofar as it is given away. Michael Maccoby's latest book, *The Leader*, describes some leaders who would accept this concept of power. Chapters Four through Seven (in *Real Power*) address these issues (Chapters Four through Eight in the third edition).

For Managers:

As a manager, you will learn how to effectively manage people at various stages of power who want and need different things from you, from their work, and from the organization. The way you would develop each type of person might be quite different. For instance, persons at the first stage will not be interested in intangibles like being invited to lunch with a client but will be much affected by your willingness to teach them concrete skills and knowledge. The old phrase "different strokes for different folks" applies here. You may also better understand the behavior of some people that was perplexing to you before. Perhaps you will also understand your own behavior and why you are more effective at managing some people than others. Chapters One through Six and Eight address these issues (Chapters One through Seven and Nine in the third edition).

For Women and Men:

As a woman or a man, you can learn about ways in which women and men are alike and ways in which they're different. One of the stages seems to be more feminine and another is more masculine, yet both sexes can move through all the stages. Some men avoid the feminine stages because they frighten these men by reminding them of the feminine side of themselves. Some women grasp onto the masculine stages because such women seek to downplay their feminine side in a masculine world. What will convince us that our differences are not so bad and that one style or the other is not better just because it's feminine or masculine? How do women keep from becoming "honorary men," as Carolyn Heilbrun so aptly puts it in her book *Reinventing Womanhood*? When men feel discontented, how do they move beyond the stereotypical roles and view of success that they learned in their youth? How do women fulfill leadership roles while maintaining a healthy balance of feminine and masculine qualities? How do we all learn about the masculine and the feminine within us? Chapters One through Six and Nine through Eleven address these issues (Chapters One through Seven and Ten through Twelve in the third edition).

For Thinkers and Problem Solvers:

As a thinker and problem solver, you can use the stage model as a practical tool for understanding organizational and personal situations that may transcend conventional logic or rational explanation. The model is based on twenty-five years of organization field research, including observation, discussions, interviews, and the meeting of hundreds of minds. After discussing the model for a time, a woman manager exclaimed, "At last I can put into words what's been happening to me for the past eight years!" Chapters One through Eight address these issues (Chapters One through Nine in the third edition).

For Powerless People:

If you are powerless, you can use the model to think of ways to move into power and avoid being overcome by the victim mentality especially prevalent in organizations. There are no easy solutions to the problems of powerlessness, but there are ways to think and act so as not to be powerless forever. An entire book has been dedicated to that topic—Elizabeth Janeway's *Powers of the Weak*. Chapter One (in *Real Power*) addresses these issues (also Chapter One in the third edition).

For Researchers:

As a researcher or student of power, you will find in the model a wealth of opportunity for further study and research. I welcome others to further refine the model so it can become more understandable and useful. I value comments and suggestions on the model from anyone and look forward to reading the results of the power questionnaire in the back of the book (not included in the third edition but visit my web site for research on *Real Power*).

What would I like this book to achieve? I enjoy trying to make abstract ideas and concepts understandable and practical. I hope I have accomplished that in this book. I hope I have made it clear how strongly I feel that a general reawakening is necessary in our country if we are to survive and maintain our health and vitality in the future. I would like this book to influence leaders to lead with more vision and less ego. I would like women to believe that there is indeed life beyond the masculine stage. I would like men to accept themselves and *be* themselves—not who they think they ought to be. I would like people of color to help us consider what implications the various stages of this model have for those who are not part of the prevailing socio-economic system. I would like powerless people to learn about themselves and the system and to gain some self-worth in the process. I would like organizations to be more tolerant of visionaries and truly wise people. I would like people to talk more openly to each other about the taboo topic of power and see that it may not be what they think it is. I would like people in organizations to see more choices for themselves as the years progress rather than fewer choices every day. I would like to see more and more healthy, innovative managers. I would like people to understand power and beyond. . . .

Henry David Thoreau sums up for me one of the underlying issues of this book when he asks why we should be in such desperate haste to succeed, and in such desperate enterprises? If we do not keep pace with our companions, perhaps it is because we hear a different drummer. Let us step to the music that we hear, however measured or far away (paraphrase, *Walden*).

Janet O. Hagberg, 1984

Acknowledgments

Although my application of stage theory to the specific concept of power is a new application, stage theory itself has been around for a long time. And while this book is the product of many years of thinking, reading, observing, learning, interviewing, and speaking, it is not the product of one mind alone.

I owe a deep debt of gratitude to the theoretical pioneers whose ideas over the years have been planted as ripe seeds in my mind. These theoreticians and teachers greatly influenced me in the final germination of the stage model applied to the concept of personal power. First is Dr. Margery Brown at the University of Minnesota, who imprinted cognitive stage theory a la Harvey, Hunt, and Schroeder on my formative mind. How I struggled in those early years to find my own developmental level and to analyze my behavior, hoping I was more developed than I feared I was! Second, my social work professors and peers taught me much about the range of complex human behavior and the motivations that drive us. Third, Dr. Howard Williams introduced me to the theories of Kohlberg, Loevinger, and Perry as well as Levinson, Gould, and Valliant. These writers opened my mind further to ways of thinking about development and life, some of which evolved into the basis for my stage model. Last, I would like to thank all those individuals whom I observed, questioned, and interviewed. I then quoted, summarized, or consolidated their responses into the case examples in each chapter. The book would be less instructive without these rich illustrations from real people.

I would like to thank several other people for being supportive and lovingly critical as I proceeded through the early drafts of *Real Power*. They listened, read, made suggestions, and encouraged me on the long journey toward publication. I am grateful to William Svrluga and Tom Thibodeau (Viterbo College) who critiqued the book and also coauthored the chapter on men, and Barry and Bradley, my stepsons, who lovingly questioned what I was up to with this "power stuff." I am grateful to other dedicated early draft readers such as Bob Bro, Knox Coit, Karen Desnick, Bob MacLennan, Ken Melrose, Miriam Meyers, Martha Myers, Susan Sands, Suzanne Sisson, and Norm Stanton. Bobbie Spradley and Norm Ferguson taught the material and gave me valuable feedback, Ella Ramsey renamed Stage Three, and Cathrien Pouw enlarged my understanding of Stage Three with her master's thesis in the Netherlands. Later reviewers were Delorese Ambrose, Bob Andringa, Kay Barber, Sue Boehlke, Con Brooks, John Cardozo, Bruce Froelke, Bill George, Marty Hanson, Hugh Harrison, Rob Harvey, Richard Jones, Duane Kullberg, Kathy Laughlin, Lisa Meyers, Paul Morrison, Elsa Nad, Betty Olson, Jeff Pope, Al Quie, Steve Rothschild, George Shapiro, and Sharon Wulf. My editors, Pat Lassonde, Kate Habib, Jodi Jacobsen, and Cindy Nelson have done a superb job of guiding the process and giving me invaluable feedback. A special thank you to Steve Nelson at Sheffield Publishing Company for a fine third edition.

Many people have inspired me on the later editions of *Real Power*: faculty members who use the material in their teaching; corporate consultants who use it in their consulting and training; and students who write papers and theses on the stages of power. Colleagues in Finland, India, Germany, and the Netherlands have validated my work and encouraged me to keep going. I'd like to thank my colleagues at the Institute for Educational Management in Arnhem, Netherlands, for their support and feedback on the new editions. I am grateful to Bobbie Spradley and Norm Ferguson for taking the time to be readers for the third edition. It is a more refined edition because of them. A special network has emerged, of people who have been particularly moved by the book and have chosen to teach it or use it in their work. I am grateful to these early network members who helped give me the vision of what Real Power still means and of how it can evolve in the future. Robin Getman is chief amongst these network members as their mentor and my dear colleague. This edition would not have emerged if not for her. The other initial network members are Delorese Ambrose, Kristin Anderson, Mary Ann Brooks, Fay Chobin, LaRee Ewers, Karen Knutson, Ann Maxwell, Sharon Stockhousen, Marla Tipping, and Rita Webster. But most of all I value individual stories; stories that describe how these ideas come to life in people's every day existence, how they validate people's experience, give them new insights and the will to grow. I am grateful to those of you who allowed me to include your stories in this edition. These stories keep me motivated to write more, to do more research, to go further into my own depths, and to speak from my own truth.

My invitation to you all as readers is to collaborate with me on the next edition of this book. Send me your stories, tell me your tales; share your ideas, disagreements, and questions. Let's learn together for a more intriguing next edition.

More (personal) power to you!

Janet O. Hagberg

Introduction

What Is This Book About?

This book is about power, real power, the kind of inner power you develop after you think you have everything figured out. And it is about true leadership, transformational leadership that allows you to go beyond ego and gender to lead from your soul.

Why did I write this book—yet another book on power and leadership? I believe our culture still misunderstands both concepts. Most books on power are written by people in positions of power or to describe people in positions of power. As Stephen Covey has so aptly pointed out, the trend since World War II is to perceive the personality traits of leaders as the key to leadership instead of looking first at the character ethic we want from our leaders and then finding leaders who exemplify it.

The model of power and leadership I propose here describes six stages of personal power which we layer one upon another as we develop. They are: (1) Powerlessness, (2) Power by Association, (3) Power by Achievement, (4) Power by Reflection, then the Wall, (5) Power by Purpose, and (6) Power by Wisdom.

People with position power are predominantly at Stage Three, Power by Achievement. This is the most externally oriented of the stages, the stage where most of our power comes from outside ourselves, from making things happen, and from external recognition. It is the most rewarded stage in our culture, requiring hard work, competence, strong knowledge of the culture, a mature ego, and political astuteness. Twenty years of research validates over and over that Stage Three is still the most common stage in organizations.

But Stage Three is only part of the way to full personal power, part of the way to wholeness. One compelling reason for writing this book is to suggest an organizational agenda for this new century, one that allows leaders to develop as whole people, as true leaders operating at the inner power stages (power by reflection, purpose, and wisdom) and to move creatively into the future.

Why is it necessary for true leaders to operate at the inner power stages? Rob Harvey, a retired corporate officer from Herman Miller, Inc., says it well.

> Leadership always comes back to the issue of character, of deep foundational values. In the current reformation this country is experiencing, and the instability we are feeling, you cannot lead by forcing compliance. It simply doesn't work. The rate of change is too high to be managed from the top down. In order to lead, one must engage followers. You will not find followers without caring, connecting and creating. Would you follow someone who did not care about you, connect with you, or did not wish to create a new reality? Mere compliance today is a recipe for disaster. As leaders, or would-be leaders, we must be vulnerable. None of us has arrived. We must recognize our own voyage. We can only lead effectively by enabling others to maximize their contribution. We are all on the journey together, accomplishing things that none of us could accomplish alone.

In the next evolution of American business, it will be necessary to go beyond the ideas that made us great world leaders initially—ideas like rugged individualism, and "the quick technological fix." The whole world is turning to new ways of operating in order to bring global stability as well as to compete in the global economy.

A corporate officer at General Mills said, "New competition is virtually rewriting overnight the rules of how entire markets function. We are facing a revolutionary shift in consumer attitudes and employee expectations."

To contend with these changes, companies are trying a variety of new and exciting programs. They are spending more time and money on developing their people, and they are encouraging more involvement, workplace freedom, and trusting environments.

All of these innovations, although thoughtful, will not work if we continue to operate with a predominantly Stage Three (Power by Achievement) mentality behind them. The innovations require people who are more internally developed and do not revert to authoritarian styles when things get tough. Stages Four and Five represent people who have integrity, can give power away, and are reflective, courageous, collaborative, and spiritual. It is not necessary to leave Stage Three qualities behind, but we need to add these other qualities in order to move to the next era of leadership in the world.

For people in the nonprofit environment, the world is a different place than it was fifteen years ago. With the division of our culture increasingly into haves and have-nots, it will take even more grounded and creative people in social service and religious organizations to work on the problems threatening the soul of the United States today. Violence, abuse, crime, poverty, hunger, addiction, and homelessness—the list goes on and on. They are symptoms of cultural neglect that are apparent in every large city in our country.

People who work on these immense challenges need to be secure themselves and spiritually grounded so they are not burned out, but transformed by contact with their clients, the people who face poverty, abuse, or homelessness. It is critical that they are a hopeful presence in the world and operate with peace under stress. They cannot do that if they cannot operate beyond Stage Three.

These are challenging times. Are you up to the challenge? Let me tell you the story of one person who learned to lead from his soul.

John was a chief executive officer of a medium sized corporation. In his mid-forties, he was excited about the future and the direction in which he was taking the company. He was a hard charger, working long hours and loving his work. His management team was equally high achieving, bringing him the results he needed most of the time even though his new task team approach with the plant managers was floundering. He even had a woman and an African-American man on his team. Life was good. Stock prices were climbing.

Then his life took an abrupt turn. His sixteen-year-old daughter stopped eating. Nothing he or his wife did would make her eat more than half a roll for breakfast and a diet soda and a few leaves of spinach salad for dinner. He tried sweet talk, rewards, and gentle prodding. Eventually he started screaming and ordering her to eat. She got thinner every week. Her hollow cheeks began to look like a corpse's.

At that point John got scared. He felt worn thin at work. He resented his family life for infringing on his heavy work schedule. He was used to having everything go his way, even if he had to resort to ordering someone else around. But his daughter was immovable. Here he had no control.

She ended up in the emergency room of a hospital after she collapsed at school one day. The doctors told John that unless she was force-fed, which would require a court order, she would die. John thought he was going to die too.

During those long months of her agonizingly slow recovery, John found out that her problem was also his problem. He was a controlling person who always got his own way. Even more devastating was the fact that his own self-image was inextricably tied to the health and success of his business and his children. John had a lot of his own work to do. And he did it. He dug into his own family issues and found a driven, rageful father image that he had suppressed for a long time. He dug into his own pain, childhood shame, over-achievement, and fear of abandonment. He struggled courageously with his inner monsters and found out a great deal about his masked inadequacies and dependencies. He also found out he was addicted to work, as many executives are.

What did all this have to do with business? Plenty. John realized, despite all his rhetoric to the contrary, that he was a top-down leader at work, just as he was at home. He felt compelled to single-handedly set the company's vision and then make sure everyone else agreed and carried it out. Sure, he involved people, but in the end his ego was always on the line.

The experience with his daughter taught him to let go of control, and now he didn't need it as much. He knew himself better and could trust himself more. Therefore he could be more vulnerable, ask for suggestions, and use them without damaging his own ego. And he could admit mistakes. His people began trusting him more. They began bringing him ideas. He was surprised. They had never spontaneously brought him ideas before. But now he didn't need to be the idea-approver. He could tell them to go back and get people around them interested enough in the idea to make it happen. If it met all the criteria the team had set up for itself, then it was a good idea.

New products and improvements in service began emerging from the very teams that had been floundering before. It wasn't all smooth sailing, but now he handled conflict by listening to people and helping them work things out among themselves rather than setting himself up as the final judge. He had learned at home that control doesn't empower anyone.

The company began operating more like a community than like several communities competing with each other. It did surprisingly well, even in turbulent times. Once, in a particularly bad recession, when the company stock fell, John almost panicked. But he decided not to take the recession personally. Instead he looked at all the factors and counted on his community to come up with suggestions. They came up with a part-time policy instead of a lay-off policy. It worked wonders in the crisis and is now an option for everyone. People were so excited about the part-time option that they even called the office on their days off to make sure everything was working all right.

John did not single-handedly change the workplace. He changed himself. That had more power than anything else he could have done. He moved from ego leadership to soul leadership. He and his people flourished.

What Is Power?

Power is probably not what you think it is. In fact, it may not even be what others think it is. Power is elusive and confusing. Perhaps that's why it is so powerful. Consider these ideas and descriptions of power from various literary sources:

> To know the pains of power, we must go to those who have it: to know its pleasures, we must go to those who are seeking it: the pains of power are real, its pleasures imaginary.
>
> (C. C. Colton: *Lacon*)

> Power tends to corrupt and absolute power corrupts absolutely.
>
> (Lord Acton in a letter to Bishop Mandell, Creighton, 1887)

> Self-reverence, self-knowledge, self-control; these three alone lead life to sovereign power.
>
> (Tennyson: "Oenone")

> He who makes another powerful ruins himself, for he makes the other so either by shrewdness or force, and both of these qualities are feared by the one who becomes powerful.
>
> (Machiavelli: *The Prince III*)

> I am more and more convinced that man is a dangerous creature; and that power, whether vested in many or a few, is ever grasping, and like the grave, cries "Give, give!"
>
> (Abigail Adams in a letter to John Adams, Nov. 27, 1775)

> Then everything includes itself in power,
> Power into will, will into appetite;
> And appetite, an universal wolf,
> So doubly seconded with will and power,
> Must make perforce an universal prey,
> And last eat up himself.
>
> (Shakespeare: *Troilus and Cressida I,* iii)

> All is gift.
>
> (Teresa of Avila)

This last quote does not refer directly to the word power, but seen from the perspective of the later stages of power, it does describe a form of power.

Is power good, bad, corrupting, polluting, dangerous, controlling, or freeing? Because all of these descriptions are true to some extent, the concept of power becomes all the more complex. Which of these statements are we to believe, and how will we ever be able to understand power?

Real Power is an attempt to set forth a simple model of power as an ever-evolving concept. In this model, power takes on different appearances at each of its six separate stages. Think of the stages as different dances. Each stage's dance has different steps from the basic to the more difficult. After you learn the basic dance, it becomes easier, and you begin to offer your own renditions. Sometimes you are content to do the same dance for a long time, getting better or just having a good time. At other times you feel like learning a new dance, and you start again on the basics of the next step. It's easier though than the first dance you learned because you understand the idea of dancing. So it is with power stages. Some people dance at the same stage forever, while others like to move on to other stages. A few are driven to learn as much and as fast as they can, while others take their learning in time.

I maintain that we all can develop personal power, and that people who aspire to be leaders need to be more concerned with internal or inner power than they are with external or outer power. For other people the need to develop more external power, due to their life circumstances, is a necessary goal. Some people seem, for various reasons, to be born with a head start. At any rate, the way in which we perceive our own and others' power affects our behavior, our leadership, and our relationships with others. Power is absent, obviously, if there are no relationships with others; therefore, it is impossible to be powerful in a vacuum. As in the dance example, we are learning the steps with others, and we are able to learn more and more complex steps as we go along.

The idea of power appearing differently in separate stages may be a new concept for many people who have come to think of power in one or two limited definitions such as control, influence, or the capacity to act.

In fact, most organizations, whether they are corporations, non-profits, or political parties, suffer from power myopia, the problem of seeing power in too narrow a vision. People are not all motivated by the same type of power, and not all power is of the Machiavellian type in which the end justifies the means. Many of the books currently available about power are designed to help us get more by being smarter, using new technologies, or by learning the games and maneuvering in our jobs to assure winning or at least to avoid losing. These theorists assume that most people in organizations seek position and status for themselves while having ever more control over a greater number of people, money, and sources of information. Although I do not discount this approach, I am suggesting that there is more, much more, beyond the traditional forms of power. The new generations of workers will teach us about these new ways of thinking if we don't already know about them. *Real Power* is about people becoming more than externally "powerful"; it is about people becoming *personally powerful.*

> **Personal power results from combining external power (the capacity for action) with internal power (the capacity for reflection).**

Personal power can be seen on a continuum, from very little personal power at one end to a great deal of personal power at the other end. Personal power at the highest stage *includes* the power derived from external sources represented by organizational and political positions, expertise, titles, degrees, control, material goods, responsibility, and authority *but combined* with the power that can be derived only from within. Inner power develops from introspection, personal struggles, the gradual evolution of the life purpose, a spiritual connection with a source beyond yourself, and from accepting and valuing yourself. If you have external power but not internal power, you have very little personal power. Therefore, some people in the highest positions in organizations are not very personally powerful. And likewise, the most personally powerful people may not have the most prestigious titles or roles in the organization. Organizational power—the "how-to-get-ahead" type of power—is represented in my model predominantly by the first three (externally-oriented) stages of power; inner, reflective power is represented by the last three (internally-oriented) power stages. At any of the stages you can be satisfied, and at any of the stages you can feel stuck.

A Model of Personal Power

Before I go further in applying power concepts to life and work situations, I want to explain more thoroughly the stages of power. This model of personal power includes six distinct stages, occurring in this order:

Stage One: Powerlessness
Stage Two: Power by Association
Stage Three: Power by Achievement
Stage Four: Power by Reflection
The Wall (a stopping point between Stages Four and Five)
Stage Five: Power by Purpose
Stage Six: Power by Wisdom

Each stage represents a different manifestation of power. In other words, power can be described differently at each stage. In addition, each stage has a symbol that describes the key idea at that stage. Since all the stages relate to the central theme of personal power, they've been graphically represented on the following page. Read over the stages and the symbols until you become acquainted with them.

This model is simple and complex at the same time. It reminds me of the oriental concept of *shibui*. Oriental art—particularly painting and pottery—looks simple from a distance, but the closer you get to it the more detail and complexity you see. Usually, if you look closely, more is revealed, and you are drawn even more deeply into the art. Much of the detail recedes when you back away and allow distance to create once again the more simple idea. The power model is similar. You can use or understand the model on several different levels. The stages themselves appear to be quite straightforward and simple, yet the more deeply you look, the more the model may speak to you. In fact, you can use the simple six-stage model to understand yourself, your relationships, your organization, your country, or the world from a personal power perspective.

Let me say a word to those who do not like to be categorized. I don't like to be categorized either. So try to have patience with me as you read along, and be forgiving of the possible oversimplification the model represents. Life is more complicated than this model makes it appear. Yet the beauty of the model is in its simplicity. It is easy to understand. And therein lies the paradox. Complex yet simple; shibui.

It will be useful if we start with some assumptions, those underlying ideas from which the model evolved. These underlying assumptions answer questions such as: Why do people get stuck? Can I be at more than one stage at a time? Do men and women see these differently? Here is the first assumption upon which the power model is based.

> *The stages of personal power are arranged in a developmental order with Powerlessness as Stage One and Power by Wisdom as Stage Six.*

This is a controversial premise. Does it mean that people at Stage Five, Power by Purpose, are better than people at Stage Two, Power by Association? No, absolutely not. But people at Stage Five are more complex. It is like our life stages; childhood, adolescence, young adulthood, middle adulthood, later adulthood. Adults are not better than children but they are more complex, have to assume more responsibility, and have a broader view of many things in life. This model differs from the age-and-stage models in one major respect. In the power model, two people who are the same age can be at very different stages due not to age but due to factors like self-image, skill, life experience, socio-economic level, and the capacity for reflection.

The power stages are cumulative. As you move to each stage, you retain the capacity to operate at those stages you have already experienced. It is like you add value with each stage you experience. And the more stages you are comfortable with, the more flexible you are. You simply have more from which to choose.

I am clearly suggesting in this model that as one's level of external and internal power increases you become more clear about what you are here for, what your calling is, and why you are alive. I am an advocate for placing a greater emphasis on developing leaders beyond Stage Three. I think that is absolutely necessary in order for our world to develop effectively into a global community and to provide us with extraordinary organizational and cultural vision. Therefore, I am encouraging development to the stages beyond Stage Three. My research shows that most of our American organizational culture is still at Stage Three. However, there has been a slight shift in the last ten years, with the second highest stage now being Stage Four instead of Stage Two. (See research on web site.) At Stages Four, Five, and Six, one can do more for others, see more possibilities, get more of the good accomplished, give away more, and ask more pertinent questions.

Since the first edition of this book I have learned that the stages are experienced as an upward journey on an ever-widening spiral. Each time we experience the sequence of stages, we have a new understanding of each of them at a deeper level. And we may even deliberately move ourselves to a different stage, in either direction (see page xxvi on "home" stage). For instance, the second or third time I experience any life-altering event (job loss, death of a loved one, divorce, illness) I know that I will survive this experience and gain a new perspective on life if I don't get stuck in the powerlessness of the current situation. I may even come to see that wisdom may emerge from the way in which I respond to these experiences.

We keep repeating the sequence of stages throughout our lives but we gain something from each turn on the spiral: we go higher and deeper, enriching our inner life with each turn.

Hagberg's Model of Personal Power

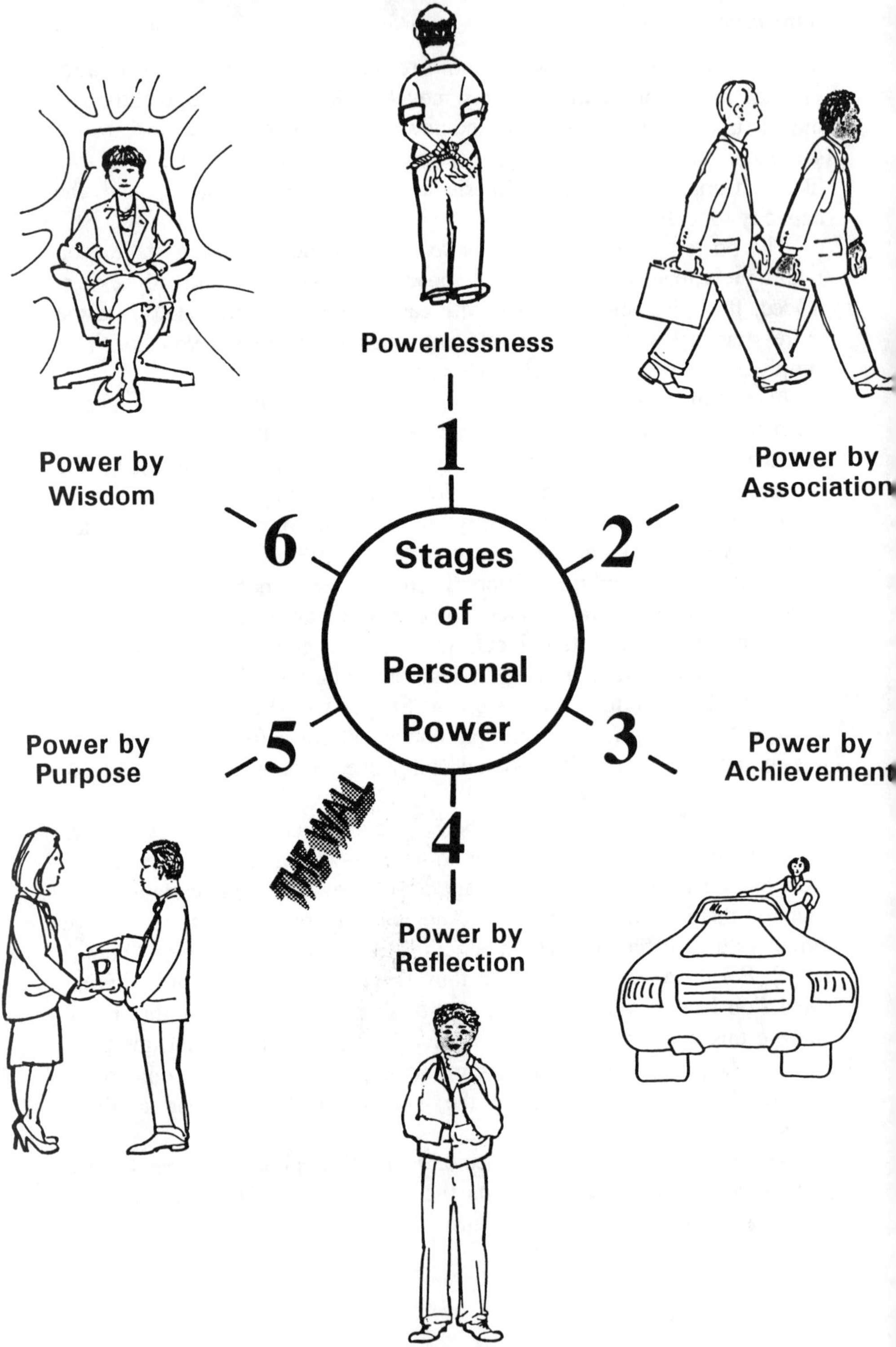

I am not naive enough to think that everyone will value this model or that all are ready to move to more complex power levels. The world is made up of people at varying stages of development, and we need that to provide a balance of interaction and interrelationships. We would not want an organization or a world of all Stage Sixes or Stage Ones. And there are some overwhelming blocks, both internal and external, that may keep people from moving from one stage to another. This matter will be addressed further in later chapters. But I am saying that individuals and organizations at the more complex stages develop greater courage and wisdom and thus have more potential for healing and revitalizing the global community.

Each stage is different from all the others.

Stage One cannot readily be compared to Stage Four because of the behaviors and assumptions that accompany each of them. A powerless person may dream of being in charge but would be intimidated by power if the opportunity arose. You do not jump readily from Stage One to Four. You can understand and experience the stages preceding your own, but it is more difficult to understand the stages beyond your own. For example, Susan is in Stage Three (Power by Achievement), has been in an organization for a while, and has succeeded in achieving titles and responsibility. Suddenly she gets passed over for a promotion and believes her job responsibilities are shrinking. For a period of time she feels as if she has retreated to a former mind-set or circumstance, that of being powerless and confused. She experiences her former feelings and behaviors once again but hopes they are only temporary. Soon she regroups, moves to another position, and feels back in balance within herself. Susan may have trouble understanding why another person deliberately turned down a promotion in favor of family relationships and more personal time. She has trouble understanding how anyone would voluntarily give up what she has worked so hard to accomplish.

People can be in different stages of power in different areas of their lives, at different times, and with different people. However, each of us has a "home" stage that represents us more truly than the others.

After hearing about each stage in more depth, you might respond as a friend did, "But I feel like I'm at several of those stages somewhere in my life almost every day." This is true because we have so many compartments in our lives and we have some of each stage within us. We may influence a decision at one meeting only to feel powerless at the next meeting because of our role with a different set of people. We may go out for lunch and experience yet another stage, let's say as mentor. Then we go home to our family and friends and experience yet another stage—all in one day. We may not act as if we are at the same stage all the time, at home or at work, but we each have a "home" stage, a stage in which we operate most of the time or in which we feel the most comfortable. We identify with it more closely than with others, and we understand its behaviors, whether we like them or not. Sometimes we feel consistently at one stage in our personal life and at another stage at work. Over time this difference can become wearing, especially if the stages are more than two stages apart.

Women and people of color most frequently report the phenomenon of being in Stages Two (Power by Association) and Five (Power by Purpose) simultaneously. Although their home stage might be Stage Two at work, they have experienced tremendous inner growth that causes them to identify with the characteristics of Stage Five away from work. The frustration is that the inner power has yet to be integrated into their work, and until that happens the dichotomy will be difficult to manage. One of the things you may learn from this book is how to translate your most personally powerful self into situations in which you feel less powerful. The more you can integrate the parts of your life into similar stages, the less split you will feel. Moving to another stage is difficult, however, without experiencing some pulling and tension.

We can tell what our home stage is in several ways: by reading each stage description and deciding which one seems most familiar, by observing what situations and behaviors make us uncomfortable, by taking the Personal Power Profile available by mail or phone (see page 305 for ordering information) or by asking other people what they think our home stage is. For example, Ahmad is not sure what stage he's in, but he's new to his accounting profession. Someone in his professional network asks him to speak at a meeting on a specific accounting concept. Ahmad is scared. He immediately envisions the other accountants at the meeting asking him questions he won't be able to answer. He's sure he'll be embarrassed. He thinks he just cannot do it until he's more experienced so he goes to his boss for advice. His boss assures him he can do it and offers to coach him on the speech. If seeking his boss's help is characteristic behavior for Ahmad, he is probably at Stage Two (Power by Association) in his work. Ahmad is being asked to use a Stage Three behavior, speaking before a group on a topic about which he has a certain expertise. But he thinks he's not experienced enough yet. In fact, in his work, Ahmad may already be approaching Stage Three, but personally he has a hard time accepting it. By giving this speech and having a Stage Three experience, and then repeating the experience again, Ahmad may eventually move his home stage of personal power to Stage Three. And Ahmad's willingness to take this initial risk will have contributed to his development.

> *One can move through the stages as "home" stages only in the order in which they are numbered.*

A powerless person cannot move into Power by Purpose (Stage Five) as a "home" stage until he or she has experienced Stages Two, Three, and Four, if only fleetingly. Each stage, in fact, leads by a natural evolution into the next, although some stages are more comfortable for individuals than other stages. Not all people stay in each stage the same length of time or move through them in the same way. We revisit previous stages all the time, for example, when we change jobs, seek new learning experiences, travel to unknown places, enter into new relationships, or uncover our fears. We move to those earlier stages and then, when we are ready to continue from that point in sequence, we move forward once again. Moving to an earlier stage gets more comfortable the more you do it, and it becomes natural.

You could think of power as a six-act play (our power play!) in which the main character (power) appears in all acts wearing different costumes—perhaps representing different parts of itself. So in each act the "power character" is the same person but looks and acts differently and, indeed, does change as the play evolves. You can't see act six and understand it fully unless you have seen acts one through five.

> *Power is described and manifested differently at each stage.*

Which of these words best describe power according to your understanding of it as you begin reading this book? Check your three top choices, one from each column.

____ manipulation	____ structure	____ fear
____ magic	____ learning	____ rules
____ control	____ responsibility	____ competence
____ influence	____ integrity	____ balance
____ vision	____ service	____ calling
____ wisdom	____ peace	____ paradox

I believe that people at each stage of personal power would describe power in a different way because at each stage we view power from a different perspective. Think again of the dance analogy: Each new dance requires different steps, a different beat, different movements, and a new synchronization. You are still dancing, but you call the dance by a certain name at each stage. I use six nouns to illustrate how power presents itself at various stages: manipulation, magic, control, influence, vision, and wisdom. As you read the chapters describing the stages, note the descriptive word appearing under the symbol at the beginning of each chapter. Then think about which word fits most closely with the words you chose just now. The first word at the top of each list is a Stage One word; the second is a Stage Two word and so on down each list.

Each stage of personal power has positive and negative dimensions as well as developmental struggles within it.

Just because someone is at a more complex stage than others does not mean life is easier or better. At the same time, those who have little access to power aren't necessarily in a dismal life situation, nor are they bad people. Each stage has different struggles and different rewards. And each stage has a shadow or dark side that can cause people to get stuck at that stage. I will describe each stage's shadow in the later chapters.

Let's look at the struggles within stages. Students, for example, are usually the least powerful people in the school (except when they unite), and most students are in school to gain more access to information or knowledge or skills that may, over time, increase their power. They are temporarily powerless, but not necessarily dissatisfied. People at other stages may be struggling to find the purpose in their lives, the meaning of their work. This search is not the same as struggling for one's equality or for recognition, but it is, nevertheless, a deep-seated struggle. Women, people of color, and certainly the poor, on the other hand, may feel more of the chronic powerlessness that can, over time, be demoralizing unless they take some action on their own behalf.

Each stage invites individuals to first enter it and taste of its uniqueness, then indulge in it, soaking in the delights of their development in that stage. The initial entry into each stage usually is accompanied by high hopes, aspirations, new ideas, willingness, eagerness, anticipation, and fear. These motivations help people look further into the stage for answers to their needs. As people develop further they take on the strengths of the stage and gain more confidence. Then, if they are willing to keep moving, there is a natural evolution out of the stage and on to the next stage. For some people, as they progress through the stage, its values, costumes, dance steps, and behaviors may cause them to become disillusioned, fearful, obsessed, or confused. These may be signs they are experiencing the shadow of that stage. The way in which they react to these feelings will determine whether they continue to move through the stage or get stuck in it. A particular characteristic of the stage may so absorb some people that they overdo that behavior and it becomes a negative trait. Vivid examples in history dramatize the shadow or negative sides of power. Take Power by Achievement (Stage Three), for example: Confident, bright, controlling, strong, charismatic, and seemingly reputable people in history have persuaded many people to do illegal things for the sake of financial gain, which soon turned into uncontrolled greed. They were really operating in the shadow of Stage Three and were not true leaders.

Women are more likely to identify with certain stages and men with other stages.

I do not intend this to be a book on women and power, or on men and power. It is, rather, a book on people and power. But I was motivated to describe different power stages when I noticed that some of the stages seemed to appeal more often to men and others more often to women. The third stage, Power by Achievement, is the most masculine and the second stage, Power by Association, is the most feminine. Stages Four, Five, and Six, Power by Reflection, Purpose, and Wisdom combine both masculine and feminine qualities.

This explanation is complicated by the fact that the more masculine qualities seem to appeal to many women at times and the more feminine qualities appeal to many men at times. I chose to explore and explain this by accepting the facts that some masculine and feminine behavior is in all of us and that we may be less comfortable with some stages because of our orientation to either our masculine or our feminine dimensions. This concept of having both the masculine and feminine at our disposal is called androgyny.

I have always felt uncomfortable with "male" versus "female" behavior models because no one fits completely into either model, even though a person may fit one more than the other. For example, I've known women who fit the "male" model perfectly, and men who fit the "female" model. I have chosen to use the terms "masculine" and "feminine" which allow for more flexibility, since they are not tied only to gender. I do think, however, that because of our socialization, we experience the world in a manner similar to others of our own gender. Other factors though, like position in the family, self-esteem, decade of birth, heredity, etc., also influence our view of the world.

The most difficult transition for women to make is from Stage Two to Stage Three, whereas the hardest transition for men is from Stage Three to Stage Four. The easiest transition for women is from Stage Three to Stage Four, and for men the easiest transition is from Stage Two to Stage Three. The only exceptions to this are very hard-driving women who identify more with men's patterns and more androgynous men who identify with women's patterns.

Stage Two appears to be more feminine.

Stage Three appears to be more masculine.

Stage Four combines masculine and feminine behaviors and Stages Five and Six go beyond gender.

Stages Two, Three, and Four are most rewarded in organizations.

> *You do not necessarily proceed to new stages merely with age or experience, although both are factors.*

If life experience automatically made us wise, then all senior citizens would be wisdom figures. Many are but equally as many aren't. Although there might be more older people than very young ones living in the more complex power stages, an equal number of older people have not moved at all. They believe they cannot move or they have become fixed at earlier stages. Feeling stuck, and at the same time unwilling to take a risk to move on, makes it hard for these people to comprehend the question, "How does one move to a new stage?" to say nothing of answering it.

So age and experience alone do not a Stage Six make. The key is what we do with our experience, how our experience causes us to see ourselves more accurately, and how we think about and learn from age and life events. In the earlier stages we build up our confidence, skill, responsibility, knowledge, and ego. We learn to promote ourselves and to expect our best. Then at some point most of us are given opportunities to become more self-accepting, to see ourselves as others see us, to get out of the perfectionist mold we may have created for ourselves. For many of us, that self-acceptance comes painfully at first through some event, crisis, time of reckoning, or rude awakening. And usually this occurs after Stage Three (Power by Achievement) has become familiar. Then as we realize that we are not totally what we had hoped to be, or that we are what we had hoped but discover it isn't satisfying, we also may find that we have the possibility of slowly becoming more than we had expected. The transformation at this point is miraculous. It is clearly apparent in some—dramatic even—and subtle in others. It often calls into question all principles and goals. It makes life appear, in retrospect, excruciatingly simple. I call it "letting go of trying to be." Knowing who we really are, although difficult at any age, is more powerful than any title or position. I believe the mind of a wise and perceptive person is like that of Virginia Woolf's creative person: "incandescent," "unimpeded," with "no obstacle in it, no foreign matter unconsumed" (*A Room of One's Own*).

There is no one right way to move or change. Some people don't even want to, and for others the timing isn't right. Probably the best thing I can do is to give you several examples of people at various stages, what they think about themselves, and how they've moved to other stages. You may identify with one or several of them and draw some conclusions for yourself. One phenomenon I've noticed is that people at Stages One and Four sometimes get confused. Ones think they're Fours and Fours think they're Ones. This is also true for people who are at Stage Two and Stage Five. Twos think they're Fives and Fives think they might be Twos. And most people at Stage Three would like to think of themselves as Sixes!! Sixes could care less how people see them.

Some folks need to be pushed and prodded to think about themselves, others need to be left alone to reflect and think. On the other hand, a crisis or external event may provide just the opportunity for a long neglected personal look. One woman told me that people in her life who ask her questions she can't answer help her to think more about herself and motivate her to take more risks. Another person imagines himself at another stage and writes in a journal as the first step in a new direction.

Another person goes to seminars, workshops, and guided retreats to think more clearly about change. One thing is certain. Mid-life or any sudden shock (illness, divorce, job loss, death of a loved one) offers the best opportunity to radically rethink your life. The internal window of our psyche opens wider during these times than at other times and gives us the greatest opportunity to let the sun into the darkened place.

> *The most externally- and organizationally-oriented power stages (Stages One–Three) show a marked contrast to the internally-oriented power stages (Stages Four–Six).*

The first three stages are much more externally-oriented, meaning that the power that is primarily sought and obtained comes from outside the person, from titles, positions, or other symbols of status. These rewards have been accumulated traditionally from the community or within the work setting. People in Stages One through Three may also be growing and developing on the inside, but the balance is clearly in favor of growth for the sake of external recognition or career movement. That's why it is possible to identify some jobs or job families with Stages One, Two or Three, although all individuals in these jobs are not necessarily in these stages.

In Stages Four through Six the *inner* journey is more critical, and the balance tips toward internal reflection. At these stages, it is more difficult to tell by external cues (titles, etc.) what stage the person lives in; therefore, the quality and character of the person takes on more significance. It is possible, for instance, for a person to move to Stage Four in a Stage Three organization, by getting support primarily from outside organizations, support groups, or leadership activities. One cannot predict with any accuracy what types of jobs or careers people beyond Stage Three will have. Living out one's life purpose, having integrity, and empowering others—all hallmarks of the more complex stages—can be accomplished in a wide variety of settings.

> *The development of one's ego and then the release of one's ego are central tasks inherent within this model. Cultural rituals are necessary in order to do that successfully.*

One of the central tasks of development from the earlier stages to the more complex stages is that of developing one's ego into a mature ego (Stages One-Three) and then gradually relinquishing that ego to a power beyond oneself (Stages Four-Six). I am reminded of the work of Carl Jung and Joseph Campbell, who describe how primal cultures handle this development in very deliberate ways, through ceremonies and personal testing. Our own high tech culture seems to have left ritual behind and that may be to our detriment. How, for instance, does a young person know when they are an adult in our culture? The primal cultures would have a religious and symbolic ritual like a puberty rite in which the child symbolically dies and is reborn as an adult. We seem to have so many different rites of passage (driving age, drinking age, voting age, college or military service, marriage, first job), no one is sure when he/she is an adult.

Perhaps this confusion about when we are mature or have arrived in some way accounts for the obsession with Stage Three in our culture. We don't know how to measure our continued growth past Stage Three so we just keep accumulating more "things." I would like to suggest that this book, with marked behaviors that define each stage, could be a way for people to tell how they are continuing to develop. I think that a ritual for entering adolescence, for entering adulthood and for surviving mid-life are absolutely necessary (beyond the "over-the-hill" birthday parties) and a ritual of "eldering" into one's wisdom years would be healthy as well. Maybe someone reading this book will be inspired to develop such rituals. I have made one small attempt by developing a teenage survival kit for each child in my life when they reach thirteen. It makes them feel special and announces that the world will be a little different for them now. Some of the items I include are the obvious things they'll need, like skin cleansers, nail polish (for girls), breath mints, and cologne. But I also like to add special things that encourage each child's gifts, like a drawing set, a computer magazine, or a special book. Each gift has a note attached to explain why I chose this gift.

These stages primarily describe the development of individuals who live and work in the United States of America in the first half of the twenty-first century.

The observations and interviews upon which this model is based were limited to current American examples and should be interpreted within that context. Several PhD and MA theses have been completed using the power model as part of the thesis. I report some of these findings, along with our own research, on my web site. Since the first publication of this book people in several other countries have studied and validated the principles or added to their richness. People in Europe and Asia seem most excited about the applicability to their cultures but it is beyond the scope of this book to explore that. However, the stages can be equally applied to American families, communities, and relationships, as I will show by cases and examples. The primary application of the model in this book is to people in organizations. Recently colleagues of mine have developed materials that apply these power stages to human resource managers, humor, church leadership, stewardship, hospital management, weight loss programs, and conflict management. And I think this may be just the tip of the iceberg.

People have inquired how I originally developed the personal power model. It is a culmination of my course work towards my PhD in adult development at the University of Minnesota, many years of business and professional experience, and personal interviews with and feedback from hundreds of people in organizations.

One warning I have for you is not to pursue the stages of power as if they were a task to be accomplished or a pinnacle to be achieved. There is wisdom in letting a natural process, a higher power, or events guide you, and there is wisdom in being open to the next thing life has in store.

If you would like to know which stage of power you identify with most and how that affects you, you might like to send for a copy of the Personal Power Profile. It is a self-scoring instrument measuring your six stages of personal power. At the end of this book, on page 305, you will find more information on ordering products related to *Real Power.* It also explains how you may contact me for speeches or workshops.

Ask yourself these questions about Stage One:

Yes No

____ ____ 1. Do you feel secure when someone else is making decisions for you?

____ ____ 2. Do you dream of possible futures (another career, higher salary) with little or no idea of how to get there?

____ ____ 3. Do you frequently question your self-worth?

____ ____ 4. Do you find risk-taking very intimidating?

____ ____ 5. Do you feel you have to ask or coax or cajole others in order to get things you want?

____ ____ 6. Do you know little or nothing about how the organization's decisions are made?

____ ____ 7. Do you feel you are just a number and not seen as an individual in your work?

____ ____ 8. Do you fear physical or emotional abuse in your relationships?

____ ____ 9. Do you think someone else is responsible for your lot in life and that you are a victim?

____ ____ 10. Do you feel overwhelmed and confused when asked to make decisions?

____ ____ 11. Do you ever try to manipulate or coerce others to get things done?

____ ____ 12. Do you feel you have a characteristic that draws discrimination from others?

____ ____ 13. Do you get so afraid that you feel frozen, unable to act?

____ ____ 14. Are alcohol, gambling, work, shopping, sex, drugs, or relationships in charge of your life?

____ ____ 15. Do you feel that nothing you do will make a difference in bettering your life?

Yes answers indicate that you identify with this stage.

Chapter 1
Stage One: Powerlessness

Manipulation

Key Question: When do you feel least powerful?

What Is Stage One Like?

We all feel powerless at times, so we can all identify at least slightly with the stage of powerlessness. As children we were all powerless, although most of us felt secure. We were dependent on other people to supply our needs—and for the most part, they did. But if, as adults, this is our home stage for a prolonged period of time, we will feel trapped—and powerless. Whole portions of our society feel they are permanently powerless as victims of the powerful "system." Just as the symbol indicates, they feel stuck, tied down with no relief in sight. Examples of people who feel powerless might be temporary workers, children, wage employees, high school and college students, floor nurses, public school teachers, clerks, waitresses and waiters, the unemployed, homemakers, taxpayers, abandoned women with few marketable skills, people of color, undocumented workers, welfare recipients, the elderly, handicapped or emotionally disturbed people, clients in the human services, even governments of Third World countries.

You might argue that some of these groups have become quite powerful in the last several years. True, they have, but only because they are no longer individuals but groups working collectively. The irony is that powerless people are usually grouped together for identification, which adds to their sense of alienation. "I'm just a number" or "Give this to the data entry people" are examples of the ways in which Stage One people are viewed. However, grouping together is the only way they can gain power for more than one member at a time. The power model suggests that anyone who resides on the lowest rungs of any ladder experiences powerlessness. For example, if you change careers at age thirty-two or forty-five, you may temporarily feel a loss of power because you are not yet familiar with the new environment. You haven't found your niche, nor have you proven yourself in the new organization. You don't know the language or the norms, and your successful prior experiences don't count for much. It takes time and experience in your new arena to gain the confidence and responsibility you once had. It's quite a shock to people who are not expecting it.

Many of us experience powerlessness when someone we know dies or develops a terminal illness. We can cry, scream, rant, or rave but there is nothing that helps take the truth away. We also experience this stage when we have a car accident, lose a friend for no apparent reason, or when we rush to a store to get something we urgently need only to find out the store is closed for the night. Most of us experience powerlessness regularly but some of us live in Stage One, thus experiencing it as our home stage.

One of the ways Stage One becomes a home stage for all of us is through our addictions. Because our addictions are in control of us, we are powerless. Until we break through our denial and understand the addictive process we cannot reclaim our power. Stage One as a home stage takes a toll on our self-esteem. We are frustrated virtually all the time, even though we cover it well and may even look very successful by external standards.

I experience powerlessness in myriads of small ways, which I have alluded to above. Whenever something happens that is out of my control and puts me at risk, whether it is in my home or across the ocean, I feel a tinge of powerlessness in the form of fear or anger. One arena in which I feel especially powerless is hospitals. I have an uncanny ability to give away all my power when I walk through the hospital door. I get so scared that I forget to ask questions, take responsibility, and take care of myself. Then when I realize what I've done and I resume my usual assertiveness, I am sometimes seen as a problem. Anyone who takes back power that they have relinquished will be perceived as a problem to someone.

Whenever I experience a life crisis, I immediately recycle to Stage One. I have had enormous losses in my life, all of which left me feeling powerless. The worst was when my mother died suddenly when I was twenty-three. I thought my life was over. It was, in a sense, because it could never be the same after that. I struggled with my identity, with unresolved anger and grief, and with my own life's presumed brevity. I found a new freedom from this legacy only in the past year when I finally lived beyond the age at which my mother died.

I have also experienced two divorces, both after many years of marriage. The loss of a love is one of the most difficult to recover from and we never do fully recover; we mend the wound and live with the scar tissue. There is the anger and disappointment, betrayal and rejection to deal with along with our cultural and religious shame. By fully experiencing all of these feelings and entering into a healing process though, there is enormous growth possible if we let the process deepen us. I married wonderful men and it astounds me to realize how far we grew apart over the years, despite our best efforts to work at the spiritual and psychological aspects of our marriage. It is a mystery to me and perhaps can only be explained from a wiser, more spiritual perspective.

I don't think Stage One is my home stage at this point in my life but when I revisit this stage from time to time, I use the same principles to move out of it that I used earlier in my life; the principles recommended in this chapter. I usually stop to calm down, think through my options, talk to friends and professionals, and move into action with a strong support base. In that way I do not stay in this stage very long. Knowing how hard it is to move forward under duress, I have enormous compassion for people who have lived in this powerless stage for years with no clear way of escape. I am certain that my own life could have moved in that direction were it not for a strong mother, the value of education in my family and several breaks I got when I was young.

The description of power at Stage One is manipulation. This has two meanings. Powerless people feel they are constantly being *manipulated by others*, pushed around, helped, controlled, duped, or taken care of, but they also find they depend upon manipulating others to get things done or to acquire things for themselves. They feel they are put in the position of making a case for themselves, pleading, persuading, cajoling, sweet-talking, or seducing in order to get what they want. They are rarely in the position of having access to resources themselves, whether those are people, information, skills, or money. They need to obtain approval for almost everything they do and usually have a limited area of discretion. This comes out painfully in organizations when a Stage One person has a good idea that is immediately squelched by a boss who claims it is too complicated or cannot be implemented in the budget. If the Stage One person is not assertive (and usually he or she isn't) it is easy to accept the verdict and become discouraged.

Characteristics of People at Stage One

Dependent, Getting Things through Others

Powerless people feel almost totally dependent on other people or organizations. Sometimes this can result in safety and security and is deemed valuable, especially if the other person or organization is trustworthy. Many women in traditional marriages are examples of powerless but happy people, secure and dependent, with their family interests and busy lives. It works well, as long as the tradition lasts. If, after having been taken care of all their lives, these women then become widowed or divorced in middle age, they may find life extremely difficult. Some have to start from scratch in areas like finances, decision-making, housing, and socializing. They often feel angry that they had depended so much on their spouse. One widow told me that she felt as if her thirty-year-old cocoon had just opened, and she didn't want to leave it.

One example of a way in which men become secure and dependent by following prescribed rules in their work is the rank of a private in the military. They become dependent on their sergeant for their self-image, their rewards and punishments. The sergeant has control over their life. Whenever someone or something has more control over you than you have over yourself, you may be experiencing Stage One.

An important struggle at this stage is to desire less dependence but not know how to become more independent without risking too much. A great deal of fear and confusion can be associated with Stage One: on the one hand, lacking the knowledge of what exactly to do and fearing the repercussions if one were to break away from dependence, yet on the other hand fearing the consequences of prolonged security. Many people remain in Stage One until it is impossible to stay there or until another person or a life event forces them out of it. But as long as they are in Stage One they are held in a powerless state, secure yet dependent on others for basic life needs.

People at Stage One understand from experience that there are two types of people—those who have power (the haves) and those who don't (the have-nots). In fact, we can all identify with this because of our experiences as children. We all chose various ways to get things from our parents: asking them, being good, playing sick, showing them affection, helping them, or threatening them. If one method didn't work, we just moved to the next one. As a child I found out that whether my parents seemed reasonable or not, they still had the resources and I had to do something to get them. They shared, but they were in charge. The resources were not mine to begin with, that is, not until I began to earn my own money and assert my own judgments. When adults feel powerless, they continually feel they have fewer resources or less access to resources than others. I heard a couple talking recently in the following manner, which illustrates this point: He said, "Well, as long as we're going to spend our vacation with my parents, I think I'll take a long weekend to ski this winter." She replied, "Well, then, I'd like to take a long weekend on the beach while you ski." He looked up and laughed, "Well, where will you get the money?"

People in organizations often feel this same sense of control by other people. If those at the top of the organization are perceived to be making all the decisions, then those on the bottom think of themselves as powerless and subject to changes over which they have no control. They feel like puppets on a string that have to respond directly to any movement of the puppeteer.

Uninformed

One of the reasons powerless people in organizations are so dependent is that they have little access to information. Because they know little about how the organization is run they are forced to rely on those who have that information; as a result, these people tend to participate only in their own world—usually limited to people who sit next to them or who supervise them. They have low-level skills and their positions are generally at the entry level, causing many of them to see their work as "just a job." For some this is acceptable, and they are proud to do a good job. Some of them shrug off efforts to further themselves because they don't believe their efforts will make any difference. This is due to low self-esteem and sometimes to reality. Some may be waiting for Prince (or Princess) Charming or for the lottery or sweepstakes to rescue them. Since they tend to be unrealistic or unaware of the rules, they may have more daydreams of get-rich-quick schemes or lucky breaks.

In organizations some powerless people can be very difficult to deal with. Some people who have very little control hoard what little bit of territorial control they have to show others that they will not be dominated on their own turf. You may recall times when you've filled out an extraordinarily long bureaucratic form under a deadline, following the instructions explicitly, only to find out too late that the person in charge wanted it another way, and you have now missed the deadline or are subject to a penalty.

Low in Self-Esteem

People feel generally confused at this stage, not knowing which way to turn and having frequent bouts of low self-esteem coupled with self-doubt. Powerless people do not know who they are as individuals largely because they are afraid to take a close look. Sometimes they don't know how, but generally they're too busy with work, or making ends meet, or escaping from life. They just take what life dishes out and they don't ask questions. They learn to accept it and hope it doesn't get worse. They say to themselves, "What makes me think I deserve better, anyway?"

Low self-esteem seems to feed on itself. The paradox of low self-esteem is that people also get some benefits out of that state of mind. They can feel sorry for themselves; they can arouse their anger at others; they can prove to themselves how much they deserve to be in this terrible spot; they can use it as an excuse to stand still. So one of the ways for people to increase their personal self-esteem is to learn to speak honestly to themselves about their worth.

People at Stage One complain a lot. They frustrate those around them. But it is critical to understand that for people whose home stage is Stage One, their underlying feeling is fear. Fear for them is a frozen feeling that is not easily analyzed. Prolonged fear diminishes self-worth and results in anger vented either at oneself or others. Even people who are otherwise confident and in control will change their behavior when they are suddenly faced with a situation in which they are powerless, such as unexpected job loss, sudden illness, or death. Colleagues or supervisors of Stage One people sometimes think these people are out to get them or are deliberately being uncooperative. The truth is that Ones are just petrified. And until that fear can be stilled, no cajoling will make a difference.

Helpless but Not Hopeless

I think of Stage One as helpless but not hopeless. There are things to do, ways to get out, further steps to take, but not if people endlessly continue to reinforce their own powerless status. Sexism and racism are certainly factors that feed into a powerless position; witness the failure of our country to pass the Equal Rights Amendment and the over-proportionate number of people of color in prison. Cultural and attitudinal barriers are almost insurmountable at times. A good example is the frustration that Native Americans have when dealing with our government. But it is possible to make some progress to other stages. The first step is the will to change, and the second step is getting support to help break out of Stage One. You cannot do it alone, and someone else cannot do it for you. It involves taking responsibility for yourself and taking some initiative on your own or with others' help. It means not blaming others or the system entirely. It means that you do something to speak out on your own behalf and get some of your self-esteem and power back.

I do not intend to analyze cultural powerlessness in this book; that is a book all its own. I am describing Stage One as it *is* in our society, not as it *ought* to be. In terms of organizational leadership, which is one of my themes, Stage One people are not effective as organizational leaders. They have little external and no internal power, and they tend to abuse it when they get it. Stage One people as leaders tend to get things done by coercion, because they have been coerced and see no other ways to lead. Examples are the revolutionaries in various countries who, once powerless and abused, turn around and kill their oppressors the first chance they get.

Spirituality and the Spiritual Connection to Work at Stage One

I will describe briefly in this book how people at each stage experience their spirituality and its connection to their work. Since this is such a large and complex topic and space is limited, I cannot do the subject justice here. If you are interested in exploring the stages of spirituality and religion, I refer you to my book *The Critical Journey: Stages in the Life of Faith*. (See page 305 for details.)

At this stage spirituality means recognizing a Higher Power or Holy Presence in one's life. Some of us entered the spiritual journey for the first time as children, others as adults. Some of us can name where and when this happened, others just know it happened. We enter this stage of spirituality either from a sense of awe or a sense of need. We are awed by the Holy, which we perceive in the miracles of nature, birth, healing, music, or love. If we enter this stage out of need, it is the result of pain, rejection, or guilt from which we seek release. Some people become aware of a Higher Power in a meaningful way for the first time when they begin attending a 12-step program. Many people experience this stage at mid-life when they embark on a quest for greater meaning in life or long for a new purpose.

Lynn is an accomplished professional woman. She is just facing the sad truth that her marriage is over after sixteen years and three children. She is feeling very unsettled and does not know exactly which way to turn. Recently she has felt a new urge growing within her—a need to connect with a Higher Power, one she left behind when she was confirmed. She's not quite sure how to do that since she's convinced that her childhood religion with its rules against divorce will not be instructive for her. She's just found a friend, however, who is a good listener and whose faith seems secure and able to withstand all her questions. She seems ready to experience the Holy in a new light.

There seems to be little obvious connection between faith and work at Stage One. Sometimes that lack of connection is what brings people to a need for faith or spirituality. We focus most of our energy on our relationship with the Holy whether that means experiencing awe, recognizing our deep need, or accepting our powerlessness. What we do spiritually at work is largely unconscious. We may even take a spiritual hiatus from work by separating our spirituality and our work, in order to concentrate on our relationship with our Higher Power.

The Shadow of Stage One

Every stage has a negative or "shadow" side. Prolonged negative behavior indicates the individual is stuck in the shadow of that stage. The result is slow deterioration in a downward spiral, no matter what stage people are stuck at. These are the behaviors that indicate a Stage One person is living in the shadow of that stage.

Holding onto Victim Stance

Victims live in the shadow of Stage One. They have a unique and difficult perspective on life. They let other people, society, family, or addictions control their lives because they believe they are powerless to change. They contend that other people are doing them in. And, of course, there is some truth in their allegations. Our society, at times, holds people down, discriminates against them, and frequently ignores their pain. And families can be abusive, dysfunctional, and mean-spirited. Sometimes the treatment has been so severe, there is permanent damage done and the person is incapable of retrieval. Victimization is a complex topic, because it occurs both on the individual level and on the societal level.

I saw case after case of sexually and physically abused women in prison. Some were so severely damaged, that it is unlikely they will ever recover. Our violent society not only does not discourage this treatment, it encourages it. Domestic abuse and violence are pervasive in our country. I believe that abuse is our biggest national family secret. Women who are domestic abuse survivors are twice hurt because our society is designed to allow denigration and then offer few opportunities for healing.

But we cannot wait for society to change when working with individual women. Each woman can be helped to reclaim her power, her sense of self-esteem, her trust in herself. It is a long and arduous path but worth the work. Thankfully there are now safe places for women to go to escape violence and learn to protect themselves.

Two stories from different occupational settings illustrate the victim stance.

Louise, the College Professor, as Described by One of Her Colleagues

> Louise is a very intelligent 55-year-old college instructor. She has worked at the same job for over 30 years and is very unhappy with it. She does not enjoy teaching and interacting with students, but is trapped by the security of her position as a tenured professor and the substantial salary she receives. Her students consistently give her poor evaluations of her teaching performance, but she appears unwilling or unable to change.
>
> Instead of being open to this feedback, she dismisses it, saying that the students are "lazy and unintelligent." When she is encouraged to attend workshops on teaching strategies she says they are a waste of time and she doesn't need them. Her fear manifests itself through the overuse of defense mechanisms such as denial and rationalization. She typically takes an adversarial stance with college administrators when they make inquiries into her job performance. Louise seems incapable of taking effective action to change her situation. Perhaps a crisis is needed to precipitate movement for her. She is an excellent amateur photographer, but does not have the confidence to pursue this as an alternative career. It is sad to watch her steadily deteriorate as a woman and as a professional.

Louise is an example of someone who is trapped in Stage One, burned out, and unable to *move*.

Joan, the Corporate Secretary

> This is really hard, um, embarrassing for me to talk about, because it's still so recent. (pause) Well, last year in the middle of a really busy time at work, my boss and I were working late to get out a rush report before a deadline. Most of the other girls had gone home and we were almost finished, just a few pages to go. My boss asked if I would get us both a cup of coffee, which sounded good to me, too, so I quickly got it and brought it in to him at his desk. He stood up, said thanks, and made a pass . . . well, um, he sort of kissed me, um, on the lips and I pulled away and left the room mumbling "You're welcome" or something weird like that. I was beet-red. I could just feel it. What a shock! I could have forgotten the whole thing and called it appreciation or something, but he started doing other things, more embarrassing and more out in the open. Now mind you, I'm no prude, no big moralist, but I just didn't want to get involved with a married man and, furthermore, not my boss.
>
> I finally worked up enough courage to sit down with him one day and tell him that I really liked working for him but his advances were beginning to get in the way of my work. He laughed and said we could talk about it another time. His behavior kept up and became more aggressive a few times. Once he trapped me in his office and started handling me. That made me really scared and angry. After that I made sure I was never in a position to be touched or trapped by him again. But I went home with headaches. And he gave me a lower-than-average performance review for that period of time. Then he told me perhaps I should see a counselor because I was not a very healthy young lady—repressed or something was what he said. Well, that cracked me. I'd do something but I think I'm too afraid of losing my job

Being trapped in a compromising work situation in which a boss is unable to face up to his harassing behavior leaves Joan in a very frightening predicament.

Addictions

Another shadow behavior of Stage One is addiction. All dependencies, whether to alcohol, drugs, work, relationships, food, gambling, sex, or money, produce victims. The addiction is in charge of our lives. Anyone who has come to terms with his/her own addictions can easily understand what Stage One, powerlessness, is like. Men frequently have a difficult time relating to this stage until they face their addictions. Then they can see it intimately.

Addictions keep getting worse if not treated. They lead to abuse of self and others, violence, self-hate, suicide, and martyrdom. They permeate the whole space in which they reside. They are never life giving, and always shame-based.

Here is an example of an addicted executive.

Todd, the Chemically Dependent Executive

What a farce I made out of my life. High roller was what I called myself. For fifteen years, my motto was "live hard, work hard, drink hard." And I did. I thought the way to reach the top was to be everything to everybody, to be the friendly guy who everybody liked. I had a lot of energy, good health, and lots of contacts. I had the world by the tail and was swinging it around. I traveled seventy-five percent of the time and was always ready for the next challenge.

The only trouble with my life, which I totally denied at the time, was that I was numb most of the time, due to my total dependence on alcohol. Alcohol gave me the feeling I could do all these things, or at least allowed me to escape the feeling that I couldn't. I was under the powerful spell of self-delusion. I wanted so desperately to be approved of and to be needed; yet I just could not be vulnerable or realistic. Now I can see I was feeling guilty and shameful for never measuring up, but my way of coping was not to feel at all—to numb myself. I was so good at the whole charade that I even had my family convinced that my behavior was benefiting them.

Thank God for my wife. After a serious illness of her own, she woke up to the fact that she was helping me toward my own destruction. She left me for a time and got help for herself. I hit bottom after several months of hell and finally agreed, for the sake of the family, to go into chemical dependency treatment. That was the hardest thing I've ever done, but it saved my life.

After a long, hard struggle back to life, I can say I would not be alive emotionally or physically if I had not taken that step. I have had to completely rethink my life and my work. It's been a real awakening. Thanks to my recovery program, I am more aware now of who I am and what I am capable of doing. I am willing to admit my weaknesses and pain and get help when I need it. Now I just live from day to day, more self-accepting, more honest, and very grateful for life. My motto has become "live more fully, love more fully."

As Todd's story shows, chemicals can cause a dependence that is every bit as powerful as it is destructive, leaving people debilitated. Chemically dependent people are deluded into thinking they are powerful when, ironically, they are powerless.

No addict will be free until they embrace their addictions. They have given up their power. Carolyn Myss wisely says that they have turned their spirit over to someone or something else. They must take it back. That means retrieving painful family or societal experiences. It means facing shame, rage, and powerlessness. It means establishing and honoring personal boundaries. It means tears, fear, and pain. It means giving up control and living one day at a time. It means taking care of us. Twelve-step programs are now the fastest growing spirituality movement in the United States. They help people get free from addictions by practicing the twelve steps of recovery.

Let's Meet Some People at Stage One

Andy, the High School Student

> I just got my first part-time job. I don't know how much I'll like working, but it's better'n sitting around in front of the tube all night. I'm working as a part-time janitor washing floors and cleaning up in offices after supper. Pay's not so hot but it's better'n nothing. Gives me a little extra money to spend on stuff I want. The way I see it, when I hit eighteen, I'll go to where my dad lives, and maybe he can set me up with something better. He's been unemployed mostly since he left us, but there's bound to be something for a guy who don't mind working. If I did better in school, maybe I could get into one of them tech schools, but school and me don't get along so hot. There's too much going on at home with the four little kids around. Makes it tough to study, and I have a hard time seeing where it will all get me anyway. Guess I'll just stick it out until I can leave.

Andy is an example of a young, unskilled student who has very little to rely on and some life situations to overcome.

Karen, Caretaker of a Parent with Alzheimer's

> At first we thought my husband's mother was just experiencing memory loss associated with aging. Forgetting names, repeating, putting things away and not remembering where. Then one incident after another showed us the truth of her condition. She couldn't drive

home from the grocery store, she paid an unscrupulous repairman a large sum of money upfront, and she burned some muffins to such an extent that two fire trucks answered the alarm. She thought her neighbor did it.

My husband and I were pressed under a heavy weight of a diagnosis of Alzheimer's. What started as an occasional blip soon accelerated. We were chasing a bullet train going south. We couldn't keep pace with the rapid decline in her memory skills. Each day we met a lady changed from the day before. And it was becoming obvious she could no longer remain at home.

We were sucked into powerlessness. The healthcare providers didn't have answers or solutions. The healthcare system seemed to have a foot on our backs. There were few lifting hands. At dinner we would obsess: "Why us?" "How will we ever have our lives back?" "How can we care for someone with whom we have a hurtful history?"

We became victims of his mother's Alzheimer's. We were rudderless. The demands for our time pressed us into setting aside our business for six months as we tried to comprehend what was happening. We were in the turbulence with no calm in sight.

Karen describes how she dipped down into powerlessness following the diagnosis of her mother-in-law's disease. She was surprised at how quickly she felt powerless.

Margaret, the Homemaker

I've been married to the same man for twenty-six years. We've done everything together. We've raised five kids, built a house, traveled across the country, suffered over deaths, taken in foreign students, laughed, fought, and loved. It doesn't seem like there's much we haven't done. I encouraged him, even knocked on doors for him when he decided to run for mayor of our town. And he won. I've lived for him and my family for twenty-six years. He and our five children are my entire life, my full-time job. Oh, I have outside interests like my sewing club, my occasional craft classes at the high school, and my garden, but these things are secondary to my job at home. Everything my husband does requires my support, and I enjoy being there when he needs me. In turn he makes a comfortable living for us all to enjoy and is the strong, decisive father for the family. We discuss all the major family decisions together, but he usually makes the final decision because of his broader perspective.

> He is very supportive of me when I want to do things for myself or for the children. If I want to take the kids to grandma's for a week in the summer, he always sees to it that we get there. When I want him to go to the children's special events, he usually makes time for them. We have had our troubles, believe me, illness, depression, fights, but on the whole, we've had a very good life. I guess we've learned to accept each other and not try to change each other any more. And our children are all grown up and either going to school or married and into their own lives. Now it's time for us to think about his retirement. I wonder sometimes exactly what we'll do because time has been more heavy on my hands these last few years, but we'll talk it over like we usually do and it'll work out somehow.

Margaret illustrates power within powerlessness. Margaret is a happy and dependent homemaker who loves her life and will meet the crises as they come.

Moving to Stage Two

There is no way to predict exactly how each of us will move from one stage to another. Some will take a direct route like this: A → B and others will take the circuitous route: A ↯ B. Each path may take the same amount of time but cover different territory. There seem to be steps in the transition from one stage to another, but we each have our own style of going through the steps. At times the transition between stages seems as long as the time spent in each stage, especially when we're in the middle of the change. I think of the movement from stage to stage as a transformation because each person has to overcome some obstacle as well as let go of something familiar in order to move. Some experience the transition as a metamorphosis, like a butterfly emerging from a cocoon. Others experience it as a death and rebirth.

Two key personal qualities will ultimately precipitate the transformation or movement to Stage Two: self-esteem and skills. People have to start feeling good about themselves, and they have to have skills they can use effectively in the world. Acquiring skill makes us feel more competent, more useful, and more hopeful. If you are new to a field and wonder how you could ever move up, look around you to see what additional skills people have that you don't. Get support from family or friends to obtain more skills, either by asking for others to teach you on the job or by reading and experimenting for yourself. For example, if you are a cook in a small restaurant, practice new recipes at home or ask the head chef questions so you can learn.

Self-esteem develops in less concrete ways. Usually there is a crisis or loss or event of some kind that stops people in their tracks or awakens them to the need to take themselves seriously enough to act in order to feel better. That does not mean that everyone acts when a crisis occurs. Some people give up, become hostile, harm others, injure themselves, or just get "stuck" at their stage. This can be due to cultural barriers, lack of access to people, money, experience, or it can represent a lack of motivation to move due to nagging self-doubt, laziness, low risk-taking ability, unwillingness to try, or satisfaction with the martyr or victim role.

Self-esteem develops when you act on your own behalf. You may not know how or why you are doing it, but you feel an inner compulsion to get out of a situation and to survive. I remember distinctly the event that forced me to act within a seemingly powerless work situation. You see, I was in a position similar to the secretary I described earlier. I was a young professional and my boss was sexually harassing me on the job. I was afraid and I knew that he had power over me, to fire me at will. I started getting severe headaches and I knew I had to do something soon. I decided to tell him that I could not work effectively under the current office conditions. He led me to believe the problem was *me* and went on to say that he needed to discuss me with his boss. In a moment of desperation I said that I would discuss the situation with his boss's boss. To this day I remember how afraid I was to risk talking to his boss's boss. I went in to that office shaking and aware that I would have to put my job on the line because I didn't know if I would be heard. And it was at a time that sexual harassment was not even talked about yet. In fact I did not tell him about the sexual harassment. I told him that I could not work with my boss, that there were two other jobs I thought I would be qualified for, and if those were not a possibility, I would quit. But I said the part about quitting in a very low voice hoping he would not hear it. You can't imagine how relieved I was when I realized he understood and appreciated my situation. Two weeks later I had a different job in the organization working for someone else. I would never want to repeat that experience, but I learned how to handle other work situations better as a result.

We all can use the help of others at these crucial times. But we also *must* acknowledge from our innermost being that we are worth the effort and that we will invest in ourselves. I think it comes down to wanting to live rather than die. Gaining self-esteem is difficult if you've been beaten down for years. How one develops it is a critical and complex issue, but self-esteem is possible with help from other caring people in your life.

The signs of increased self-esteem are different for all of us. Think back, if you're over twenty-five, to the first time you decided to take yourself by the hand and make a go of it. Perhaps it was running for a high school office, studying for a test, asking for a raise, going back to school, or buying a car. It could have been ten years ago, forty years ago, or yesterday. This experience of going beyond feeling helpless, beyond blaming others for our lot, beyond the dependency stage is one we face on a major or minor level periodically, even if our home stage is elsewhere. The seduction of the "poor me" syndrome plagues all of us from time to time because our powerlessness feels so real. It takes enormous energy to move on, but it feels good to have the safety of avoiding change as well. Sooner or later we realize it is time to move on and to get out of our debilitating powerlessness.

Whole groups of people who experience powerlessness (the poor, people of color, women, elders, the disabled) due to structural blocks in our society need to experience the individual change described above, but often they can do this only by identifying with each other as a group and by fighting "the system" together in order to make change occur. Some of the ways powerless people who feel victimized get together for their common good is to form collaborations, to form coops, or to form labor unions.

Here is an example of one woman who took her life seriously and made a decision that changed her life. The experience catapulted her into the next stages of power.

Nancy, a Survivor of Domestic Violence

> Nancy had been married less than a year when her husband choked her until she passed out. "Ironically, that's when I woke up to the fact that if I didn't leave Robert, he would kill me," she says. After regaining consciousness, she managed to run out into the night, find a pay phone, and call 911. When police escorted Nancy home, she noticed Robert's car was no longer parked in front. But when a policeman searched the apartment, he found Robert hiding; he had moved his car to lure Nancy back inside and was lying in wait. Robert was convicted of domestic violence and stalking and was sentenced to a year of probation. Nancy received counseling for the first time. "I had always assumed men just treated women like that," says Nancy, whose father had verbally abused her mother. She was able to pick up the pieces after her divorce, but never truly healed until she started volunteering for the Silent Witness National Initiative, an organization dedicated to healing domestic violence. She found herself the organizer of the Rhode Island exhibit of red life-sized figures representing the women who had been murdered in her state in acts of domestic violence.

> She organized the volunteers in Rhode Island to take the Silent Witness figures to the national march in Washington. While at the march, she heard a man speak to the crowd about how he stopped abusing his wife and salvaged his marriage. She realized for the first time that she needn't blame all men and it changed her outlook on her work and on domestic violence. Now she speaks regularly to groups about domestic abuse and she always has people come up afterwards willing to talk about their experiences. She is no longer a victim. She is a healer and is making a big difference in the world.

Nancy's story shows how women can move forward from a desperate situation by getting help themselves and then getting involved with a project that helps others to heal.

Listed below are activities that may help you develop more fully through Stage One and on to Stage Two. Some of these will seem appealing to you and others will not. Different people make the transition in different ways, and these are a compilation of the ways in which others have moved to Stage Two.

One program we know of is especially successful in working with people who experience powerlessness in the form of anger, anxiety, depression or fear. We would like to highlight it here:

> Self-Mastery Program: Rose Mary Boerboom, a colleague of mine, has developed a program that uses the latest in brain theory and emotional intelligence. She teaches people how to go underneath the surface anger, fear, or mistaken belief about oneself and heal the wounds underlying that feeling or belief. It is an amazing program. It has shown success with perpetrators and survivors of domestic violence, as well as with people in organizations who have anger or anxiety issues. Her STOP skill, used to regulate emotions, can be learned easily and, when used consistently, has been proven to be successful in changing people's behavior. Contact information for her is listed on page 305.

Other ways in which you can work yourself out of Stage One are:

- Build your self-esteem by exploring who you are and how you get yourself through crises in your life. Consider becoming part of a supportive group who will help you along the way. Resources would include friends, community centers, YM/YWCAs, churches, synagogues, family counseling agencies, and other non-profit organizations.

- Find allies in your organization or in the community who can help you with information or referrals: a network, employee relations people, a community center, advocates of all kinds, other people you know, or support groups.
- Name some skills you could develop that would help you become more qualified for better jobs. Talk to people who have these skills to find out how they developed them.
- List five things about yourself that other people like. List five things about yourself you like. Do something in the next ten days that shows that you appreciate your qualities, e.g., tell someone about something you have done that was satisfying.
- Talk to someone about your life so far. What major events led you to this point? How do you feel in your life now (happy, sad, afraid, angry, trapped, excited, sorry, joyful)?
- Think of ways to overcome or live more comfortably with your greatest fear. Get help from your support person or group on this one. Listen to others share their fears, and give them examples and support for overcoming their fears.
- If you always feel someone else is to blame, ask yourself how you might be "buying into" the issue or letting it happen to you. What can you do to make changes? Discuss the guilt and resentment you feel when attempting to break out of a situation.
- Talk with your boss, if you are comfortable doing so, about the skills he or she thinks would be useful for you to develop in order to grow in your job and in the organization.
- Do you need to get out of your present job in order to gain more personal power? If so, look around for three other jobs that you are or could be qualified for within the next year. Talk to others about the steps necessary to make a move, e.g., go to a career workshop, tell others you want to move, post for the job, prepare a history of your work, or develop a new skill.
- Are you in a life or work situation in which you are being abused physically or emotionally? If so, talk to someone about your feelings and move yourself, with help, toward getting out of the situation. You may need to tell someone in authority about the situation.
- Find a model or ally in your organization who can teach you about the operation of the organization and how you can become better prepared to move along within it.
- Decide which of your characteristics seems to draw the most discrimination—that you are female, a person of color, young, old, overweight, bald, unskilled, uneducated, or short. Name several

features about that characteristic that are pluses or that could be turned into positives for you.
- Go into treatment for your addictions or seek counseling to learn how to move out of your powerless place in life. Frequently people who experience mental/emotional illness feel powerless. Counselors, support, and mediation may help them move forward.
- Close your eyes and imagine yourself as a more powerful person. What are you like? What are you wearing? What are you doing? Who are you with? Who among your family and friends supports you most? Who disapproves? How do you feel?
- Watch familiar people who you think have more power than you. Observe what they do, ask them questions, or try out some of their behaviors for yourself. As you change, see how it affects you, and observe how others respond to you.
- Band together with other people, especially if you are being discriminated against and have tried consistently to solve the problem using other means. Be prepared for the response by trying to share your concerns as a group rather than threatening the other party. Negotiation is a long, slow process.

Todd's story of chemical dependency shows how someone else who cared nudged him to take care of himself.

Joan talked to two other secretaries confidentially and found out that she was not the first person her boss had bothered. She talked to her personnel representative, and with the help of other managers she had met previously she found another job in the company. Her boss has been put on probation for his harassment and has been sent to a professional for counseling.

Karen and her husband moved beyond being victims. She says, "One of the benefits of dropping down into powerlessness is that one day it dawns on you that you don't like being there. The cry is: 'Enough of this.' With new resolve we were determined to get the help we needed. We went to counseling at the Alzheimer's Association. We worked with an assisted living placement service to narrow the search for a new home. We chose not to discuss his mother at our dining table. With the help of friends and counselors we are no longer victims, but strong advocates to guide her as best we can on her remaining journey. We created a motto. *Our job is to make it work.*"

"We don't have answers, but we have a process to partner with the day's opportunities. We may from time to time still say, "Why us?" Now the difference is that we see more quickly how to move through the situation to the other side. We are not powerless in a powerless disease."

I'm sure others are in situations like Joan's or Todd's or Karen's, and they will not find a way out or a worthwhile person inside. That is perplexing and saddening as well. Sometimes the impetus for change occurs only when a crisis arises. What do you think will happen to Margaret when her husband dies? What will Andy find when he joins his father in a distant state? Will Louise ever find fulfillment in her academic career? Are they building up enough skill and self-esteem to be resourceful?

What Holds People Back?

What do you think will hold people at Stage One back from moving on to the next stage? Probably the most consistent deterrent for them will be fear. And that fear can take several forms: fear of physical abuse or punishment if they strike out on their own, fear of the unknown, fear of success, fear of being afraid, fear of being done in again, fear of failing because of the "system," fear of finding out what they can do if they try, fear of peer disapproval, fear, fear, fear. These fears are real, whether or not they are justified.

The fear itself is not the deciding issue, though. *How they deal with the fear is what determines whether they move forward.* For Stage One people to overcome their fears, even partially, they must get support from others in some form. That does not mean other people should do things for them but that they realize they are not alone in the struggle. That support provides validation that they are capable of doing something for themselves and that they are good people.

We should also remember that for every person who moves out of Stage One, there is someone else who wants to move but is not quite ready. When they are ready, people at other stages need to be available to help them, as others were for them. It's like passing on to others what we received from someone else at an earlier time.

Woody Allen expresses my sentiments about the fears of Stage One people when, in the last scene of his classic movie, *Annie Hall*, he is talking to his psychiatrist.

> "My brother is in bad shape. What can I do to help him?" Woody sighs.
>
> "What seems to be his problem?" asks his psychiatrist.
>
> "He thinks he's a chicken."

"Why, that's ridiculous. Just tell him straight out that he's not a chicken."

"It's not going to be that simple."

"Why not?"

"I need the eggs."

Hagberg's Model of Personal Power

SUMMARY OF STAGE ONE
POWERLESSNESS

Symbol

Key Question: When do you feel least powerful?

Description
Manipulation
Trapped stage

Characteristics
Secure and dependent
Low in self-esteem
Uninformed
Helpless but not hopeless

Shadow of Stage One
Holding onto victim stance
Addictions

Catalyst for Movement
Self-esteem
Skill development

What Holds People Back?
Fear

Spirituality at Stage One
Recognition of the Holy/Higher Power

Ways to Move
Build self-esteem, find allies, get support, develop skills, appreciate yourself, share yourself, confront fears, take responsibility, talk with your boss, change jobs, get out of abusive relationships, confront yourself, get into treatment or counseling.

Ask yourself these questions about Stage Two:

Yes	No	
____	____	1. Do you love to learn, absorb new information, and have new experiences?
____	____	2. Do you watch other people to consciously imitate their behavior?
____	____	3. Do you have a mentor or role model?
____	____	4. Is your self-concept dependent on how other people feel about you?
____	____	5. Are you new to a job, relationship, or body of knowledge and feel you have to prove yourself?
____	____	6. Do you feel that you are learning "the ropes"?
____	____	7. Are you intensely loyal to a boss whom you would like to work for as long as possible?
____	____	8. Are most of your social contacts friends of your spouse through his or her work?
____	____	9. Do you like being around people who have powerful positions, listening to and watching them?
____	____	10. Do you feel you can see power around you but that you don't have it yourself or at least you have very little?
____	____	11. Are you aware of specific skills and knowledge that you are striving to develop in order to progress in your career?
____	____	12. Are you just beginning to find out who you are inside?
____	____	13. Do you seek information and advice from as many people as possible?
____	____	14. Do you feel trapped or stuck in your job as a result of a boss who isn't interested in your development?
____	____	15. Are you an apprentice?

Yes answers indicate that you identify with this stage.

Chapter 2
Stage Two: Power by Association

Magical

Key Question: Who made you feel worthwhile before you were 25, other than your parents? What did they do? How did it affect you?

What Is Stage Two Like?

Do you remember Star Wars? When the young Luke Skywalker was learning to be a Jedi knight he was an apprentice to the wise Yoda. Luke tried to model his behavior after that of his mentor, and his training took him on a long adventure, to a new place within himself and within the larger community. The things that he longed to be capable of doing, like fighting successfully with the dark side, looked magical when he first observed it; but later, as his apprenticeship moved along, he realized what he was being asked to do and who he was being asked to be. His apprenticeship is a good example of what it feels like to be at Stage Two. Luke doesn't have the power yet, or at least he doesn't feel the power, and there are things he needs to learn in order to live into his power. He has power because of who he is associated with and because of the journey that he is on.

Stage Two people do not have much external or internal power yet, but they can feel the power moving through their office or through their hands. They are apprentices to power, which is similar to the apprentice phase of a craft or a trade. They just can't grasp power yet. It is elusive, like magic. So power manifests itself at Stage Two as magic, not quite real or yet available. At Stage Two we are not at all sure how those other people got power, nor are we sure what we would do with it once we have it, but it certainly looks desirable and worth seeking.

Thankfully Stage Two people love to learn. They can absorb things, ideas or techniques like a sponge. In fact, even if they have been at other home stages, they may deliberately change jobs or assignments so they can get a new challenge and feel like they are learning new things again.

Stage Two people believe that certain people in the organization have the power, usually defined as control and influence, and they hope that these people will notice them, lead them, nurture them, and reward them. For people who have been victims in Stage One, and have taken back their power, this can be a "coming out" stage in which they genuinely learn from other people and discover more about themselves. In this stage, people tend to emulate mentors or role models, hoping that by being around them, the power may rub off a little. This may be overt like the dress-for-success syndrome, or it may be entirely subconscious. It might even take the form of intense loyalty to the person or the organization, like hero-worship.

Bosses take on more significance for Stage Two people than for those in other stages and can have the most long-term positive or negative influence. Since this is such a formative stage, your boss can be very active in a teaching or coaching role and can guide you into developmental opportunities on the job and elsewhere. Supportive bosses at this stage may be the most significant factor in whether or not you pass through the stage. Early in my counseling career I had a supervisor who really believed in me and wanted me to grow as much as possible while working for him. He always gave me cases I didn't think I could handle and then worked with me each step of the way to help me gain confidence. At that point in my career the more responsibility he gave me, along with his support, the more I learned.

On the other hand, non-supportive bosses (distant, self-serving, afraid, unfair, racist, or sexist) can cause you to wither developmentally and to start feeling insecure or self-critical. They can erode your self-confidence by subtly giving the impression that you are invisible or not capable. There is nothing worse than being ignored when you are in need of development or training on the job. Every effort should be made to work with these bosses through suggestions, employee relations, or heart-to-heart discussions. If nothing seems to work, the person at Stage Two must consider finding another boss at some point.

The spiral concept of power is especially applicable at Stage Two. The second or sixth or tenth time we re-enter this stage it feels very different from what it felt like the first time we experienced it. We know that we will not stay here forever, that this is a learning stage, and that we will get more power eventually.

Having valuable mentors is one of the finest experiences of Stage Two. They have appeared, like angels, at low points in my life to either guide, direct, or challenge me. I remember vividly the mentors I've had over the years. One early mentor, my college advisor, was so instrumental in my life, she actually changed the way I think. Once I went out to Oregon to visit her after her retirement. I was discussing my newest writing project with her. After hearing about it, she asked me, "Do you really want to write this book?" I had never been asked that question before. I thought for a moment and said, candidly, "No." And she asked me the obvious question, "Well, what book do you want to write?" I told her and that was the beginning of my journey to my most exciting writing ever.

Another mentor helped me gain the confidence to start my own business. He provided the space for me to teach my first seminars. All I had to do was recruit the people! Other mentors have asked me the right questions, helped me heal from devastating experiences, and shown me a much larger perspective on the world. Most of the time they teach me most effectively by the way in which they live their lives. Behavior speaks louder than words and I "listen" well. Some day I hope I can be the kind of mentor to others that these wonderful mentors have been to me.

I revisit Stage Two more often than any other stage. In fact, it is my favorite stage. That's because I love to learn. And I like change. And I get bored easily. Every several years I take a new direction in my work or I write on a new topic. I experience this stage once again each time I embark on something new. I feel new and insecure. I am eager and afraid. I feel awkward and full of anticipation. And I learn by my experiences and my questions.

Several years ago I took up drawing. In my fear of the unknown I brought a ruler to class, in order to make each drawing exact, since I couldn't imagine recreating an object or picture any other way. No one else in the class had rulers. They just drew. I looked around and felt anxious. I wondered how they knew how to draw so easily. Where were they getting that skill? Was it innate? Would I ever be able to do that too? My teacher, bless her heart, never said anything about my ruler. She just encouraged me to draw using it as I wished. Gradually my confidence grew until I left my ruler at home.

The only danger for me in Stage Two is that it becomes too comfortable. And I can get stuck here because I like the learner role and I have gotten tired of taking risks. Taking risks and responsibility move me to Stage Three.

If leadership, stated very simply, is the way in which people get things done, then people at Stage Two lead by modeling others. By this I mean that they look to others' leadership style or behavior and try to practice it. Because it may not yet be their own internalized style, they suffer from inconsistency and lack of inner confidence. But they are sincere and want to lead, even if leading frightens them.

Some examples of possible Stage Two occupations or situations are trade apprentices, associates in law offices, instructors and assistant professors, marketing assistants or assistant product managers, secretaries to groups or individuals, seminary interns or assistant ministers, women who are married to men more powerful than they, men who are married to women more powerful than they, bureaucrats, people in human resources, appointed officials, new counselors in human service agencies, engineering assistants, or cub reporters. It can be dangerous to describe people's stages by their occupational level because people at the same job can be at different stages from each other. But frequently people in these jobs feel that their jobs prescribe their stage. It means they must work harder to move to another stage internally.

In addition, anytime people move from one job to another, or from one career to another, or from one relationship to another—even though it's their third or fourth move—they still go through an apprenticeship stage, in which they are learning the ropes. Anyone who's decided on a particular field and is willing to learn and grow to gain full admittance to that field is in the apprenticeship stage. Apprenticeship involves learning a new language, a new set of assumptions, and new behaviors. It means cultivating new people, joining new associations, adopting new skills. It means gaining respect in a whole new arena.

Characteristics of People at Stage Two

Apprentices

A good description of this stage is the apprenticeship or mentorship stage, in which people are learning the roles, trying on new behaviors, testing assumptions, wearing new uniforms, trying out skills, exploring possibilities, setting up dreams, and beginning self-exploration, all as a result of watching and working for others. For some, it's the first time they've really been recognized for being an individual instead of one of the crowd. As apprentices they are open to others' teaching, influenced by others' ideas, able to absorb and grasp new things. They may even reach out for more experiences, because at this stage, they are eager to learn as much as they can and build a solid foundation.

Many now have a clearer sense of their own identity in the organization than they had at Stage One, perhaps even a sense of belonging. Sometimes the belonging feeling is aimed more at a leader than an organization. Some leaders are such strong personalities that they almost demand a following of loyal supporters; and there are many people who like to be part of a loyal contingency. This is most apparent in sports, politics, and show business, but it is also true of visionary leaders who have ideas that others want to help them fulfill, whether it is in education, religion, architecture, business, social work, or government.

And at still other times the belonging feeling may be aimed at a belief system such as security, political aspiration, religion, or love. Along with the infatuation with power comes the disillusionment phase that people experience in Stage Two when they discover that their mentor makes mistakes, their boss is self-serving, their security falls apart, their religion has no easy answers, their politics fail, or their love fades. This is all part of the process, part of the understanding of power. And this too shall pass, as the saying goes.

For many people in large hierarchical organizations this apprentice idea has become a life-long learning philosophy. Since there are fewer jobs to move up to as you progress, at some point creative people choose a different strategy, that of gaining their identity through broadening—moving laterally and learning as many new things or having as many new experiences as possible. On each new job or with each new experience they strive to learn as much as they can to become skilled. Then when the apprenticeship stage is over they gradually find themselves getting bored and wanting to learn something new again. They gradually lose interest in moving up, and they find new strategies for moving around, to satisfy their curiosity for new learning. It also keeps them renewed. A new philosophy of advancement for these organizations could be this: that every five years everyone moves at least two chairs to the left!!

Learning the "Culture"

The first few experiences of Stage Two as a home stage can be exciting, scary, and fun, but also tentative. It is a newness stage as well as a loss-of-innocence stage. Along with the acquisition of skills and techniques comes a realization later in the stage that there exist rules, games, barriers, hidden information, informal networks, and a bigger world. At Stage Two people are mostly operating in their own department with a limited group of people, a closely defined job description, and little job discretion or access to information about the larger organization. They gradually begin to see that there are many other departments, fields, and organizations, and they recognize that they are in very circumscribed jobs. That is not bad, but it opens their eyes to a much broader world of people, ideas, and contacts.

This is the stage at which being in a network of similar people—a professional association, trade association, women's or men's network, athletic club, Jaycees, or a golf club—starts to make sense, if for no other reason than support and perspective. Many organizations now have groups for women or people of color started by employees for the purpose of self-education, information sharing, and support. In order for these groups to be successful it helps to have the support of senior management and to have people from many parts of the organization as members. These groups generally have their own governance structure and are self-supporting, not sponsored by the management.

One of the issues at Stage Two that is definitely clearer for white males than it is for women and people of color is the issue of learning the culture. White men experience this stage as an uncomfortable place because they have been primed to get on to Stage Three. They are eager to pay their dues and get on with real work. Women and people of color more often are learning a new culture at Stage Two. It's like going to a foreign country and trying to fit in. So the learning role is especially critical for newcomers, and bad experiences at this stage can stunt their personal and professional growth. That is why a wise supervisor or manager is so important.

Dependent on Supervisor/Leader

Supervisors and managers are the main or usual source of information for people at Stage Two. For that reason, employees depend on the supervisor's knowledge of the system in order to function successfully. That is why it is important to work for a good boss during the apprentice stage. (If you learn golf from a duffer, it takes a lot longer to unlearn your bad habits later.) People who have good managers tend to outperform those who don't, and they are more satisfied with their work, according to several management development studies.

But some people get so attached to their first manager that they become fearful of ever moving on. That situation may work well for a while, but at some point the manager may leave, retire, be passed over, become disillusioned or ill, and then Stage Two people can find themselves in a real crisis. This is particularly apparent for administrative assistants who move with the same person throughout their career. They are intensely loyal, but when their boss leaves, no one knows quite what to do with them.

As I said earlier, this is a time in which one's boss is central, so it sets up a difficult situation for people who want to progress but feel forever like apprentices, even to a good boss. One man I talked with had worked with the same political figure for twenty years, ever since he had joined the man's staff out of college. In his mid-forties himself, he foresaw the possible retirement of his boss, so he spent a year thinking, reading, and talking to other people about job possibilities. It was frightening because, even though he was highly respected, he had never had to wage a job campaign for himself before. He moved to another state and became head of a non-profit educational organization and is happy and increasingly confident. He still keeps in touch with his former boss and friend, but he has made the necessary break.

I have also seen this happen with graduate students who stay in school for ten years studying with the same professor because of a good working relationship and perhaps the fear of the next phase, that of finding their own niche. Others stay on the staff of a well-known person acting as his or her right-hand person for years, making the person look good and getting satisfaction in the staff role. Many enter a very uncomfortable phase after a time, combining loyalty with some confusion and perhaps resentment. They begin to realize just how much they are needed and how much of the work they do for the other person, who appears to be reaping most of the benefits. Sooner or later they leave, either to join another organization at a different level (on their own merits), or they start something on their own. This is particularly true in consulting firms, political staffs, advertising agencies, small businesses, and counseling agencies.

New Self-Awareness

Internally, Stage Twos are just beginning the first phases of self-exploration, trying on the one hand to distinguish themselves from others and, on the other hand, learning how they are alike in their struggles. They also learn their strengths and limitations as they relate to good performance on the job. Given the definition of personal power as the combination of externally derived recognition and action, as well as internally-induced reflection and wisdom, Twos are more externally than internally powerful, but are beginning to develop a stronger ego as a result of recognizing their competence and skill.

This can be an excellent time for Twos who want to open themselves up to new awareness for the first time and try out new behaviors. It is best done within a known or relatively safe environment, one that allows for mistakes and sees them as learning tools. In fact, not for a few power stages will mistakes be seen again as good learning experiences. That is why membership in trade or professional associations, health, social, or athletic clubs is so useful for Twos. They are good places to practice personal power.

Some Stage Two people go around hunting for advice from as many sources as they can possibly find. In fact, they go from one to another, looking for ways to transform themselves into success models. They go from experience to experience, trying to conform in order to be accepted or admired. Perhaps we can all identify with the intense desire to be loved, or at least admired, by others for what we are.

This need became abundantly clear to me during my single days following my divorce when I was once again faced with the issues of dating. My need to be cared about was as strong as my repulsion for the singles clubs. I was caught in a dilemma: Do I try to meet people or just decide to remain single forever? Of course, at that time I saw no middle ground. After eight unforgettable months of "dating," during which I generated some life experiences I can only laugh at now, I decided to give it up and spend the time on developing myself into the kind of person I wanted to become. I became much more relaxed and relieved not to be in such confusion, and soon meeting people was a secondary issue.

A lot of people at this stage take the advice of other people rather than trust themselves. The following fable adapted from Aesop, describes the possible results.

A Man, a Boy, and a Donkey

A man and his son were walking on a road toward town with their donkey. They met a man who chastised the son for making his poor father walk when the donkey could carry him. So the son encouraged his father to get on the donkey and off they went.

Soon after, they met another man on the road who chastised the father for making his young son walk while he rode the donkey. So the father set his son on the donkey with him and they continued on.

After traveling a few miles, they came to a bridge and met a group of people who chastised them both for riding on the poor donkey who was old and weak. So they decided to get off and carry the donkey.

In their attempts to lift the donkey to their shoulders they got too close to the edge of the bridge, and the donkey toppled into the river and drowned.

People who live their lives according to the prescriptions of others run the risk of losing their "donkey."

Self-exploration can take the form of volunteering for new assignments on the job that will test and push you into new or risky skill areas. One young woman set up an internship with her supervisor's help so she could find out what a first-line supervisor in another department did, thus helping her decide what kinds of skills she would need to prepare herself for that job eventually. Job-related self-exploration can also include reading, conversations, and classes or workshops on topics that will help you learn more about yourself personally. These might include areas such as values, communication, skills, life planning, personal growth, assertiveness, family dynamics, attitudes, personality styles, and group dynamics. Many people say that these experiences of finding out more about who they can be, open their eyes for the first time to the ways in which they defeat themselves or hold themselves back in the organization. They also find out that they have many more good qualities than they have given themselves credit for.

Still another way to find out about yourself is to put yourself into environments in which you are the stranger or the inexperienced one. This could include travel to other countries where languages and customs are very different from your own, travel to the inner regions of your psyche through counseling, or travel to the wilderness or the mountains to explore the world around you and the wilderness within. My belief is that the strong urge people have to explore canyons, woods, mountains, and rivers brings them closer to nature and thus closer to their own inner nature. Thoreau said so wisely, "Dwell as near as possible to the channel in which your life flows."

Many Twos experience the career dilemma of feeling stalled in the organization for a variety of reasons: the age of their boss, the number of positions available, the unavailability of further education or training, their own unwillingness to move or change jobs at the time, or politics. For whatever reason, they probably will not move to any positions of increased responsibility for a long time. In many companies, this is becoming more the norm than the exception. When people feel stuck, they often begin to give up, to be disappointed, or to lose energy in their work because of the loss of motivation. When this occurs the whole organization suffers, and the individual suffers the most. This problem occurs primarily because people have become too dependent upon the organization for their development, their recognition, or their self-esteem.

One of the most important things people can do for themselves at Stage Two (or that organizations can assist people in doing) when the stuck feeling occurs is to continue to develop themselves personally and professionally on their jobs, and more importantly, outside the organization. While it may be impossible to chair an important committee inside the organization, it may be very possible to become the program chair for a professional association or to work on a community action project. Or it could be an opportune time to develop hobbies that are self-fulfilling. If another degree may not be useful, then further broadening of oneself through liberal arts classes or just reading widely can be a major developmental move toward becoming a broader thinker. If the external skills and behaviors are as developed as they can be, then the internal realm may be fertile territory for exploration. Knowing oneself better may result in different career moves, like moving laterally, moving down temporarily, or moving across to other divisions instead of just moving up in the organization as I alluded to earlier. Changing the attitudes of people about upward mobility—which presently means success—will be very slow in coming.

Two specific groups of Stage Two people illustrate how differently people view themselves at the same stage of apprenticeship. I call the first one the "sky's the limit" group. These Stage Two apprentices firmly believe that Stage Two is but a brief stopover on their way to the top. Some new MBAs, for instance, or fast trackers in the computer field feel they are actually being "reined in" by having to learn the ropes. Those in fast-growing organizations all think they will make it to the top, or that they will become wealthy at a young age because that's what has happened to their predecessors. At Stage Two they can be viewed as training for the stiffly competitive stage to follow in which they find out whether they "make the cut" or not. Observed from the outside, it appears that the young thoroughbreds are racing each other for their shot at the big time a few years hence. They are enthusiastic young idealists who are out to make a mark on the world, seeing this stage as the starting gate, and waiting impatiently for the starting bell. For many of them this is the most exciting, though perhaps not the most satisfying, time of their careers.

The other group of strong apprentices appears in the professions of law and medicine. The newcomers are tested, tried, and then initiated into the "brother/sisterhood" with all the long-standing norms, values, and privileges associated with membership. Those in the middle of the initiation sometimes complain bitterly about the treatment they are being subjected to, but as soon as it is over they seem less eager to fight for change, and some even watch enthusiastically as the next group is subjected to the same treatment.

Spirituality and the Spiritual Connection to Work at Stage Two

At this stage spirituality develops out of living a life of discipleship. This includes learning about the spiritual journey you are on and learning about the Holy or your Higher Power. We apprentice ourselves to others now, taking in everything we can to grow in our spiritual life. Our meaning comes from belonging to groups of like-minded people who teach us about our spirituality. We seek answers from our leader or a cause, feeling secure and right about our faith journey. We are excited and energetic, eager to engage with others and to keep learning.

We would like a concrete connection between our work and our faith journey. We want to learn and then share our experience by serving our Higher Power within our own group, our community, or our work place. We strive to study, build our skills, and get support from others. Our exact faith-work connection differs whether we come from conservative, mainline, Western, Eastern, or liberal traditions. Examples are working on justice issues at work, striving to use our work talents wisely, being creative on our jobs, witnessing to others about our faith, striving to be ethical, focusing on prayer or meditation, working within religious organizations, finding our right niche, or attending meetings of spiritual co-workers.

Susan is an example of this stage. She is a nurse in a children's hospital. She has been thinking for a long time about how to bring her faith and work closer together. One day following the surgery of a child, the parents were experiencing fears about the child's recovery. She suddenly realized that she could pray quietly over the child when she was attending to her. She decided to hold the whole family in her prayers as well. Now this comes routinely for her and it makes her work much more rewarding.

Mark is a financial planner. He feels his greatest witness of his spirituality is to be a competent and honest professional, treating each client with utmost respect and care. Each morning he spends quiet time asking his Higher Power to guide him through the day. He has a calmer day and feels it helps him view his clients' needs more clearly.

The Shadow of Stage Two

Recyclers

I see another group of people who are quite different from the "sky's the limit" group and represent the shadow of Stage Two. This group I call the "recyclers." They enter a career and try to take on the norms, behaviors, and skills of that job or profession. They find people who they think are successful and try to be around them; they use the jargon of the field, even dress the part, yet they do not "make it" in that field. They do not become accepted, get promoted, or become well-enough recognized. In short, they fail to catch the spark. Or perhaps they get impatient with the process too soon. They move on, continually looking to each new career or job as a magic wand that will somehow touch them and make them satisfied. They have not discovered that a career does not make a person—a person makes a career. They are confused about who they are and how their skills, values, and interests fit into various careers. If the magic doesn't happen, they leave to pursue the next possibility, like Don Quixote chasing windmills. During this erratic process, they fail to accumulate knowledge and experience, and they see no need for behavior change.

We could look at this another way as well. If careers were hypothetically made up of four levels: (l) apprentice, (2) practitioner, (3) expert, and (4) muse, recyclers would always be at level one, unwilling to commit their time, energy, or money to move to the next level. Perhaps they fear success. Or perhaps they fear the self-exploration necessary to find out who they really are and where they fit. The cause of their discontent may go back as far as childhood, to traumatic experiences and messages or early school memories. Clearly, it is a complex and frustrating situation. Most recyclers are not hiding their dilemma, even though they may think they are. Other people can see their patterns more clearly than they can, but others can't do anything about it. Recyclers are not unskilled, just mismatched in jobs or careers that are not congruent with who they are.

The Counselor, Ray, an Example of a Recycler

> I'm one of those people who could never decide what I would be when I grew up! In fact, I wondered if I would ever grow up. First, I was a seventh grade art teacher. I did that for three years and thought I had found my life's work, but then the sameness of teaching got to me. I also had the feeling of being tied to the school all day with little adult conversation. The third year, the seventh grade class was made up of fifty percent delinquents, it seemed. So I got out and decided to try selling for a while. There was more money and lots of freedom. That's what I thought. Well, I was selling educational materials on a salary plus commission basis and the pressure to make salary was enormous. And did I get to travel, to every school district in the state! It didn't take long to realize I wasn't cut out to be on the road. I liked the idea of making money, though, and selling is the way to do that. So I switched to insurance sales. I took all the training and then I beat the bushes, as they say, for clients. I called everyone I had ever known. The turndowns were hard but I kept on going. In fact, I had a really good record for number of appointments booked. But I had a lot of trouble in that first year actually closing the deal, asking for the sale. I was embarrassed to tell anyone, so I said the appointments were missed. I felt trapped by that mess so I decided to switch. Besides, a real deal came along.
>
> A guy I met was starting a new venture. He was going to produce wildlife reprints that he claimed every office in the state would buy if they could just see them. He promised me salary plus lots of extra bonuses if I would give it a try. It sounded better than educational material to me so I took it on. Little did I know the volume he was expecting in the first six months. It would have been impossible for a superman. After six months and what I thought were good sales, he closed operations and there I was, out in the cold. (It was February in Michigan.) Now I'm trying something new that might not pay as much money but it's more secure. I'm working nights and going to school days to learn to be a counselor. I'm not sure how I'll like it but it's sure worth a try.

Recyclers can be found in any occupation. By their very nature they seem to be always looking for themselves outside of themselves.

The recyclers should not be confused with people who seek new challenges and new levels of accomplishment on their jobs and in each new career. These people have a wide variety of interests and enjoy entering into new challenges. They need variety and change to keep them fresh. They tend to do the job well and to complete their goals or to reach a certain level, and then they are bored, needing the next challenge. They are more like entrepreneurs within organizations, higher risk-takers than most people.

Chameleons

Chameleons, people who shift their behavior to the prevailing mode, no matter what it is, are another example of the shadow of Stage Two. They have very little consistency in who *they* are. They hurt other people, sometimes unconsciously, by not appearing to be trustworthy. They gauge their worth by how much they are like others who they admire. There is emptiness within. In fact, sometimes you can sense the inner vacuum in their eyes. It feels to the viewer like there is nothing behind their eyes. They are confused and hurting.

I knew a person who tried to find himself by wearing the trademarks of his mentors. He dressed and talked like several different people. The problem was, no one knew who *he* was. On him the mannerisms were not authentic because they didn't fit him, but he had convinced himself that this acting was necessary in order to be accepted. No wonder he was surprised when people had a hard time trusting him.

Naïve People

Intensely naïve people are yet a third shadow manifestation of Stage Two. They resist the loss of innocence and view the world as if it were already the way it should be—good, just, and beautiful. They are not willing to acknowledge and grapple with the other side of life, which includes evil, unfairness, and ugliness. They may seem like very sweet, child-like, happy people, but one gets a funny feeling that deep inside of these people there is a great explosion or a rude awakening just waiting to happen.

Stage Five people may behave in some ways that are similar to the "innocent" person but with a completely different base—that of understanding the evil in all of us but choosing to go on trusting and living—with eyes wide open. I elaborate on these similarities and differences in the chapter on Stage Five.

Let's Meet Some People at Stage Two

Lenny, the Police Officer

Ever since I could remember, I've dreamed of being a policeman. Every time the kids in the neighborhood played cops and robbers I was there in the role of the cop, protector of the neighbors against the tyranny of the lawless. I felt it was my duty in life to be strong and to help others. As soon as I graduated from high school I went to school in police science. It was the happiest day of my life when I was accepted as a rookie patrolman in my city. I remember wanting to jump up and down, but I knew it wouldn't fit the image. Well, I set out to be the very best patrolman in the precinct and did it with zest. I thought you just did all the things we read and talked about in school. I had another think coming! It's not quite the same to read about domestic calls where there are weapons involved as it is to be on the front lawn of a home where a man has just beaten his wife and is threatening you with an old shotgun if you don't leave. So much for trying to get the couple to calm down and talk things over. Oh, I don't mean I didn't learn a lot in school, but it's just more real on the streets. And it can be really boring a lot of the time too. We're rarely in chase scenes or gun battles, or even in grave danger. It's just that anything could happen at any time, and we have to be constantly alert.

Lucky for me, one of the more senior officers on the force took me under his wing the first year and taught me some of the rules before I had to learn them the hard way. I did have one very difficult lesson, though, which I will never forget (or live down). I was assigned to a stakeout, to keep tabs on a suspect that we had been watching for weeks. I was alone in my unmarked car just having to while away the time. Well, it started to get pretty warm in the car and I got a little bit too comfortable. I started to have a harder and harder time keeping my focus on the house. My eyes were very heavy. The next thing I knew I was shocked back to reality by a tap on my window. It was three hours later. The suspect had been picked up and no one could get me by radio, thus causing all kinds of worry. I was embarrassed and frightened by my mistake, falling asleep on the job. What would this mean for my career, for my future? Well, I did get reprimanded and lectured to by my sergeant, and my older buddy explained what to expect and how to act in the future. But the razzing from the other officers was the worst. Lullaby Lenny they called me. Thank God my mistake didn't put anyone in danger. Needless to say, it's never happened since, but it was undoubtedly the most memorable event of my rookie year.

In this example we learn the value of making mistakes and learning from them while in the role of apprentice.

Jane, the Fledgling Photographer

For a very long time I have wanted to be a photographer and take beautiful pictures. The only mechanical thing I knew about a camera was to point and shoot. I took infrequent snapshots. I wanted to do more. I wanted pictures that were not only beautiful, but that also told stories of a thousand words. I signed up for Photography 1 at the local college.

The class was an art class. We would compose pictures, develop our own film, and print our enlargements. I strongly considered dropping the class. How would I conquer f-stops and shutter speeds? How would I put film onto a reel in total darkness?

Gone were all the illusions of spontaneity that come with point and click. Gone were all the expectations of an easy, fun-filled summer of taking instantaneously beautiful pictures. I felt as though I was in water over my head and going under. I didn't know how to rewind my first roll of film and exposed it to the light. I put the film on the developing reels incorrectly but learned to pull the reel apart and start over.

Gradually the mechanics made sense. I was learning—learning from the instructor, my classmates, and from trial and error. My confidence grew. At the end of the course I knew I would never be able to take a snapshot again. Now I compose my pictures. Now I can read a picture worth a thousand words.

This example shows how difficult it is to put oneself in the role of a new learner when you are used to a different kind of performing.

Martha, the Assistant Professor

It is abundantly clear to me which stage I am in at the university. The only power I have is my identification with my discipline of history and with my department. Since I have not yet received tenure, the main activities I engage in are those that will help me to get there, teaching, publishing, and committee work. I feel almost as much an apprentice now as I did when I was writing my dissertation, except now my salary is a wee bit better. I know my department

> associates are willing to help me, but they also will be involved in my tenure decision. And if I don't make it, I must leave. So I feel pulled between wanting to do a better job at teaching, which I love, and having to keep up with research and committee work, which I am less fond of, having had my fill for a while after my dissertation. And historical research in my specialty, Tibetan manuscripts, is not very applicable to Introductory History 101. I know people say that you must get some visibility in order to have a more favorable tenure position, but it feels like I am being told to be excellent in all three areas (teaching, research, service) at a very early stage in my career. I have a lot in my favor, though. My educational background is superb, from one of the best schools in the country, and my department chair seems to be supportive. All I can do now is press forward with my work and make a decision about the next phase of my career when I know about tenure in a year or two.

Martha is a good example of a professional who knows the written rules but is not yet knowledgeable about the unwritten ones or the politics of tenure.

Joyce, the Computer Apprentice

> I feel like soaring, I'm so excited. Here I am, young and eager to learn with nothing stopping me. Right now I'm in the technical side of the computer area of our company, and I'm learning new things every day. I have moved up two grades in fourteen months, and my future looks fabulous. It took me a few years to figure out that computers would be my career, but now all I have to do is put in a lot of time and effort to finish my degree in computer science. That's my next step, and I'm starting back to school this fall, three nights a week at the state university.
>
> I know I can do it, thanks to the wonderful support of my supervisor who is also my mentor. She's really responsible for my new lease on the future. She pushes me and encourages me to go beyond what I'm doing and to try new things, knowing I will make mistakes. And I've made some over the last few years. But she says that's how I learn, as long as I don't repeat them too often. She is such a fantastic manager that I'd like to be just like her myself someday. She is energetic, respected, bright, and savvy. In fact, I plan to work for her as we both rise right to the top. But that will take a few years yet!

Joyce feels like she has really found herself, thanks to her supervisor who is also her mentor.

Sam, the Assistant Director

> The economy certainly has a way of changing my career plans. Two years ago I thought I was next in line for a Jewish Community Center director's job, only to find myself on permanent hold because of the cutbacks in social service funding. Everyone became security conscious all of a sudden, and no one moved at all, not even to retire. Well, I thought about the situation for quite awhile, considered my other career options, and decided on a path that I am very pleased about, now that I can see its effects.
>
> I decided to develop myself as much as I could additionally on my job through skill-based seminars and directed conversations with my boss. At the same time I chose to move into a few select community activities, such as serving on the board of a community health agency and joining a citizen's information group. I also made a conscious effort to meet personally with all the long-term members of our community center to get to know them better.
>
> None of these outside experiences seems to be directly related to my job, but I think I am showing more leadership already after one year on the health agency board than I could get the opportunity to show in my own center. I'm learning new things about myself and I'm meeting some fabulous people. Now, as a result of people I've met and ideas we've shared, I not only have a new vision for our community center, but I have other possibilities for my own future. All this happened when I thought I was stuck.

Sam is a good example of someone who used his own "stuckness" as a way to renew himself in his career.

Moving to Stage Three

Not everyone wants to move to another stage nor should they. I have known people over the years who are satisfied and happy in their lives and work who really have decided that the amount of responsibility they have at their stage is about what they can handle and still maintain the balance in their lives. A free-lance legal secretary comes to mind. She likes her work, is very competent, has the opportunity to move to a variety of work settings, makes enough money to travel, has close family ties, and wouldn't change for anything. She has struggled to arrive at her decision, thinking she should be doing something else, but she knows her needs, energy level, interests, limits, and aspirations, and she is content. Her hobby of oil painting brings her some extra cash and her free-lance status allows her time to paint and travel. She is developing more on the inside than on the outside. Single working parents with young children often feel that they do not want to take any extra time away from the family for a few years so they choose to put their career in second place for a period of time. One young musician turned down an internship with a fine chamber orchestra in a distant city for love! He decided to stay in his present job and spend more time with his girlfriend.

We all make choices and live with them. The major factor to address in thinking about moving or staying in our present stage is whether or not we can accept ourselves or be satisfied at our stage. There is a propensity in all of us to grow and change but at different rates and at different times in our lives. Some people push themselves (or allow themselves to be pushed) faster than they can handle. We call it getting in over our heads. Others do not push themselves at all and end up being stuck forever. Both can be detrimental.

The crisis that people experience in moving to Stage Three is one of confidence. They know they are doing a good job or that they have certain skills, techniques, or knowledge to do their jobs. They may feel fairly secure or safe in the shadow of their boss, spouse, or mentor. Or they may be trapped in their job with an unsupportive boss or little information about options. The questions in the back of their minds when they are presented with opportunities are, Can I do it? Will I let my boss or mentor down? Am I confident enough of myself to take the risk? Do other people believe in me more than I believe in myself? Will I be able to compete? Am I in a rut? Is this a balloon that will burst? Do I want to make the investment in myself? If I wait, will someone do it for me?

Moving to Stage Three requires you to learn self-confidence and how to take risks on both the personal and the work side. In addition, moving to Stage Three will mean taking on more responsibility for yourself and making a bid for recognition in the organization. It could mean gaining visibility, taking risks, volunteering for new things, competing, being evaluated against others more regularly, working longer hours, achieving more, learning the games and politics of organizational life, getting degrees, leaving the cocoon, depending less on other people, investing in yourself, proving yourself, possibly leaving your boss/mentor, and being exposed to the realities of organizational life. Many of the popular books on the market about power are written for people who want to be Threes. They observe Stage Three people who are in positions of power, describe their behavior, and encourage us to emulate that model. Only in the last few years has there been a selection of books that encourage behavior beyond Stage Three.

For most women, the movement from Stage Two to Stage Three is the most difficult move in the entire personal power model. For men, the most difficult is the move from Stage Three to Stage Four. Stage Two is the stage at which women, traditionally, are most comfortable. It can be satisfying as well as secure. One can be competent and responsible without having to be in control or to control others. You can just work for good people. The dilemma at this point for women who want to move up is whether they want to do what is necessary: develop their masculine side in order to successfully navigate the somewhat tempestuous waters of Stage Three. Women need to understand their own masculine behaviors and how they can be useful in the organization. The most obvious example is assertiveness, including the ability to say no to or disagree with colleagues or bosses. Other examples are making decisions on one's own, confronting conflict straight on, showing individual achievement, not showing outward emotion in times of crisis, competing with other people, keeping a distance, being rational and analytical, quantitative in thinking, being task-, fact-, and detail-oriented, directed, short-run-oriented, active, verbal, linear, scientific, orderly, objective, and critical. These masculine characteristics seem to come easier to most men and must be deliberately learned or reinforced by women who want to be able to use them. Although women as individuals are socialized differently from each other to a certain extent, we still do have many characteristics in common, some that come much easier for most of us than they do for most men. We will call these the feminine characteristics, recognizing that men, too, can have some of them without being a female.

Many women balk at having to learn to flex the atrophied muscles of their masculine side, saying that being feminine is fine and they don't want to buy into the male-dominated behaviors. They would like to leap mysteriously into Stage Four, or preferably Stage Five, and spare themselves the pain of Stage Three. And they are justified in their reluctance. Far too many women have flirted with their masculine side only to let it completely overpower them, turning them into "honorary men" and losing the essence of what it means to be feminine. The pendulum can swing too far, and for many women it does for a while, a most uncomfortable period of time. Some of my own most embarrassing and awkward moments were those in which I was holding on so tightly to my masculine image that I almost smothered. I remember telling a business client once that I preferred to do business in a certain way, and that if that didn't suit him, perhaps he needed to find someone else. He found someone else.

For "honorary men" like me at that time, the transition from Stage Two to Three is not very difficult. That is because we already have developed the masculine side of ourselves. Obviously, I am not advocating that women become men and accept all the norms of the male-dominated organization. But in order to enter and move through Stage Three and towards more leadership in the organization for the future and for the long run, women need to accept and be able to use masculine characteristics when appropriate, understanding the role those behaviors play in organizational life, while never losing touch with the feminine. I will further develop this theme and introduce the concept of flexibility in sex role behavior in the chapters on Stages Four and Five and in the chapter "Women and Power."

The other more critical task for women in moving to Stage Three is to strengthen their ego. An insightful colleague in the Netherlands describes this as the major issue for women in their self-development and calls the result a "grown-up ego." The self-confidence required at Stage Three comes most satisfyingly from within. It cannot be superimposed from outside for long.

One other task at the juncture of Stages Two and Three is developing confidence in yourself. Find out who you are, what makes you tick, what you are good at, what you like, and what others like about you. Try out new behaviors and find out what fits you. Take the risk to leave aside what doesn't fit you. Take other risks, like asking for what you want, volunteering for assignments, putting your own ideas into your work. Spread your wings so you can fly at Stage Three. I have a piece of wood sculpture by Brian Andreas in my home, made to look roughly like a bird, but with a human face painted on it. It reminds me of some women I know. It says, "For a long time, she flew only when she thought no one else was watching."

Sometimes these two tasks, developing your own confidence and taking on your masculine side, seem insurmountable. I can tell you the task is not insurmountable but it will take time, support, and practice. That is why it is the most difficult transition in the power model for women.

This poem, written by Veronica Shoffstall, was given to me by a woman in an organization who realized the struggle that people go through to find themselves amidst all the pushes and pulls of contemporary life. It represents the struggle to move beyond Stage Two.

After a While

After a while you learn
the subtle difference between
holding a hand and chaining a soul
and you learn
that love doesn't mean leaning
and company doesn't always mean security.

And you begin to learn
that kisses aren't contracts
and presents aren't promises
and you begin to accept your defeats
with your head up and your eyes ahead
with the grace of woman, not the grief of a child
and you learn
to build all your roads on today
because tomorrow's ground is
too uncertain for plans
and futures have a way of falling down
in mid-flight.
After a while you learn
that even sunshine burns
if you get too much
so you plant your own garden
and decorate your own soul
instead of waiting for someone
to bring you flowers.
And you learn that you really can endure
you really are strong
you really do have worth
and you learn
and you learn
with every goodbye, you learn...

The dilemma of Stage Two men is somewhat different from that of Stage Two women. From the perspective of the organization, men must accept and buy into the norms of power, control, and the cultural pressures to achieve and move into Stage Three, or they will run the risk of feeling alienated by the society. Most men are so schooled into the image of achievement that they don't even question it. They just learn a trade or go to school to become a satisfied and successful employee, manager, boss, or expert—whatever is within their grasp. For men, the greatest loss of ego and loss of face would be never getting to Stage Three.

Doing Stage Three differently is a reality for another group of men who grew up rejecting the prevailing masculine norms as their only option. They are, as the title of the book by James Kavanaugh suggests, "men too gentle to live among wolves." They grew up with the space age, women's liberation, and gay rights among other things. They have been faced with a difficult dilemma: either losing face and being deemed failures by society if they accept the less-than-competitive nature they have cultivated, or being disillusioned and unhappy in the traditional roles passed on by their parents. They are men whom I would describe as "caught in-between." They do not subscribe to the acceptable norms of men nor do they consistently use their masculine behaviors in relations with others off or on the job. We put men into tighter boxes than we do women today. These men have just lived through a formative time in which their values were developed differently, and so they want different things from life. As a result they may provide some vital links between the traditional male model and emerging male options.

Listed below are activities that may help people move from Stage Two to Stage Three.

- Find a mentor. (A mentor is a wise and trusted advisor who can be objective with you about your life or work.) Ask that person to be a guide for you while you seek out your direction.
- Have a long talk with your friend, boss, spouse, and mentor about your skill areas, strengths, values, personality traits, blocks to effective work, and possible directions in life or in work. Get feedback on your performance that is realistic and that gives you some direction for improvement in the future. This will help you overcome your crises of confidence.
- Work hard on doing a very good job at what you are currently doing. One of the best ways to be seen as a capable and competent person is to be one. Do not rely totally on being discovered for being so competent, but certainly do not overlook it.
- Find out what knowledge and skill you need to move into jobs at the next level in your field or other places in the organization. Look into degree or credential programs that will help you obtain that skill and knowledge. Find programs that work to your schedule and expect time to be very tight for a while. It's worth the effort in the long run if you've chosen the program carefully.
- Get to know your organization in depth. You can do this by talking to people, looking at printed material, and getting yourself into a broader network. Name the top people in your organization and the department in which each is working. What path did each person use to get where she/he is? What are the unwritten norms of your organization? Who really makes decisions? What kind of behavior is rewarded? Whom do you need to know? How can you get extra assignments that will give you access to more people in the organization, e.g., committees of all levels of employees, a centrally located department, a volunteer activity?

- Name some things about your organization you like and some you don't like. How can you capitalize on those you like and work around those you don't like? A complaining person without solutions is not appreciated in organizations for long.
- Decide to do at least two new things that you have never done before and that constitute some kind of a risk for you. Record how you felt in preparation for them, during the event, and after. What were the results? What did you learn about yourself, about taking risks?
- Develop your network. Name three professional or trade associations that you could join to meet more people or learn more about your profession and its leadership. Absorb as much as you can from the meetings you attend and stay around afterward to talk to people who work in organizations other than yours. Name some people you know already who could be information sources or supportive people in your life and career.
- Take care of yourself. Try not to be disappointed when you realize that there is no magic in the world and that most of what people get they work for. If the magic has left your life, get with other people who can help you bolster your own self-confidence once again. Practice making your own decisions and learning to live with the consequences.
- Start your own business. One good way to find out how you would function in a risky environment is to run something on your own. Many people who are very unhappy in organizations because they feel uncreative or unappreciated are frustrated entrepreneurs. Look into what it would take to start your own business by talking to others who have done it.
- Examine your dress, language, and habits to see which of these may be getting in the way of imaging yourself as more satisfied or powerful.
- (For women) Name the masculine behaviors. Check those that you are comfortable with, circle those that you aren't comfortable with. Plan ways you can develop the behaviors you think are most important on the list. Talk to other women and men about this. Take some courses, model other people, practice the behaviors in safe settings, and get feedback on your results.
- Increase your confidence by learning as much about yourself as possible and then take risks with supportive people coaching you.
- Work out to the best of your ability any relationships you have with bosses, spouses, or friends who are unsupportive. Use every means you can to remedy the situation. If all else fails, remove yourself from the situation and learn how to take responsibility for yourself.

Martha, the assistant professor, decided that she was not progressing toward tenure in her all-male department as she wanted to, so she joined a women's faculty club. By discussing her situation confidentially with some insightful tenured professors, she formed a plan for tenure that included both the objective and subjective sides of the issue. She joined some different committees, co-authored articles with some people, had candid conversations with others, became a board member in her professional organization, became more collegial with her peers, worked diligently on her teaching, and sailed confidently through to an affirmative tenure decision. Lenny, the rookie, is now in his tenth year with the police force and chooses to remain a street patrolman: "I don't want to sit behind a desk or go out on raids. I like being with the real people, the average person who needs me and appreciates what I do at least once in a while." Ray is wondering what to do with his counseling degree, and Joyce is in the middle of her college work, still glowing with enthusiasm. Jane, the photographer, is now taking her third class and has given her photos to family and friends as gifts. Sam wonders why he ever wanted to be a director. He has much more time in his present job to do the outside things he wants to do.

What Holds People Back?

People at Stage Two will have to overcome their need for security if they are to move to the next stage. It's so comfortable to be learning from others, to have the way paved by another person who believes in you. Now it's time to try out the unfamiliar, the new—the next step. Most find it helpful to do so in familiar territory, though, with others' assistance. That way you have change within some security, and you can examine your fears realistically. Others find the only way for them is to change abruptly, to move or leave in order to get going. Whatever you do, find and use resources and start taking risks, small risks and then larger ones. Try one new thing and see how it works, like going to a professional group meeting in your field. If you go again it will be easier. Before you know it, you'll be an officer. Try to move the sense of security from outside yourself to inside yourself without being overwhelmed. Think of yourself as a butterfly emerging from a cocoon that has been holding you. Remember, you can usually go back to the place you left (in some form), so ask yourself "What's the worst thing that could possibly happen to me if I move ahead with my plan?"

Above all, don't try to do it alone. Get into a supportive environment or with a group of friends or associates who believe in you and will help you grow.

Hagberg's Model of Personal Power

SUMMARY OF STAGE TWO
POWER BY ASSOCIATION

Symbol

Key Questions: Who made you feel worthwhile before you were 25, other than your parents? What did they do? How did it affect you?

Description
Magical
"Be like Yoda" stage

Characteristics
Apprentices
Learning the culture
Dependent on supervisor/leader
New self-awareness

Spirituality at Stage Two
Learning about our spiritual journey

Shadow of Stage Two
Recyclers
Chameleons
Naïve people

Catalyst for Movement
Confidence
Risk-taking

What Holds People Back?
Lack of confidence
Need for security

Ways to Move
Find a mentor, get feedback, be competent, get credentials, get more involved, find solutions, take risks, develop networks, develop your ego, take care of yourself, do something on your own, examine your image, take on the masculine if necessary, work out relationships.

Ask yourself these questions about Stage Three:

Yes	No	
____	____	1. Do you feel competitive about most things?
____	____	2. Are you developing a stronger ego?
____	____	3. Do you make a conscious effort to appear confident?
____	____	4. Do you feel that you now have to prove yourself because you have been given responsibility?
____	____	5. Do you think that power is finite, i.e., there is only so much to go around?
____	____	6. Do you think you've acquired a lot of knowledge and now you ought to make use of it?
____	____	7. Do you understand the political games that people in organizations play?
____	____	8. Do you sometimes think that you have "arrived"?
____	____	9. Do you usually ask yourself first, "How will this affect me?"
____	____	10. Are symbols important to you, like salary, titles, material possessions, office placement, or number of people you manage?
____	____	11. In the game of life do you feel someone has to win and someone has to lose?
____	____	12. Do you think success will make you a better person?
____	____	13. Do you believe power involves being in control?
____	____	14. Do others look to you as a success model?
____	____	15. Does your main satisfaction come from your work?

Yes answers indicate that you identify with this stage.

Chapter 3
Stage Three: Power by Achievement

Control

Key Questions: What are your gifts? What kinds of things come easily for you? What are your skills?

What Is Stage Three Like?

Stage Three is the dynamo stage, the success stage. It is exciting, challenging, rewarding, competitive, and oriented to self-development. People at Stage Three are in the thick of things. They know how the organization works and they help make it work better. The threes are in charge. They have the feeling that "this is it!"

All Stage Three people have one thing in common. They like to achieve. Their forms of achievement vary. Some like to be experts or show their knowledge. Others like to set and achieve concrete goals. Others achieve through their products. We arrive at Stage Three by varying routes; degrees, competence, experience, self-confidence, being in the right place, having a sponsor, taking risks, or developing our egos.

Along with the achievement of Stage Three comes the symbols of success. These vary widely, depending on the arena, but we all yearn for symbols and we all have a need to fulfill our yearning. The most predominant symbols in organizations are:

positions	titles	degrees
salary levels	bonuses	office size
type of uniform	office placement	size of budget
number of employees	parking privileges	offices with windows
awards	recognition	

Secondary symbols are:

cars	boats	homes
travel opportunities	clothes	body shape
club memberships	collections	athletic prowess
achievements of children		

Some people love to show others their symbols by displaying them or photos of them in their office, wearing them, driving them, putting them on business cards, or living in them. Others are subtler about them. We all have them.

It is not necessary to reach the top of an organization in order to achieve satisfaction and symbols. But there is a certain level of outside recognition necessary to affirm oneself at this stage. This is the most externally oriented and externally rewarded of all the stages.

Most organizations also function at this stage. Their goal is to be the best at what they do, in order to meet their goal of selling more, servicing more people, making social change, or educating better. The words or programs that represent the standards of achievement change in each decade but the goal underneath them is usually the same, to be more productive.

The only compelling problem with this stage is that our society deems it the top, the best, and the achievement most worth pursuing. Our competitive and individualistic culture is just beginning to recognize Stage Four, a stage that represents inner power, but Stages Five and Six are still seen as less familiar and therefore either unreachable or suspect. So once people arrive at Stage Three, our culture encourages them to strive for more of that stage all the time. This is especially true for men and puts them in much more constricted boxes in our culture than it does women. Then when something happens to break the spell, or stop the Stage Three upward progression (job loss, demotion, being passed over for promotion, illness), there is a tremendous loss of ego and prestige. It is the death of a dream. And there is nowhere to go, no one to talk to. When the symbols become men's identity, and they lose these symbols, their self-worth crumbles at the loss. At that point it feels like life is over. Ironically, it may have only just begun.

The paradox of this stage is this: it contains the best and the worst of our culture. It is organized, competent, technologically advanced, and successful. On the other hand, every scandal we can remember evolves from the shadow of this stage, the misuse of power. The scandal can be in politics, on Wall Street, in foreign policy, in religious leadership, in sports, or in families. All scandals develop from greed, misuse of external power, or self-serving behavior. If one is not alert, Stage Three can plant the seeds of its own destruction. It is both appealing and frightening to us at the same time.

The description of power at Stage Three is control. It is the word that comes up most frequently (along with influence) when I ask an audience to say the first word that comes to mind when the word "power" is mentioned. Control suggests that one person has more of it than others, that the buck stops somewhere. Control suggests discipline and persistence. Control suggests well-thought-out responses and having strong defense mechanisms. Control suggests regulation and comparison against standards.

So who exactly are Stage Three people? He or she can be anyone who has achieved some sought-after external recognition or reward, whether it is position, status, credential, material possessions, salary level, or stage of expertise. And these are obtained by a variety of methods: hard work, degrees, luck, inheritance, being in the right place, connections, or competence. The prize is external and recognizable and makes the person feel that she or he is more worthwhile as a result. The person is achieving the prizes for being successful in our culture. For many there is even a sense of initiation into Stage Three. Sometimes a ceremony occurs to mark the occasion, e.g., public recognition, an award ceremony, or graduation. More often the initiation consists of the first meeting of the new managers, the purchase agreement, the letter of promotion, the diploma, or the first results of the election.

People may experience Stage Three in a wide variety of ways; so if you find yourself thinking, after reading this chapter, that you don't fit the examples and therefore couldn't ever get to Stage Three, look more closely at what this stage means in your environment. What does it take to feel success in your work? There are others who will read this chapter and say they don't need the symbols and can skip right over this stage. My experience says this response may suggest fear of facing this stage.

There is a group of people in our culture worth noting because they are so frequently left out of this stage and suffer loss of self-esteem as a result. They are people who do not work for pay and contribute to our society in other ways. They, too, can operate at Stage Three, through volunteer activities, expertise in various fields, athletic prowess, raising healthy children, or speaking out for social change. But in a culture that measures so much of our worth by salary and paid positions, we have difficulty recognizing their worth. Retired people, homemakers, and children feel this stigma most and as a result, we as a culture are missing out on a wealth of expertise and talent that could be better cultivated.

These people need to recognize their own worth and expect to be treated with respect.

My experiences at Stage Three are wide ranging. I admit to loving the symbols as much as anyone. In fact this is the most seductive of all the stages for me. I am a high achiever. My public side is mostly Stage Three. I have a few degrees, have been a college professor, and have run my own business for many years. I like getting recognition and respect, especially for my ideas. So my published books are very important to me. I am a risk-taker and can rise to a good challenge. And my satisfaction at having arrived at this stage is doubled by being female, since only twenty-five years ago I could not get a business loan without my husband's signature. He was unemployed at the time!

I have been very comfortable in the male-oriented world of business. I think I was raised more like a boy than a girl and I had the self-confidence required to take risks. I love sports and can keep up with most Monday morning post-game discussions. I keep score at baseball games and have been to several NCAA Final Four Basketball Tournaments. One business highlight during the height of my Three-ness was sitting in an outdoor heated swimming pool with my business partner under a full moon in Vail, Colorado in the winter saying, "We ought to be paid for doing this." My partner laughed and said, "We are." We were there training the ski school instructors how to use different learning styles in their teaching.

It is harder to admit the symbols I love because, having written this book, I am very aware of how the symbols can lay claim on your psyche. But I also have to confess that I like the symbols of success as much as anyone. My yearnings are still alive and well. I value a comfortable home, a pleasing personal appearance, and travel. But my two favorite symbols are fountains pens and fast cars. Fountain pens stir my soul. When I write I like to see the ink dry behind the beautiful gold nib. Ink from a fine fountain pen. And driving fast cars makes my blood race. I like knowing I can accelerate to sixty miles per hour in under six seconds. Driving the autobahn in Europe was a peak experience as was watching the fighter jet take-off scenes in the movie Top Gun. So now I have confessed. It is good for my soul.

The seduction of success and recognition are almost irresistible for me, especially because of my personality. Not that success is wrong, but I have a hard time knowing when to draw the line, when I've had enough. And the cultural rewards that go along with success at this stage are so appealing—money, recognition, awards, travel, and fame. So my challenge is to appreciate the power of this stage, appreciate the skills I have developed that allow me to operate at this stage, and use these skills wisely, but also be aware of the seduction of this stage visited on me by the voices that whisper more, more, more.

Characteristics of Stage Three People

First of all, let me reiterate that Stage Three is the most masculine of all the stages; so, many of the characteristics described may apply more to some males and may disturb some females. Many women think, however, that in order to move up in the organization, they must become just like men, usually Stage Three men, and that is why they get stuck at this stage. Stage Three is the most representative of our culture, of what our culture strives for. We must gain the respect of this stage even though our personal ways of behaving at Stage Three may vary. It is probably the easiest stage to understand because it is so much more predictable than the rest, and the expectations on the surface are so much clearer. Stage Threes are rewarded for being strong, decisive, expert, organizationally savvy, and competitive.

Stage Three is somewhat unique in that the development of people *within* the stage, as they move through it, is more obvious than in the other stages. Perhaps this is because it is the most visible stage in our culture. We are clearly different when we enter Stage Three than when we prepare to leave it. It is as if there is an entry behavior, midpoint behavior (behavior depicting the heights of Stage Three), and exiting behavior. I'll try to highlight these three levels briefly as I describe each of the characteristics of Stage Three.

Mature Ego

When people first experience the move from Stage Two to Stage Three they do not yet have a strong ego, and are not self-confident. They are new to this bigger world, the world that a new job, a fresh degree, or a new skill invites them to experience. But they need time to hone their skills and to live into this new level of responsibility. Over time their confidence usually grows, and with that their ego starts to develop as well. Everyone knows what it feels like to be in a position where you are in "over your head." It is uncomfortable—but it is also challenging.

The behavior most characteristic of the maturing Stage Three is a strong ego. This means that people exhibit confidence and a unique sense of themselves. They know what their skills and competencies are and they are not afraid to use them. Our culture generally rewards this behavior so it gets reinforced. Strong egos feed our aspirations and fuel our desires to succeed.

At the height of Stage Three people show that they have learned an important lesson somewhere along the way: you must believe in yourself in order to expect others to believe in you. They have learned to develop self-respect. Another way of saying it is their egos have begun to mature, develop, to "grow up." Once you have developed a degree of self-confidence you are more willing to take risks, lead other people, and try new things. Confidence breeds confidence. Strong people usually attract others, just by their persona.

If you remain open to new growth, another level of ego development starts to emerge. I call this the mature ego. It is characterized by a more attractive strength that reaches beyond you. This strength spreads to other people around you. It is a great leadership tool. Strong people can inspire others to follow their direction because others believe in them, and want to be influenced by their ideas and vision. These leaders leave an impression on people they meet. They can even become bigger than life if we project onto them qualities that we long for in ourselves.

A mature ego is backed by a long history of competence and skills. This requires hard work in honing strengths and overcoming weaknesses. Others tend to trust these people and depend on them, looking to them for leadership. Even if these people don't happen to be in formal leadership positions, they are the foundation, the rock upon which the organization depends because they are organized, reliable, and have confidence, no matter whom they are speaking with.

Of course, we expect that most people in the traditional power positions, such as CEO, president, chairperson, vice president, director, will be Stage Threes, but there are many others in other positions who can be at Stage Three because they have developed their ego and self-confidence. Anyone who is willing to give honest feedback to his/her boss, speak their minds without being intimidated, and who can disagree with others without trying to boss them around is likely to be operating in Stage Three.

Realistic and Competitive

One of the most exciting aspects of Stage Three is its energy, pace, and motivation. There is a lot of action at this stage. Most of the production that occurs in our lives comes from the Stage Three part of us.

When we first enter this stage we may need to get accustomed to a heightened level of activity and competition, which we may have been shielded from at Stage Two. Competition is there whether it takes the form of fundraising for a non-profit or developing a higher market share for a product. So we may experience a steep learning curve around competition at this stage—and this may be truer for women, unless they have experienced competitive sports. But usually we are so eager and excited to be at this stage that we are up for the challenge.

As people develop into the heart of Stage Three they know more about the rules and the games by which the organization functions. They make it their business to know. And it is important, because they have external power now and must take their responsibilities seriously. The rules at Stage Three usually involve playing to win, beating the competition, and being the best. It is an exciting and heady feeling, whether it involves being the best university, selling the most products, or eliminating a social ill.

In order to effectively move up in the organization, Threes must know these two simple rules: there are people who you need to keep informed and there are definitely people you need on your side. It reminds me of the old union leader who was talking to a younger member. He said, "I don't care if you like the board members or not, but you've got to get them on your side to pass a motion." Stage Three people operate on the reality, not on what ought to be. Some people call this company politics, while others refer to it as the only realistic way to get things done.

Men used to be totally in charge of this realistic and competitive environment. They still are, for the most part. But many more women and people of color have entered this arena in the last few decades. This change has caused more than a little confusion amongst those who were quite a homogeneous group just a few years ago. But along with new faces, we frequently get new ideas and a broader perspective on the world.

Depending on what sector of the economy you work in, there are two other groups of Threes in the competitive environment. The first group is the "suits" and the second group the paid volunteers. The first group consists of people who play by the prescribed rules, say all the right things, wear the right clothes, go to the right places, entertain the right people, join the right clubs, chair the right community committees, cover the right mistakes, and take the right risks. They know the rules of the game and they are understandably out to win. Without rules and roles they would flounder.

An executive who has worked with these people coined a wonderful term for rule players, whom he says he can always pick out at a meeting. He calls them "suits." He says the suits always say the expedient thing. They follow the dictates of the prevailing organizational culture and they are very predictable. A few years ago I heard a "suit" give someone advice on her doctoral dissertation: "Do whatever your committee says. Write exactly what they want you to write, even if you hate it. Pick something that you can finish in a year and grit your teeth. The important thing is to finish and get the piece of paper." The more prescriptive the career ladder, the more likely you are to find "suits."

The other competitive group—a product of the nineties—is the "paid volunteers." They are mostly young and very talented people who are displaying different values towards the workplace than their predecessors did. They are willing to work really hard for a couple of years and make a lot of money but then take three months off in their mid-twenties to see the world. They are willing to move from one career to another, taking what seems like extraordinary risks, because they like the challenge and because they have extraordinary amounts of self-confidence. Some of them have made a lot of money at a young age and wonder what else there is besides money, so they try something else just to see how it feels. A human resource professional told me recently that it is really difficult to know how to put together employee benefits and incentive packages for them because they act more like volunteers than employees. They take the jobs they want, enjoy working on what gives them a challenge or meets some personal goal, work more or less the way they want to, quit when they get bored, and do not stay if they are not treated well.

As people move into the latter part of Stage Three there is a subtle shift in the way they experience their achievement motivation. Now instead of being focused on the competition, they switch their focus to achieving excellence. Whereas competition emphasizes winning and an external comparison (I am better than or stronger than someone else), achieving excellence can be done without competition and with an internal focus, not an external one. Examples might include a runner who is trying to beat his or her own best time, or a tenured professor who takes joy in developing new ideas for publication.

Expert

Many people move into Stage Three by accumulating knowledge or expertise. They obtain degrees or develop competitive skills. In order to stay at this stage they need to keep on gaining more knowledge and skill or learn how to capitalize on what they already have. Their symbol is the capacity of their mind or their level of expertise. They gain control because they know more than others do about certain subjects. And they often use this to their advantage, for instance, by asking detailed or specific questions of others at meetings or by citing facts and concepts from their store of knowledge. Lawyers, doctors, college and university professors, technical experts, scientists, and ministers generally rely on this symbol for their power. In corporations engineers and financial analysts generally consider themselves the professional experts. Experts tend quite often to be responsible and hard working because that is what they have always been rewarded for. They can put out volumes of work and come up with intricate plans in a very thorough manner.

It becomes apparent sooner or later, however, that expertise in a particular subject does not suffice if one wants to gain more decision-making power (control and influence). People who can manage well usually run organizations. Experts frequently find that in order to move up in the organization they must move to the management side and they fear losing their expertise. Sometimes it is not the best move for them since not all experts enjoy management and they may not be good at managing either. Most organizations also reward technical expertise quite highly, if it's kept up to date. At any rate, it is a key decision in their career. Choosing to remain in an area of technical expertise is, in many cases, a better decision, but it represents a perceived limitation in organizational power and takes reflective and introspective thinking to accomplish successfully.

Ambitious

This is an intriguing characteristic of Stage Three because it can show up in such a variety of ways. Many people show their ambition through their work lives but an equal number reserve some of their energy for their avocations. One middle manager I met at a Fortune 100 firm said he was very satisfied with his place on the corporate ladder because he found his work interesting and challenging, but he was not interested in moving up to the next level. He wanted to have enough time and energy to devote to his other pursuit. He had the largest collection of baseball memorabilia in the state and he was an avid trader.

Many people in organizations get involved with volunteer activities, taking on roles and leadership positions they would not have the opportunity for in their jobs; like project leaders for civic events or serving as chairperson of a non-profit board.

People at the heart of Stage Three seem to be perpetually in search of new challenges. This is as true of their personal lives as it is of their work. They love being given a problem that looks insurmountable, for it means that the opportunity as well as the reward will be greater. And the more visible the challenges the better they feel. They even thrive on taking risks. It gets their adrenaline going and gives them energy. In fact, they take enormous pride in their energy level and their ability to handle many projects or problems simultaneously.

Sometimes their drive and desire for a challenge permeates their choices in leisure, and they participate in many unusual, demanding, or visible sorts of activities. Each new event presents a new challenge. Canoeing is more fun in whitewater; hiking is more attractive in the mountains or some exotic place; being in nature can become a survival challenge; running turns into marathons; driving quickly evolves into racing; reading means devouring best sellers. The event itself is exciting to Threes, but just as exciting is the opportunity to tell others about the experience.

There is a group of people who take this challenging approach to its heights. They are the "fast trackers." They particularly identify with this idea of becoming the best and taking risks. This group is made up of people who move in the fast lane. They are highly visible, and they stand apart from other Stage Threes because they have been selected or programmed to move up. The pressure is on them to maintain their momentum, to take risks, to perform at a high level so they will not disappoint their sponsor or someone else, but most of all themselves. Since many of them are bright and well-trained, they will not be satisfied until they have gone as far as they can go. It's as if they marry their work. They probably received their success programming as children. For the boys, it was not enough to play football, they had to be the most valuable player; not enough to be good, they had to be captain; not enough to be a good player and captain, but chosen all-conference; not enough to be chosen all-conference, but given a full football scholarship to a prestigious school. For the girls, it was not enough to get good grades, they had to be popular; not enough to be popular, they had to be athletes or cheerleaders; not enough to be athletes, they had to be homecoming queen; not enough to be a queen, they had to date the football captain. It goes on and on, and carries over into their adult life. The pressure is enormous. But many fast trackers seem to thrive on it. For them, the more action the better.

Success or perfection programming can be readily observed in the behaviors of parents. For instance, two fathers of high school students were talking to one another at a prep school basketball game. The one said to the other, "Where did your son do his earlier work?" Another example comes from a newspaper article on sports, from the father of a ninth grader who had just pitched his fourth no-hitter of the season. He said, "It was a good game, but I told Arthur not to let it go to his head. He can always do better."

In many ways the fast-lane people are the most ironic of all Stage Threes because they appear to be the most successful, yet they have the most to lose. What happens to those who don't hold up, who break under the pressure, who suddenly get passed over because their sponsor fell out of favor? They may recoup, but generally the bruises are worse because they also have a longer way to fall. For all those who make it to that supreme goal—whatever it is—there are just as many who don't. The death of the dream is a very difficult experience to come to terms with. Sometimes their dreams fade when they lose their families due to neglect along the way, or the dream may die when their health fails them. Perhaps the most confused group consists of those who do make it to the top of the ladder and look out over the landscape, only to discover the tops of other ladders and a lot of emptiness, as described in the wonderful little classic by Trina Paulus, *Hope for the Flowers*.

At the end of Stage Three a person still feels ambitious but begins to shift the focus more to the organization's best interest or thinks of other people's best interests as well as their own. This is one subtle sign that the person may be ready to move into Stage Four.

Women and Stage Three

Women are certainly capable of operating at Stage Three, but they have had to make a conscious choice, a deliberate move to develop their confidence and take on their masculine side in order to do so. For many women this is frightening, even a bit distasteful. They may think of it as giving up part of themselves rather than taking on a new part. As a high-ranking woman in a Fortune 500 company said, "Act like a woman, but think like a man." Unfortunately, some women also act like men at this stage, and they buy totally into the rules and games of the organization, thereby losing some of their own most worthwhile qualities. This is not to say that women cannot compete with men, but that they can do it in a style that represents another model, another way of being. Otherwise they are once again dependent upon men for their acceptance; being one of the boys is their goal. Women need to step back and look at themselves periodically to see if they have outwardly become incongruent with their inner selves.

Women need to understand the games—perhaps even respect them—but do not need to play all of them. They need to understand the men in the organization, but do not need to become one. It is difficult because sometimes women feel they may fall behind if they don't get in there and "do battle." In the short run that may be true, but not in the long run. An example of this comes from two women managers in an organization who both worked for the same male boss. He had confided in each some disturbing news about the behavior of the other woman towards her. They were both confused because the behavior did not seem like that of either of them. After several days of thinking, one of the women went to the other confidentially to ask whether what she had heard was true. The other woman was very surprised and then related what she had heard about her colleague. They then figured out that they had been pitted against each other deliberately. It was one of the organizational games, or at least their boss's game. They decided they didn't like to operate that way, and both went together to speak with their boss. His initial reaction was, "I can't believe the two of you talked to each other about this!" Now he would have to find a different way of managing them because the old ways were not sufficient.

Women need more than anything else to keep their self-respect at Stage Three. It may not be their favorite stage—or it can surprise them and be very invigorating. But it is a good and necessary stage, that of competence, a maturing ego, and self-respect in a male-dominated world.

Stage Three is the biggest struggle for women in organizations, but they really can't afford to get stuck there. One way to avoid that is to talk regularly with women who see the larger picture, who have not lost their feminine side, and who are respected in the community and in the organization, no matter what their positions are. Test out ideas with them, ask for their advice and counsel, and thank them for their leadership. Listen and learn. Resist the urge to know it all. Because women have not been pressured as strongly as men have to "arrive" at Stage Three, women may be the greatest hope for helping organizations to move their leadership on to higher stages.

People of Color and Stage Three

In many ways people of color face the same issues women do. They are not the predominant culture of Stage Three—white men are. So it is an achievement just to get to Stage Three amidst all the obstacles built into our culture. One African-American man said to me at a speech on power, "I have set my professional and personal goal to get to Stage Three in my career."

But there is an additional factor facing people of color in trying to achieve success. While women face sexism, people of color face an inherent racism that is built into our culture. And it is deadly. We lose so much richness when we do not cultivate diversity. And fear of facing differences keeps so many people immobilized. Now that our country is truly diverse, we will not move ahead as a whole society unless we can embrace our diversity and mine its riches together.

People of color find new issues waiting for them when they begin to achieve at Stage Three. Do they buy into the prevailing culture more or do they hold on to what makes them unique? In order to get to Stage Three most people have to emulate the prevailing culture, but do they forget who they are and become "honorary white males" or do they work to stay in balance? Who do they go to as role models? By attending to these struggles and by reflecting on who they are becoming in this culture, people of color, as well as women, will do us a great service by bringing us into new forms of leadership.

Men and Stage Three

Most men have been taught that they should "arrive" at Stage Three. It is considered the epitome of success. For many it is indeed a satisfying juncture. They have attained what they were aiming for. They fought the good fight, obtained the degree, achieved significance, and won the race. They are ready for a different challenge, the next salary level, and stiffer competition. Sadly, for many men reaching Stage Three, climbing higher and higher is their whole identity. Since they were small boys they've been scripted to work hard, carry all the burdens, make good, and leave no time for relaxation. They go to school, work long hours, exercise strenuously to keep stress in check, take minimal time off, retire at 65, and die within three years after retirement. The facts don't lie. They are in tight boxes. And in our culture many men *are* what they do. So, if you are what you do then when you don't, you aren't.

For these men, work success is the only thing in life that matters, and one hears the tired and sad line, said to a lonely spouse, "But I'm only doing these things for you." That is difficult to swallow when it means one's spouse is never home, never has time for family events, always lets organizational priorities prevail. "Doing it for you" really means doing it for me, even if I think I'm doing it for you. Some men work to make a living, rather than making a living work.

Other men in Stage Three acknowledge that there is much more to life and many other arenas in which to achieve success: family, community, personal, intellectual, emotional, and political life. This is harder for men in our culture to do, but it puts one's life in more balance in the long run.

And then there are the gentle men discussed in Chapter Two who struggle with the societal pressures to achieve Stage Three when it holds little appeal. Some of them truly are afraid and need to be supported to learn how they can be Stage Three men without totally buying into the predominating rules. Their issues are different from women's because women were mostly socialized to be at Stages One or Two, and to go beyond represents progress in our society even though some women would disagree. For men not to strive for Stage Three, which they've been pushed towards, means to settle for less or not to have succeeded in society's eyes—a more difficult pressure to withstand.

Spirituality and the Spiritual Connection to Work at Stage Three

At this stage spirituality means being productive in one's spiritual life, working for your spiritual group, the Holy, or the cause. We have arrived. We feel special to our community now that we're finding our niche. Responsibility and leadership roles interest us as ways to use our gifts and talents. We value the symbols of the spiritually fruitful life, whether those are the fruits of the inner spirit, respect, recognition, or reaching spiritual goals. We want to teach others how to live out their spirituality as we have learned it for ourselves.

Living out this stage varies according to one's tradition and current spiritual practice. For people with a social justice preference it may mean teaching others how to work on issues like homelessness; for those with evangelical leanings it might mean speaking out about your personal faith and encouraging others to as well; for twelve-step or recovery group members it might mean becoming a sponsor; for orthodox people it might include a pilgrimage to a holy place.

We value a concrete connection between skill, competence, and our spiritual journey. We practice our faith regularly through our kinship groups, causes, churches or synagogues, twelve-step groups, or our outreach to others. Our competence and confidence are high so we can move to new levels of responsibility or to new arenas, like advanced study or acting as a mentor to others. We are in the position to teach others what we have experienced about faith and work. Conscious of ourselves as role models, we monitor our work decisions, practices, and treatment of others. Our management and leadership styles represent our faith values. We believe what we are doing represents the will of the Holy in our lives and we strive to do our work as competently as we can. Success is one measure of our faithfulness, especially if we have been raised in the classic European religious traditions.

Sarah is an example of Stage Three spirituality. She runs a law practice and for years she has been on a journey to make her spirituality a strong part of her work environment while still valuing the diversity of her employees' religious beliefs. She gathered her twenty employees together during one of their planning retreats and asked them to devise a set of principles for the treatment of their clients and each other, based on their own spiritual/religious beliefs. She set up a few case studies of tricky situations they might encounter and the group talked through how they would approach these situations. Out of the discussion emerged a set of principles they refer to regularly in their planning meetings and their work with clients. These principles have become their North Star, their guiding light as a law firm.

The Shadow of Stage Three

Stage Three lends itself to shadow behavior more readily than any other stage because our culture so highly rewards achievement. We aren't sure what is enough. And no alarm automatically goes off in our heads when we've had enough. I will describe three characteristic behaviors that depict the shadow side of Stage Three.

Use of Bravado to Cover Addiction

Addicted Stage Three people are often in positions of power in which others expect them to behave in a mature, competent fashion. On the surface they look strong and have the right credentials and experience. But under the surface they are addicted. Anyone who works for them finds them intolerable. You feel like you are walking on eggs all the time. They are unpredictable, moody, easily wounded and vindictive. They hide their mistakes or worse yet, blame them all on others around them.

Their behavior is intimidating, even threatening, but under the surface they are really fragile and petrified of being found out. They are in denial about their hurts and fears so they will not resonate with any facts about their behavior that are brought to their attention, or they will acknowledge them and then do nothing about them. They wreak havoc in organizations because they can cause so much destruction without being found out. They abuse others, most often emotionally, which is much more difficult to decipher than more obvious physical or sexual abuse.

Their addictions are diverse; work, sex, money, danger, control, alcohol, drugs, relationships, or gambling. In reality their addiction spirals them inwardly to Stage One but they use their position power to cover their addiction. They are lethal to anyone working for them or around them. They infect organizations like viruses attacking computers. The best thing that can be done for them is confrontation and treatment. They need radical inner healing.

Here is an example of a bully boss who is stuck in the shadow of Stage Three and is at a top level in the organization. It is told from the perspective of one of his intended victims who ultimately got free. But the bully boss syndrome is an all-too-frequent scenario in organizations today.

> I was a young lawyer for one of the big international law firms. I was being courted for a transfer to a larger office. The partner in charge of the tax law department said all the right things to convince me I wanted to work with him.
>
> He was the head of a very successful tax practice. He was involved in all the right community, civic, and charitable organizations. He wore privately designed suits. His monogrammed shirt cuffs barely covered his Rolex watch. He always exceeded annual goals.
>
> At the end of my first day I was taken out by many of the other managers for a 'welcome' drink. They began to tell stories about this man. I couldn't believe what I was hearing. The bottom line message was that he was a tyrant. I was cautioned that I was on a honeymoon with him. The grace period might last a few weeks, but not longer than a few months. Everyone would know the day I met the person beneath the exterior.
>
> Why had none of this come out when I interviewed with these same managers? I later understood that abused people often do not reveal the abuser. Their victim-hood becomes a brotherhood.

Before my honeymoon expired I began to see the signs of his tyranny. He yelled at people, threw things, slammed doors in people's faces, stood on desks to make his points, and attacked people in front of others. He delighted in saying that there was not a person in the office he had not made cry.

Then I met the tyrant head on. I was told I was inferior. He had never met anyone as incompetent as me. I was absolutely clueless. There was nothing I could do that met his approval. The only meetings with him were one-sided confrontations.

The straw that broke the camel's back came a couple of years after enduring this ugliness. (I had turned into one of those silent victims.) I had sent free customary tax guides to one of my clients. He was outraged as this client only billed out at 80% of actual charges. He wanted me to write him a personal check for the guides. He told me I would pay or that I could go to the partner in charge of the office and discuss the situation with him.

I went to the partner in charge of the office. I told him everything I had seen and experienced in this man's department. He was sympathetic to my story and told me I would not be writing a check.

I was hoping that something might happen that would stop the abuse. I now understood that as long as the man exceeded his profit numbers he was a protected boss. The other partners may have had difficulty confronting him because they were all benefiting financially from his tactics.

He was told of my tell-all session. He made me invisible in the office. I was taken off the agenda at manager meetings. He wouldn't look at me or acknowledge my presence. I was not called to his office for reprimands. It was great! The other managers wanted to know what I had done to cease being his target. He continued to bully the others at his whim.

Then he didn't meet his numbers. He made some aggressive investments in local tax practices that ended in litigation. He was fired.

I'm not pleased that I endured this mistreatment for as long as I did. At the time, I was committed to working for the 'best tax department.' Initially I thought I could tough it out. Besides, when he was in good humor it was a great place to work. It made the bad episodes less painful. Oh, what we can tell ourselves to justify our choices.

> The most important lesson this angry man taught me was: my thoughts about me are more important than anyone else's thoughts of me. This was a huge awakening. It freed me to expand my definition of who I was. I understood how important it is to define my boundaries for others to respect. I saw how I show others how I want to be treated.

Egocentric

Some Stage Three people have learned an important lesson somewhere along the way; discover your strengths and capitalize on them at any cost. They adhere to the power of positive thinking philosophy, and they are always trying to become more powerful. They have achieved such an unusually high level of confidence that they are willing to take on the world. In fact, it may appear as if they are, at times, proving to the entire world that they are strong and powerful. They have worked long and hard to get where they are and they are proud. Partly as a result, they have a consistent characteristic—to think about themselves first in any situation. How will this decision, program, or person affect me? Will this be good for my career? Will this get me recognition or visibility?

Most Threes have highly developed egos that tend to affect the way in which they view themselves and other people. But these folks spend a lot of time thinking about themselves and how others view them. They can run the risk of being unusually self-centered or driven. Sometimes their egos appear to be strong but are indeed fragile, which may cause them to do such things as hide their mistakes or weaknesses in the organization, or make it look as if the mistake is someone else's fault. Making mistakes is hard on them. They really like, more than anything else, to be right, which ultimately means for them to be perfect.

Greed

The third group is perhaps the most difficult to work with because greed can be covered with such outwardly respectful behaviors. And greed starts in small ways. If I can beat out someone else on the freeway I feel like a better person. If I get more change back than I deserve I keep it and make a little money. Then I take organization merchandise. It starts with dishonesty and builds to greed.

As it builds it gains momentum. The greedy always get overzealous. The more I get the more I want. The more I want the more I will do to get it. Threes in this shadow behavior play subtle games in organizations, setting people up against each other to make them look bad. Sometimes they just play the game for the thrill of seeing what they can get, or whom they can bring down. It doesn't even seem real to them. Who they hurt is just part of the game. It's a game about power. The more power I get, the less you get, and the better I am. It is such a sad story, and leads to nothing but an emotional dead end. But greedy dishonest people wreak havoc on organizations before they crash, just like addicted people do. Only truly courageous people can name and put an end to their behavior before it destroys others.

Let me tell you an old story representing how subtle greed can be and how easily it can distance us from our own goodness.

The King's Seamstress

Long ago in a faraway land lived a young woman who gained a reputation far and wide by being the finest seamstress in the country. She could make rags look like velvet and thread look like golden strands. She was very happy with her family and friends and loved her work. One day the king, who had heard of her fine work, asked to see her and some samples of her most elegant garments. She was elated and scurried to find her most superb coats and gowns. They were strewn with beautiful jewels and cords and were soft and luxurious to the touch. The king was pleased and asked the young woman to become one of the court seamstresses. Her dream had come true. She would be famous and would be able to serve the king and queen directly, with all her needs attended to. She was told that her family could not accompany her, and it was a great distance to her home from the castle. Still, after long thought, she could not pass up an offer to sew for the king. She packed up, said a tearful goodbye to her family, and started her new life in the castle of the king and queen.

All went well for several years. She was busy and made new friends among the seamstresses in the castle. She was so busy that she did not have time to visit her family, but she was in a different world now and they would have a hard time understanding her life. After one particularly complicated robe project she began to notice that her fingers were stiffening in the joints. It was harder and harder to do the fine detail work she had been known for. She became less and less adept at even the regular sewing. Eventually, the king had to make the difficult decision to dismiss her because she could no longer serve the court well. He was very kind and thanked her for her work, telling her that she could now return to her family and friends in the country.

When the time came for her to return home she was nowhere to be found. The whole court searched for the woman but to no avail.

Finally a young boy who was playing among some remnants in the corner of an unused room came upon the woman wrapped up in a ball as though she were hiding. He told her that people were looking for her and that it was time for her to go back to her home. She tucked herself desperately under the fabric saying to him, "Please don't tell anyone where I am. Just leave me alone. This is where I want to die. Leave. Pretend you never found me. Please! Please!"

"But why?" the young boy said. "You can't stay here. It is time for you to go home."

"That is impossible," she wept. "I don't remember where I came from!"

Let's Meet Some People at Stage Three

Pierre, the Foundation Executive

I love my work. I feel like I'm married to it in all honesty. I eat, drink, and sleep work. What happens to this organization while I'm the director will mold my image in this community for the future, and I know the top jobs in the big foundations only go to people who have a strong track record. I intend to have more than that. I want a strong track record at a young age. I want to usher in a new era of foundation philosophy, but I can only do that when I have enough power to pull it off. Right now I feel very successful, and I need to really capitalize on the areas of foundation work that will give me visibility. Right now that is in the area of evaluation models. The board is very interested in this, and I intend to become even more of an expert along the way. After we try out some models successfully I'll give a presentation at a national meeting on our experiences with evaluation. That will help the foundation, and it can't hurt me at all.

You know, I like being the head of something—in charge. I enjoy the challenge of managing other people and working with clients, the board, and employees. A clear distinction I've noticed about being at the helm is that other people's image of me changed. People listen more when I speak, and some try to stay on my good side more. I also get more flack, just because I'm the one who is in charge and who gets the blame for things. But I especially like the position I play in the community. I represent an enormous amount of power that can change things for the better. If others' causes fit our mandate and the criteria we have for funding projects, we in turn will persuade the board. That very fact gives me a great deal of control, too much at times, over the direction of events and organizations. Sometimes what I say goes just because of my position. Now there is a discomforting side to that too. I can't tell

> from how people treat me whether they're being nice to me because of my position or because of who I am personally. Would they be different if I were not in a powerful position? I don't know, but as long as I like it, why worry about it?

Pierre gives us a glimpse of the still unquenched drive for success. He is confidently and hastily climbing the career ladder and will not stop until he reaches the top. You decide whether he best illustrates a maturing ego or an egocentric person. What would people who work for him say?

Andrea, the Entrepreneur

> In a lot of ways my story might be typical of most business ventures. I was working for someone else in my mid-thirties. The work was OK, but my ideas went beyond where that company was at the time. It just so happened that I inherited a very small amount of money, but enough to suggest a risky venture. It was now or never, I thought, and the ideas I had for new products were sure to sell if I could get the capital to back me. I got my business plan together with the help of some financial wizards and started manufacturing a prototype in my basement because I was still working on my old job. I worked for months getting all the investors (including the bank) informed and relatively secure about the success of my venture. I recruited a management team and we waited and talked and persuaded. I'll never forget the day we signed the final agreements and we were official. I thought I had died and gone to heaven. Not for long though, because the real work was ahead. It took years of blood and sweat to make a success of our product and we did it. That was nine years ago. Now the whole situation looks different to me. We grew pretty fast the first years, and, as many companies do, we sold out to a larger corporation. Now I'm miserable. All those years I'd been my own boss, making my own decisions, and getting instant feedback and rewards. Now I'm working for someone else. They have the last word and have to approve all major financial investments. There is no challenge left for me, and I'm too stubborn to kowtow to bureaucrats. After all, I made this company what it is. Now I feel like I'm being gently put out to pasture. That's not for me. I'm looking for something new to dig into, a new and bigger challenge, another mountain to climb. As soon as my obligation is over, I'm on my way.

This entrepreneurial success story exemplifies how much success can breed a thirst for more. Some people get success only to be bored and eager for new challenges.

Susan, the Minister

> No one told me in seminary that churches were so political. It makes corporations look mild by comparison. I was expecting to come and teach, preach, baptize, bury, and counsel people who would thank me and tithe generously. Those ideas were shattered during my internship year. Now that I've had my own church for a while, I must admit that I thought I could change some of the factors here that lead to politics and strife. I'm beginning to believe that it is the nature of life in the church. Now don't misunderstand, I like the ministerial functions very much and feel quite competent in them. It's just the extra administrative duties, heated committee and board meetings, budgets, and personality clashes that I wasn't ready for. There is always a small vocal group that disagrees, and that really wants control. I'm learning quickly how to listen better, negotiate, and stand firm in cases where I need to.
>
> It's further complicated for me because there is a faction here that doesn't believe a woman can be a senior pastor. They don't expect me to stand up for myself, to challenge them, or to be able to have a true sympathetic ear. Yet when critical events occur in their lives they are forced to involve me because I am their minister. It's a clash of traditional and new ways and it's difficult. Another example is that some men withhold financial information from me because they don't think I'll understand it. My ministry is giving me real opportunity to show my people that I am up to the challenge. I've got a plan and I'm determined to follow through with it. Right now, I'm just very conscious of being competent but different, capable yet outside. I know it'll just take time, but it can be exhausting along the way.

Susan gives us an example of some of the questioning that occurs about new careers and risk-taking at Stage Three. She is breaking new ground and testing whether her values and ways of solving problems fit with the organizational culture.

Pete, the Engineer

> I consider myself a top-flight engineer. I've had many good job assignments here and I am very loyal to this company. After all, I put in a lot of my time to prepare for this and I wouldn't want to change now. There is too much water over the dam to do that now. But I'm at a real decision-making point in my career. I have always identified myself strongly with engineering. I've received recog-

> nition and rewards for my expertise in this field. Now that I've had success I look at what's happened to other guys like me in the past. If I continue to pursue the engineering route I will become more specialized and narrower but more of an expert in my work. And that track, even though it looks inviting, is not rewarded as much nor looked on as highly as the managerial track. At least that seems to be the perception. On the other hand the managerial track is more of an unknown and more of a risk because it requires people management skills and less technical expertise. It feels like I'd have to start over in another field. And if I don't do well, I'll be obsolete as an engineer. I'm confident though that I can manage well. I'm just not sure what I want and what will be best for me. I want to weigh the risks but go beyond where I am to new challenges, whether that means I'll be on the engineering track or the managerial side.

Pete is an expert who is at a turning point in his career, wondering whether he ought to go the technical route or the more rewarded managerial route that arrives closer to the top.

Marsha, the League of Women Voters President

> When I first joined this organization I did it to get out of the house, frankly. And little did I know that lurking inside me was a leader, wanting to get out. I quickly moved through the committee structure the first few years, doing a good job at every position and finding out all about the power structure of the organization. (I learned early on how to have a say in the league: be in charge of a project that people support and which has high visibility, and do a good job.) Next thing I knew I was elected to the board and now had a role in the policy-making and financial aspects of the league. There was a tricky year in there in which I wanted to run for vice-president (president-elect), but I didn't want to come out and ask for it. What happened was partly luck, partly planned. I had lunch with two influential board members, and during our conversations I briefly outlined for them my personal plan for the organization's future. They both figured strongly in my plan. When the discussion came up several weeks later about appropriate vice-presidents, one of them asked me if I would be willing to consider it. I said it looked like a lot of responsibility but I would like to give it a try. Now that I'm in the middle of my term, I look back and wonder how I could have considered anything else. The question now is, where do I go from here?

This example points out the joy and excitement that occurs when a person discovers new areas of confidence and learns to capitalize on them.

A Turning Point in the Personal Power Model

The movement from Stage Three to Four and beyond marks a distinctly different move from any that have preceded it. The first three stages have many trends or characteristics in common, and the last three stages do as well. It may be useful here to illustrate the main differences between them, so that as you begin to read about Stage Four you will understand why it will seem like such new territory—or a turning point.

Building Up, Then Letting Go

The first major difference between Stages One through Three and Four through Six is called "building up, then letting go." In Stages One, Two and Three you work quite diligently at getting to know who you want to be, acquiring basic self-esteem, feeling good and confident, and seeking recognition and affirmation. You find, capitalize on, and promote personal skills and strengths as well as any new skills and experiences you can accumulate. All these things build normally and naturally into the self-confident image of the Stage Three person. It's as if you've been filling a pitcher all along the way and now it is getting full.

Carl Jung and Joseph Campbell both write extensively about the idea that the first task of life is to develop a healthy ego (Stages One through Three) and that the other task in life is to let go of one's ego (Stages Four through Six). Both Jung and Campbell claim that many primal cultures handled this development much better than our high-tech western cultures do. That is, young people went through training and then a religious ritual (puberty rites) in which the child symbolically died and then was reborn as an adult. Today some people still go through church confirmation, but there are a great many "rites of passage" in our culture now so it is difficult for many individuals to know when they have become true adults. Perhaps, this may be one reason why our society seems to think that Stage Three is pretty much the be-all and end-all. From a sociological perspective, our present society may not promote an individual's continued growth to the degree that many primal societies may have. To the extent that this is true, what kind of rituals might we need to develop in order to move beyond Stage Three and into the inner life of courage and wisdom?

We hope to give a number of these rituals in this chapter (techniques for moving beyond Stage Three).

In Stages Four through Six the story changes. Stage Four people begin to go deeply inside and encounter intense personal questioning and reacquaintance with their true selves. They begin to question the value of the full pitcher and even the value of the pitcher itself. After this crisis of integrity is understood they can proceed, as they move to Stages Five and Six, to letting go of having to be seen as strong, confident, perfect, and competent. They have found a deeper source of self-esteem that does not depend on external signals. Again, this reiterates that Stages One through Three are more externally-oriented even when it comes to inner journeys, while Stages Four through Six are more internally-oriented, but in touch with the world.

Finiteness of Power

Another major difference between Stages One through Three and Four through Six is the "finiteness of power." At Stages One through Three, power is seen as finite. Remember the gold coin analogy? There are only so many to go around. If I have twelve coins and you take six, I will have only six left. I've lost power. Someone wins; someone loses.

At Stages Four through Six the idea of power is changing. It now appears to be infinite. Accepting infinite power may take a little doing, which is why Stage Four is a transition stage in this respect. But infinite power suggests an ever-filling well from which to draw power. Another analogy, an earthy one, describes infinite power too. Let's say I have planted twelve lily bulbs. I can divide my bulbs and give you twelve and I will still have twelve left. Then you can plant your bulbs and eventually you can give away twelve more. Power multiplies. Everyone gets more. It is infinite. The win-lose status of power is lost.

Empowering other people is a way to increase the total potential of power and spread it around. No one loses. Stages Five and Six people see themselves as conduits only, as channels of power to other people. They have no need to hang on to any of it themselves. It is like love: The more you can channel it to others, the more it multiplies.

From Tangible to Intangible

Another main distinction between Stages One through Three and Four through Six is that the first stages result mostly in tangible rewards, while the later stages reward people with intangibles. Skills, degrees, jobs, titles, material possessions, elected positions, salary, and homes are examples of Stage One, Two, and Three rewards. They fit neatly on a resume. As you gain each new experience, your resume builds. Intangible Stage Four, Five, and Six rewards might include understanding one's life purpose, integrity, empowering others, enjoying quietude, peace of mind, and long-term thinking. If, in the section of your resume marked "career objective," you write peace of mind, you probably won't get an interview. That is why it is difficult to motivate Fours, Fives, and Sixes in traditional organizational ways. The motivations and rewards do not have the same meaning they used to.

Cultural Encouragement and Discouragement

Lastly, the culture is a strong influencing factor in the decisions of most of us when it comes to personal power. We are either trying to meet the cultural expectations and aspire to the positions that our socialization encourages, or we are trying to rebel against the culture and deliberately change the goals that have been instilled in us. Either way we are still controlled by Stage Three ideals and models in our advertising, in our family, and in our social lives. Beyond Stage Three the situation gets more confusing. Because the predominant culture (laws, mores, customs, rewards) is just now beginning to recognize or reward Stage Four, Five, and Six behavior, moving to these stages becomes more of a personal decision, a commitment to purpose, to service, to inner principles. It is a lonelier and less charted course, and most of the work goes on inside long before the behavior is apparent to people on the outside. It feels as if you are being asked to give up many of the things you've learned to want and strive for all these years. It's an about-face in many ways. And you have to look inward before you can look outward again, not in a narcissistic way but in a self-healing way as is elaborated in the chapters on Stages Four and Five.

Moving to Stage Four

Contrary to what many of us would like to believe, you don't just sit down one day and decide to move or grow into Stage Four. Moving to Stage Four is more of a process than it is an achievement. Usually a change of this magnitude requires a crisis to precipitate it, especially for men who've been taught all their lives that being successful, strong, rich, competent, expert, and masculine is the highest goal and reward in life. The crisis in moving from Stage Three to Stage Four is one of integrity, inner and outer congruity in life. The event that initiates it can be of internal or external origin, but it triggers a whole series of deeper, more serious questions, which are extremely painful to answer. They are questions such as, who am I, really? What am I doing here? Where do I fit at work, home, in the community? Do I want to work? Can I trust myself? Can I remain (or get) married? Do I have more capability or am I on a plateau? Who cares? The event may be a major or sudden illness (heart attack), being passed over for a promotion, losing at sports, discovering total boredom in life or on the job, falling out of love with your spouse, a significant birthday, losing energy, chronic depression, or it can be developing a strong case of burn-out. Whatever the event is, it invites or propels the individual to enter the inner realm of self-knowledge and integrity. Integrity is simply a quality or state of being of sound moral principle, honest and sincere. The move from Stage Three to Four, because of the nature of the crisis, is perhaps the most critical turning point in one's life.

One man told me that he didn't realize, until he was lying in the intensive care room following emergency heart surgery, that he never wanted to be in the successful family business that he had been in for twenty-five years. For the next several years he twisted and turned his life around, trying to find out who he was and what he wanted. Everything was up for grabs. He tried another line of work, had an affair, sold his house and lived on a beach, read a lot, wrote a lot, and tried a variety of counselors in the attempt to peel back all the crusty layers that had grown up around the real person he was inside. He caused himself and others a great deal of pain in the process. But he was determined to get his questions answered before it was too late. He and his wife, who was, of course, having her own struggles during this time, survived these events and are now building a new life for themselves, more realistically and more genuinely than ever before.

I have just described one man's mid-life crisis. Not everyone will experience the events he did during the transition, and dramatic outward events are not required to prove what's going on inside. Nor can a midlife crisis guarantee that everyone will take that opportunity to look inside and allow that experience to really change them. However, the mid-life crisis often coincides with being stuck at Stage Three—the inability to get out of the trap and the added confusion of not knowing which questions to ask. It can be a frustrating and bewildering time for people who've ordinarily been competent, energetic, reliable decision makers. They don't trust their own judgment any more because they can't seem to focus enough to make decisions. They don't know what they really want or where they want to go. And the more others push them to get the answers, the worse it becomes.

It takes a courageous person to take on the struggle of knowingly moving from Stage Three to Stage Four. Men sometimes think just the opposite. They believe that introspection and discovering fears and other emotions are women's traits and are soft and weak. Being out of control is one of the worst things that can happen to a man. Many men will fight, ignore, shun, or ridicule the whole idea of discovering the fearful and wonderful world within. They will choose to stay in Stage Three by diving into their work to reach a higher level of success or by pushing themselves physically to prove their prowess. Or they will become drained and bitter over the confusion and lock up the inside, never to hear from it again. The pain of feeling is so great they turn off their feelings altogether. They withdraw from life and work; and then they die from the inside out, both physically and emotionally.

There is a tendency in all of us to look at what the transition to the next stage requires, and then go back to earlier, more comfortable stages. The move forward is too scary, too new. And there are few role models for us to follow into the stages beyond Stage Three. To move to and through Stage Four men need to let go little by little of their stereotyped view of themselves and their prescribed roles in the world and cultivate their true feelings. They need to develop the qualities that they have not understood or have undervalued, qualities such as the ability to have deep relationships, to nurture others, to reflect, to see longer-range issues, to empower others, to give to and collaborate closely with others. Men tend to negate personal growth, quality-of-life questions, values, feelings, intuition, flexibility, and adaptability. These are the qualities that will help men balance out their masculine side with their other side (the feminine side) that has been dormant for so long. *This does not make them weak; it makes them whole.*

Recently two male college students interviewed me for their adult development and leadership class. One asked me a very interesting question: What is an example of the crisis of integrity for college students? I thought for a second and then used this illustration; suppose that you are part of a group of guys or a fraternity that promotes heavy drinking as a social norm, almost a rite of passage. You have been an active part of that social life on campus. One weekend you get a bad cold and although you decide to go out with the guys, you are just too sick to drink. So you get a chance to watch how your friends behave when they are drunk. You see how they treat each other; you see how they treat women they are with; and you see how they treat the wait staff. You are, frankly, appalled. Something inside of you just clicks. You think to yourself, I absolutely cannot do this anymore. But now over the next days and weeks you are faced with a huge dilemma. What do you do about the situation? They are your friends. How do you socialize with them? Do you say something? If so, what do you say? How do you say it so it doesn't sound sanctimonious? What kind of inner development will be required of you to work your way through this inner crisis? What a crisis of integrity!

A man shared his transition story with me illustrating another view of the change in moving from Stage Three to Four. He felt that he was being controlled in a negative way. He was possessed by his job and his habits. He noticed this one night when he couldn't get himself up from watching TV, even though he wanted to. He observed the same things about work. He set appointments to do recreational things and then let work infringe on them frequently, even though he didn't want it to. Success at work and the power it brought compensated for the lack of meaning in his life.

First he gradually withdrew from TV, newspapers, and other controllers like coffee. That only made matters worse because now he craved TV and coffee constantly. Finally he had to admit the craving was overwhelming. He went to talk to his priest about the escalating problem. He recognized that his was a spiritual struggle, that power for him covered the fear of confronting death. Now he had to let go of his expectations for his life and start afresh. It was difficult, he says, " but when I totally let go, everything came back in a fresh form, my work, my life, my family." He spends more time alone now, is better balanced, understands his other side better, has moved to a new position with more responsibility but less weekend work, laughs at himself more, is calmer, and is excited about life.

This man created his own crisis. He asked the question, how much is enough? And he decided he had had enough of Stage Three and its outward success. We can create the transition to Stage Four. It is just more difficult, because Stage Three is the hardest stage to give up. These are a few of the ways I have observed people get started on it: act like a person you know who is at Stage Four; experiment with new behaviors; put yourself in an introspective experience like a silent retreat; go to a therapist; start reflecting on your behavior in a journal; ask yourself before each statement you make at a meeting, why am I saying this?

To move to Stage Four women have to reconfirm themselves. At this point they have had some recognition or success at Stage Three and have been acknowledged by the system sufficiently to feel they can compete in it, but not so much that they drown in it. They may have felt the stress of Stage Three acutely (the glass ceiling, loneliness, health issues) and now they need to reassess their lives. They need to balance the behaviors they took on at Stage Three with the inner qualities of being a woman and find the style that suits their real selves. Some women have told me that this means they have to move to another company to capitalize more effectively on their competence. Or it may mean splitting off from a mentor or model that is no longer necessary. More often it means being involved in a broader sphere of activity in which they can develop their style without so much pressure from their part of the organization. It means getting a broader view. It's time to establish who they are, apart from everyone else. Some women may experience lingering doubts at this stage because they may wonder whether they are the token woman or whether they really are respected for who they are and what they can do. At this point it is helpful for women to seek leadership opportunities inside and outside the organization that will broaden their visibility and base of influence, like community boards, organization-wide committees, professional groups, or broadly-based civic groups.

One Woman's Crisis of Integrity: Time to Move on to Stage Four

January 1988 I began a career in public accounting. Within my first hour I determined that I was going to be a partner in this firm. And from that moment on I was obsessed with this goal. I did whatever I was asked. I always exceeded expectations. I watched the political machinery. I knew the right dress, the right outside activities, the insiders.

Slowly and methodically my blood turned into company blood. Silently I marched into twelve-hour days, sometimes seven days a week. I was in a gerbil wheel cycling from work, to eat, to sleep, to work and on and on. A life outside of work was an illusion.

In January 1995 I was a participant in a tax seminar in Houston, Texas, when the voice of the instructor faded out as my mind was back in my office in St. Petersburg, Florida. I was busily creating an imaginary worry list: What fires were building up in my office? Would there be enough time at the break to return all my phone calls? Was the staff working on my projects or were my projects getting bumped?

Then, I was interrupted by my next thoughts. My own internal broadcaster began to shout. This is what I heard. *I'm stressed, out of balance, gaining weight, losing sleep, and not exercising. I'm road kill!*

This is not a good personal inventory. Why was I stressed, out of balance, gaining weight, losing sleep, and not exercising? Why was my self-worth so flattened, so run down that I was a tasty tidbit for the circling vultures?

Because I was too busy being the person my husband wanted me to be, being who my family wanted me to be, and especially being

> the soldier my employer wanted me to be. And I was busy being the friend my friends wanted me to be. There simply was no room for me to be who I wanted to be.
>
> In 10 seconds I lost all certainty of who I was. One moment I am a CPA and then snap—I now know in the very core of my being I can no longer be a CPA. And I don't have a clue who I do want to be. Ten seconds and I am thrown into suspended animation. Who am I? What is my purpose? How may I serve?
>
> The panic subsided and I thought, "This is only Monday. I am here for a whole week. By Friday I'll have this all figured out." The biggest project of my life and I think I can do it in five days.
>
> Well, on Friday, I didn't have any of the answers—kind of depressing for a person who thought she always had it together. I was an illusionist. But, I am also fortunate. I have some friends I call people of wise counsel. People of wise counsel always see the big picture and in a few carefully chosen words they do not tell me what to do, but send a message to help me find my own wisdom.
>
> Monday morning I sought the advise of one of my friends of wise counsel. I raced into her office screaming, "I think I need a shrink."
>
> The response back was, "No, you don't need a shrink, you are just shrink-wrapped. Everything you need is packaged within you. All you have to do is unwrap your gifts."
>
> Only a few words; she was right. The answers are within. Then, I couldn't name my gifts. I only knew I had to be different. I had to walk away from the path I was on. I have never looked back with one moment of doubt. I have stepped forward into my evolving personal power. I am learning it is through my personal power that I am able to live the life of my truth, my meaning, my vision, and my passion. Right now, my journey is filled with unnamed and unlimited possibilities. I am being me the best I know how to be at this point in my learning. I no longer call myself road kill.

This young woman had developed a strong enough ego to know she needed to leave and she was developing enough courage to do it. Her integrity crisis was becoming who she was, as opposed to what everyone else wanted her to be.

At Stage Four, both men and women move beyond jobs and titles to credibility, respect, reputation, and experienced judgment. You begin to develop and trust your own personal style, which capitalizes on strengths and acknowledges weaknesses, for both are there. Your spheres of contact become broader because you are less afraid of people who are different from you. You see them as people to learn from, not people who might be trying to outsmart you.

Here are some specific ways to move to Stage Four:

- Become an observer of yourself and detach from ego-involvement. Put your personal philosophy into action. Several practices allow you to do this. One of the most useful is called Practical Spirituality, a course offered by William Kemsley that includes a set of practices derived from various religious traditions. More information may be obtained from Kemsley at wkemsley@yahoo.com.

  Review of practices:

  1. Observe what state you are in at any moment: sattva (serenity), rajas (action), or tamas (lethargic). If in a lethargic state, you need to move to action before you can get to serenity. These states are not all-or-none. We can experience two states at the same time: lethargic and action or action and serenity. Remember that detachment brings humor.

  2. Use the sense of touch to bring your focus to the present—touch something with your hands.

  3. Say, "Is this me walking or am I observing my body walking?" You can do this while drinking a glass of water, brushing your teeth, lathering up in the shower, etc. The intent is to become an observer of your own behavior.

  4. Do a two-minute exercise where you sit quietly and focus your attention briefly on each of the five senses, one after the other, and just notice what you experience without thinking about it. Just concentrate on the sensory experience.

  5. Pause between activities—give yourself time to be quiet.

  6. Say, "Not this, not this!" to yourself when confronted with a stressful or frustrating situation. This will help you detach from it and, therefore, have less ego involvement with it.

  7. Say, "Is that so?" when someone is being obnoxious with you.

  8. Listen to the sounds of someone's words (voice) without focusing on comprehending and have a different experience of them. As an example, the same activity may be draining, energizing, or relaxing

at different times—like washing the dishes while listening to someone's voice.

9. Recognize that you have a choice of whether your attention will be focused/absorbed by a situation or detached from it and not captured by the pathos. For example, think to yourself, "I am uncomfortable, but I am bigger than this discomfort." Attachment takes a lot of energy. Calm down.

Practice these strategies whenever possible.

We limit ourselves through bad habits, fear, and worry about outcomes. So, stay in the present and you will experience liberation, clarity, calmness, contentment, and depth. We are not looking for ecstasy, which is a short-lived high.

- Perform a ritual that will help you move out of Stage Three. This ritual needs to be something that has meaning for you. You can do it alone or involve friends. Rituals usually involve something tangible along with words or actions.

  One example might be to give away or give up a symbol that has been especially important to you but is not something that you want to cultivate any longer. One ritual for me was giving my sports car to a non-profit organization. I told the car how important it had been for me and said that now that era was over. I drove the car reverently to the drop-off place and actually felt like a part of my life was leaving with the car.

  Another example might be to spend time with friends reflecting on what it would be like to live a simpler life and then commit to them what it is you will do to move toward that simpler life and in what period of time. Report back to each other about your progress and have a (simple) party when you have met your objectives.

- Start a long-range plan for life change. If you are serious about moving beyond Stage Three and you don't want to wait for a crisis to happen naturally, commit yourself to the long-term process I suggest in Chapter 12: Leading from Your Soul. Be prepared for adventure, pain, and change. It will take you inside and help you find a new person there. But first, it will rock your boat.

- Learn from a life crisis.

  Allow for vulnerability and other feelings that arise. Hold them as a sign that a window is open for you to find out more about yourself and to grow from this.

  Talk with someone you trust and let the process take you to a new place inside.

- Learn how to be alone with yourself. Go on a long day trip by yourself and see whether you fill it with activities or have some quiet moments to think about larger issues.

  Learn to sit quietly and listen to your thoughts without having to get anxious.

  Learn to express yourself through a journal in which you can write anything and everything.

- Do some serious self-assessment.

  Ask yourself whether you want to be the person you represent at Stage Three. If so, fine. If not, admit to yourself that you aren't who you want to be.

  Read classic books or attend seminars on the mid-life reassessment time: *Seasons of a Man's Life* (Levinson), *Legacy of the Heart* or *How Then Shall We Live?* (Muller), *When Work Doesn't Work Anymore* (McKenna), or the classics, *In Her Time* (Sangiuliano), *Fire in the Belly* (Sam Keen), *Transitions* (Bridges), *Iron John* (Robert Bly), *Making Our Lives Our Own* (Marilyn Mason), *Transformations* (Gould), *Passages* (Sheehy), *Middle Age Crisis* (Fried), *Against the Grain* (Moitland), *The Inventurers* (Hagberg, Leider).

  Make a list of the things your parents would want you to do with your life. Circle the items you don't want to do. Think through the implication of this for your present life/work situation.

  Learn to be honest with yourself.

- Try new things that will make you think differently. Read widely in the arts, literature, and science to stimulate your creative mind. Keep an open and active mind, especially about things you think you know a lot about.

  Create a crisis or ask someone else to create one in your life to get you "off the dime."

  Push yourself into an experience that requires you to act beyond your normal comfort level. Try a workshop, a trip to another country, or a physical experience. Do it quietly, not with the gusto of a Stage Three. Examine its effect on your thinking. Reflect on it, write about it, and let it sink in.

  Get out of the rut of daily activities. Develop a hobby, read in new areas, get on a board in the community, or write a column for the newspaper.

- Get support if you need it.

  Start a men's group or a women's group to talk about work or personal issues.

  Find a new mentor or begin being a mentor to others.

  Seek out a counselor, priest, minister, rabbi, or a good, patient friend to talk through the things you're feeling. Choose someone who is beyond Stage Three in your opinion.

- Build on your networks.

  Broaden your range of contacts in the organization and outside the organization by getting yourself on broader organizational committees and tasks. Think quality, not quantity.

  Keep track of old friends and contacts in the organization so you can help them out whenever possible.

  Test your leadership skills in professional or civic association leadership positions, being who you really are, and then let your management see how you are respected outside the organization too.

- Concentrate on what you are doing now instead of concentrating on the future.

  Build on the reputation you have secured in order to work on projects you like. Don't take on things that will move you ahead in your work if you sincerely are not good at them or do not like them.

  Accept the challenge of broadening your job and deepening yourself rather than complaining about not moving or looking around for other jobs.

  Have a long talk with your boss about what you do best, like best, and can learn from on your present job.

- Reflect on the types of people who are at Stage Four.

  Write the names of people you know whom you respect the most for the quality of their judgment and their personal integrity. Are these the same as the people in your organization who have the best jobs? What qualities of the most respected people would you like to have that you don't have now? Talk to one or two of them about how they acquired those qualities.

In an article entitled "The Things You Know After You Know It All," John Gardner says:

> The things you learn in maturity seldom involve information and skills. You learn to bear with the things you can't change. You learn to avoid self-pity. You learn not to burn up energy in anxiety. You learn that most people are neither for nor against you but rather are thinking about themselves. You learn that no matter how much you try to please, some people are never going to love you—a notion that troubles at first but is eventually relaxing.

As you can imagine, Andrea and Pierre, the entrepreneur and the foundation executive, are still concentrating on the climb to success. Marsha, the league president, has decided to go back to school to study public administration. She enjoys the practical side of running an organization and now sees her children getting to the age where she can invest more concentrated time in school. She hopes to manage in government or be a director of a non-profit agency someday.

Pete, the engineer, got himself involved with a management assessment center and found out that his people skills would have to be developed extensively to compare with his fine technical expertise. He decided it would be too much of an effort to do that at this stage when he is just getting into the enjoyment of his expertise. He's decided to stay in project engineering and broaden his professional base by presenting more papers and getting on the board of his professional group. He's also going to take a month-long vacation to Europe with his wife this fall.

Susan decided to have a series of long-range planning sessions with her church board to help get her plans implemented. There were some very tense times along the way when she sensed people's doubts about her abilities, but enough strong people supported her to turn the tide. Now she has to get the plan implemented.

What Holds People Back?

People at Stage Three are most frequently stuck because they think they aren't. They think they've made it or they are on their way, so they don't need to move anywhere but up. They are very comfortable and do not want to be upset or stopped. They simply have not had enough of Stage Three or do not want to think there is anything else beyond Stage Three. One man said, after hearing the stages, "I don't want to know anything about Stage Four or Five. I like it at Stage Three."

The second major factor that interferes with the move—but only after they know they are dissatisfied with Stage Three—is confusion. They have hidden their weaknesses for fear they will be found out, and covered their other side (males especially) for so long that the process feels, at first, like excavating in a very old and deep mine. The confusion is perplexing; it lasts far longer than their patience or time permits; the solutions seem to come only from inside; and no one else can tell them what to do. The only redeeming quality may be that others have been through it and usually find themselves better off after it's over. One woman said, "One of my friends reminded me when I was in the middle of all this that it was a great growth experience. It's hard to see that when you're in the middle of it. Ask me in a year whether it was a growth experience or not." Eventually the confusion becomes more acceptable and life takes on a vastly broader potential.

Hagberg's Model of Personal Power

SUMMARY OF STAGE THREE
POWER BY ACHIEVEMENT

Symbol

Key Questions: What are your gifts? What kinds of things come easily for you? What are your skills?

Description
Control
The dynamo stage

Characteristics
Mature ego
Realistic and competitive
Expert
Ambitious

Spirituality and Stage Three
Spirituality is being productive on our chosen faith journey

The Shadow of Stage Three
Bravado
Egocentric behavior
Greed

Catalyst for Movement
Embracing integrity

What Holds People Back?
Not knowing they're stuck
Confusion

Ways to Move
Accept the potential change that crisis can bring; learn to be alone and to seriously reflect on yourself; try new things that make you think differently; design a ritual; create a crisis; get support from a Stage Four, Five, or Six person; build networks; concentrate on the present; be reflective about the next stages; consider a long-range plan for true leadership.

Ask yourself these questions about Stage Four:

Yes No

____ ____ 1. Do you take pride in your solid record of competent work?

____ ____ 2. Are others consciously choosing you to be a mentor to them?

____ ____ 3. Do you feel as if you have a life going on inside of you that is distinctly different from the one on the outside?

____ ____ 4. Have you consciously chosen to act with integrity, despite the consequences?

____ ____ 5. Do you think beyond your current job and peers as part of your base of influence, i.e., community, professional leadership, political arena?

____ ____ 6. Is it important for you to have a natural and personal style that is yours and not what the organization expects?

____ ____ 7. Have you had a major crisis or triggering event in your life that has challenged the way you think about life and work?

____ ____ 8. Do you feel a loss in moving away from the center of the action?

____ ____ 9. Do you find that the symbols of success do not motivate you the way they used to?

____ ____ 10. Have you learned to admit weaknesses and mistakes readily, without putting yourself down?

____ ____ 11. Do you acknowledge both feminine and masculine behavior as useful, depending on the situation, and use them appropriately?

____ ____ 12. Do you ever feel you are different from or out of touch with other leaders in the organization?

____ ____ 13. Do you speak out when you are asked to do something you don't believe in?

____ ____ 14. Do you feel confused about who you used to be and who you are now?

____ ____ 15. Do you enjoy collaborating with others even though you could easily be in charge?

Yes answers indicate that you identify with this stage.

Chapter 4
Stage Four: Power by Reflection

Influence

Key Question: What was the moment of keenest insight in your life and what happened when you acted?

What Is Stage Four Like?

Power by reflection. What does that mean? What are reflective people like? Where do we find them? What can they offer? What are they reflecting about?

Stage Four people have influence in organizations, not because of their position power but because of their reputation for sound judgment, fairness, and a listening ear. These qualities have developed as a result of their own inner struggles and reflection on their values and purpose. They are coming to know themselves in a new way, a more intimate way. And they can be more honest because they have less to lose. Their security comes from within. The important focus with them is what is going on inside. In organizations they are more adept at handling crises involving others because they have experienced their own inner turmoil.

Seasoned and trustworthy, they are the people others choose as confidants and mentors. Power is not their issue and they can encourage win-win solutions. They are more integrated themselves and have no need to find fault in others or themselves. They are congruent. What this all adds up to is that they have *integrity*.

But, Fours do not arrive at Stage Four with all these qualities intact. The transition from Stage Three to Four is a difficult one and it doesn't just happen. The entrance to Stage Four frequently involves a painful confusing experience and only gradually do Fours move on to the strengths that show publicly. The entry is masked with confusion, grief, and ambiguousness. Fours have no answers to their pressing questions of meaning and purpose and they have to learn to live with the questions.

Reflection, the description of this stage, means contemplating or pondering. Fours are entering into a self-reflective stage that will not be readily apparent on the outside. As a result of whatever experience or crisis they had in moving out of Stage Three, they will never be the same. In fact, the more accepted and respected they feel for what they are doing, the less important it becomes and the more confused they are. This is a stage of confusion on the inside and assuredness on the outside. I think of it as the sandwich stage, because Stage Fours feel caught between their own outward show of competence and their inner dilemmas, just as they are caught between clear and straightforward Stage Three and mystifying Stage Five. And so the problem that needs to be addressed is one of integrity, i.e., soundness or wholeness.

As people enter this stage they no longer want to play by all the rules, for they realize the rules don't mean what they used to mean. Now that they are developing their own style and way of being, they wonder if they are out of touch, too different, or fooling themselves. They have not yet emerged as inwardly confident people, yet they look very polished and competent to others. They are undergoing a reassessment, which causes them to be a bit more humble and tentative. A good analogy is that of a trapeze artist. A Stage Four person is in the precarious moment of the trapeze act when she or he has let go of one swinging bar and is floating through the air, waiting for the other bar to come swinging along. He or she has not yet completed the act and is filled with expectancy, a bit of anxiety, and confidence.

Stage Four people have become more secure primarily because they have established a record, a long history of competence, expertise and respect. They are not living from one promotion to the next, because life seems too short for that. They generally trust themselves and others much more and rely on informal contacts within the organization more than on any formal reporting structure.

One symbol for this stage is the reflective thinker, which emphasizes the importance of spending time reflecting and thinking, listening and questioning—mostly inside. It is a time for deeper exploration, for raising questions about self, life, and work that may have been lying dormant or have never been raised before. Stage Fours may even appear at times to be taking a sabbatical from work or life. Fortunately, this does not go on forever and the Four reemerges slowly as a more integrated person. The greatest changes are going on inside as part of the reconfiguration process. As the issues gradually become clear, the outer and the inner begin to integrate through this struggle. Delorese Ambrose writes about this journey to the inner life in her book, *Leadership: The Journey Inward.* "To transform our organizations, our communities or our lives, we must first transform ourselves. Leadership development, then, becomes a process of self-reflection aimed at personal growth: a journey inward."

Stage Fours have influence, and that is the definition of power at this stage. People respect their advice, come to them for counsel, want their recommendations, and invite them to plan with them, no matter what level they happen to occupy in the organization. They give people straight answers, are more caring, are better listeners, and do not use their position in the organization as a lever.

However, the appearance of influence or reputation alone should not be mistaken for Stage Four behavior. Stage Fours influence people because of their fairness, follow-through, honesty, and unwillingness to be self-serving.

Compare this wise-counsel type of influence, for instance, with the type of influence that we call political clout, which is obtained through large contributions to political candidates or by rubbing elbows with those in office. Although that is one form of influence, the more substantive influencers in politics are those who keep themselves out of the limelight and help the candidate see both sides and the long-term implications of issues so as to make the best decision for the greatest good. Partisanship can get in the way of making difficult decisions, especially for politicians who seek the good of the constituency over their own parties or egos. One governor recently stated, "Until I decided not to seek reelection, we could not get the two parties to work together on some difficult budget decisions. I decided it was the price I had to pay to get a fair solution."

It is impossible to describe Stage Four people by the positions they hold within the organization. They cannot be identified by symbols or specific status but by how they interact with others. For instance, it would not be unusual to hear this comment about a Stage Four person regarding an important committee assignment: "If you are serious about that committee's objective, make Jane the chair. She won't be shoved around, but at the same time she is fair and listens to everyone. She always seems to forge win-win solutions that everyone can live with because she has no flag of her own to wave." We've all heard words similar to these. Someone else may be technically more qualified or have more prestige, but if you want it to be done fairly, give it to a person who is not unduly biased and who will listen.

Think of Stage Four as a value-added stage. Until recently our norm for organizational culture has been Stages Two and Three. Now the organizational culture is reflecting Stage Four more strongly than it has in the past. So if we can operate at Stage Four it will add additional value to us and to the organizations with which we associate. And the stages are cumulative. Fours can operate at Stages Three, Two, and One because they have experienced those as home stages in the past. It will be a real advantage in the coming years to have versatile Stage Four people in our organizations.

At Stage Four true leadership occurs, separate from position or status leadership. People in status positions *can* be leaders but are not automatically leaders because of their positions. Stage Four people are known for being natural leaders, but are not the self-promoting types. Fours emerge as leaders because they have integrity as they plan, organize, listen to others, help work out solutions, and think up good ideas. True leaders must have true followers, people who will follow because they trust the leader's integrity, not because they are manipulated by threats, theatrical persuasion, or by the power of a position that forces them to follow. True leaders have long-term followers because they give more and more of the power to the followers. Stage Four people lead from the middle. Stage Three people lead from the front. And you guessed it; Stage Five people lead from behind.

My experiences of Stage Four have been excruciatingly wonderful. I've been in and out of this stage several times but I'll relate my first clear memory of entering this stage. I was at the height of my career, writing a book, working with Fortune 500 companies, traveling around the world doing seminars, actively involved in the community. My life was full. I went to Europe with a friend one summer to find my family roots in Scandinavia and arrived back home to find that my fifteen-year relationship with my husband was over.

All of a sudden my world changed. I was no longer the carefree businesswoman for whom crises were merely new learning experiences. I had failed. I felt ashamed that we had grown so far apart and that I couldn't keep my marriage together. And nothing seemed to make a difference in my life anymore. I was forced to stop, listen, cry, ache, grieve, and also reflect on my life, my values, and my work. I had to change something. The formula for success was not working. It was like someone changed the problem so my formula was not relevant. It was hell.

I knew I had to change. And not just change the surface, like my clothes or my hairstyle or the wallpaper on my wall! I had to reassess my priorities. I had to consider "doing life" in a new way. I engaged in more meaningful volunteer work, reduced my travel schedule, and spent more time with family and friends. But my work was still essentially the same—and much less satisfying. Then I read a quote from Henri Nouwen, which haunted me. "I used to complain that my work was constantly being interrupted, until I slowly discovered my interruptions are my work." What a different way to think about work. But what did it mean for *my* work? I knew I had to change my focus. I needed to give more attention to relationships. As I was healing from the pain of the divorce internally I decided to change the nature of my work. Even though I continued doing career consulting, my "work" changed to developing meaningful growth-oriented relationships in the work place. So my focus became the people who hired me, not the content of my work. I wanted to see what kind of influence I might have on their lives by focusing on our relationship. I was still able to deliver the product, but I shifted where my heart was.

It transformed me. It transformed my work. I am still feeling the satisfaction of that decision made years ago. The changes in my life and in the lives of my clients are still testimony to the miraculous experience of that change in focus. And that crisis and resolution lead me to the initial writing of *Real Power.*

I move among the power stages regularly. In fact I spend a lot of my work life at Stage Three since I am a public speaker and author. I also spend a good deal of time at Stage Two because I change work emphasis and book subjects regularly. Now I think more of the stages as choices and I can decide which stage I will opt for at a given time. If I want to learn about a new way of being, I can move my home stage to Stage Two. It gives me more flexibility. Of course, unexpected events catapult me into Stage One at a moment's notice. Like several years ago, when the co-author of one of my books died unexpectedly at age fifty-two while I was unable to be reached in Eastern Europe. I was devastated. It takes a long time to work through the tremendous grief that comes with the loss of people close to us. And so it goes. Life is about surviving—and thriving. Life is about living at each stage and experiencing the wholeness of life—the pain and the joy.

Characteristics of Stage Four People

Reflective/Confused

Few are aware of the battle that goes on within Fours. It is fought between their outer reputation and their inner questioning. Since the movement from Stage Three to Stage Four was precipitated by a reassessment, Fours find it difficult to escape the gnawing internal questions: why am I doing things this way? Who am I? Now that the old goals are less intriguing, what do I want next? What will my peers think when they find out I'm more vulnerable? How can I find more balance in my life—to let family, friends, and community become more important and to relegate work to a more realistic place? How will I live up to the trust that people have in me? Do I want to stay here? How will this new person within me behave? Can I admit my weaknesses now or even laugh at them? Can I be helpful to this organization with my newly emerging sense of self, or will they think I have lost the spark? Am I too driven? These and other questions will continue to be asked all through Stage Four despite the competent behavior that may appear on the outside.

There is mass confusion inside Fours. As they look at Stage Three they see what they no longer want or can no longer have. It is clear what that was. But as they look ahead, everything is a shade of gray. It is not clear who they are, or what they will be. And they don't even know how to approach the issues. A cartoon mournfully expresses their dilemma. A middle-aged manager sitting at an empty desk with a never-ringing phone as it's only adornment asks, "What the hell am I doing here?"

Lots of people at Stage Four are asking that question. And they don't mean *here* at this desk. They mean *here* in this world. What am I doing HERE? Who am I? There is grief, loss, and ambiguity in the emergence of this stage. Am I losing everything? Do I have a place here? There is a great deal of uncertainty and it is part of the growth process, despite feelings to the contrary. Reflection or inner pondering is necessary to move with this intense growth process. It takes time. A personal journal as a companion can be very consoling. It is also useful to have someone you trust who can talk with you about all the things that are going on inside, the doubts and the fears, the pains and the strange exhilaration.

The armor has cracked. The true self is beginning to emerge. The old rules are changing, and the new rules are being written from inside. Most of the growth and change occurring at this stage is on the inside. And it can be a roller coaster experience: One day the world all fits together; the next day it all falls apart. The consistency on the outside is mocked by the confusion on the inside. It's like being in a revolving door with one half going out and the other half coming in. The outwardly firm direction and decisions are backed by a cloud of gray at times inside, yet the balance for most people is maintained, and the debate is largely a silent one. This is especially true for men who, while feeling more open and questioning, have not been taught how to discuss it nor been given permission to talk about it. The results are brooding, moodiness at times, seduction by distractions that will help to avoid the issue, easy solutions, frequent change of plans, long fantasies and daydreams. People tell me that if their peers knew what they were thinking, they would be shocked and amazed. Some say they feel they're losing their stuff, shrinking, drying up, or dying. They believe they have nowhere to turn and no one to understand them. Admitting to limitations, truths about self, pain, sadness, fantasies, need for care and love is extremely difficult for us all, but men struggle more with themselves at this stage.

This ability to admit to human limitations and to be able to let go of the need to be in control is one of the major factors that distinguish Stage Fours from the previous stages emotionally. The impulse to be in control, to take charge, is still strong, and Fours constantly struggle with it. Running things has always been their practice, and it has worked well most of the time. But now they are learning from a slow inner process that life and work are really not controllable ultimately, and they are beginning to feel there is a different way to be. Unfortunately, Fours are not certain what that way is; so they let their reputation speak for them while they sort it out. (We'll see later that the obstacle is mostly a matter of ego.) But eventually a slow acceptance of humility and patience appears that has never been felt before. One man said, "I felt as if I had a flat tire and no way to fix it, so I had to learn to walk or take the bus. I couldn't race around as much, and I learned a lot about myself and other people in the process."

Men are going through a process that includes taking on their feminine side, accepting themselves as whole persons with the warmth and emotions, intuition and inner strength of the feminine as well as the analytical, competitive, intellectual qualities of their masculine side. When men take on their more feminine qualities—sensitivity, nurturing, intuition, thoughtfulness, long-range thinking, caring, giving—they sometimes feel as if they are "going soft." This is a particular dilemma until they realize that there's nothing wrong with having softness in your repertoire. They're afraid that people will think of them as wimps. Our culture is tough on men who seek wholeness. And being vulnerable is especially difficult for men. There are few role models beyond Stage Three. Our cultural heroes are usually excessive Stage Threes. So it is lonely at Stage Four for many men. At times, the pendulum seems to swing toward the feminine so far that they fear they will lose their identity in a world that rewards the masculine so strongly.

For many women, another movement is taking place. Women have lived longest in the most feminine stage (Stage Two), have taken on the masculine (Stage Three), and now they must reaffirm or accept in a different way the balance of both in them to avoid becoming "honorary men."

Again like a pendulum, women make a swing to the masculine side in Stage Three, then at Stage Four they struggle to return to a more comfortable place. It may feel to them as if they must give up some of the rewards of Stage Three, but women find the rewards of Stage Four more satisfying. If they were able to manage being in Stage Three but not caught up by all the trappings of Stage Three, they can now move on and restore their balance more quickly at Stage Four. They are now able to use both masculine and feminine behavior appropriately, depending on the situation. This comfort with flexible behavior does not occur in men until Stage Five.

I would like to add a note here about women as mentors. Whereas men were teachers or models for women at Stage Three, women are teachers and models for men at Stage Four. The wisest men I know have said they learned the most important things about themselves—both personally and interpersonally, as adults—from women. Some say this is because it is less threatening to talk to a woman or that men do this to feel taken care of. These are possibilities. But also many men seek or crave inner strength in women at Stage Four and beyond. Men know there is something more there that goes beyond the stereotyped roles in which they can get stuck, but they truly do not know how to find it on their own. This is why it is so sad to see women content to be honorary men, stuck at Stage Three forever. It's an interesting case for choosing different counselors and mentors for different stages of one's own development. For example, female mentors might understand better how to move from Stage One to Stage Two, whereas male mentors might be more helpful when learning how to move to Stage Three. Beyond that, the most critical consideration is that the home stage of the mentor be beyond one's own.

This struggle for identity at Stage Four can be equated in some ways to the powerless stage (Stage One). One may again sense the feeling of confusion, dependency, fear of the unknown, risk aversion, or tentativeness. With Ones the outward skills and behaviors need to develop, while with Fours the newness is deep and internal. Fours are in a training period preparing them for another real turning point, but they have the advantage of an organizational front that shields them from vulnerability.

This thought from the poet, Rilke, in his book *Letters to a Young Poet,* expresses the stance necessary for Stage Fours.

> Be patient toward all that is unsolved in your heart...Try to love the questions themselves...Do not now seek the answers, which cannot be given because you would not be able to live them. And the point is to live everything. Live the questions now, perhaps you will then gradually, without noticing it, live along some distant day into the answers.

Competent in Collaboration

Stage Four people have proven beyond most doubt that they can be counted on to get the job done well. They follow through on tasks, they are honest and sincere, and they do what they say they will do. They do a good job mostly because it is a mark of personal pride. They do things because they are the "right" things to do, and because, at the same time, this behavior brings its own rewards. If they feel strongly that they are being asked to do something they don't believe in, they have enough courage to speak out. On the other hand, they are not petty perfectionists, who never finish anything because it could always be better. Because of their history of competence and their developing inner strength, they are the best at collaboration, the art of working *with* other people, sharing power. They have little to lose by encouraging others to be the leaders. Their egos are not as involved. Who they are, not what they do, is beginning to emerge in their persona.

Stage Fours are respected because of who they are over the long run. Someone has said they're like high-quality classic cars. They may not be the most glamorous cars, but they are made better, last longer, and don't go out of style. And this stage gives a good return on one's investment over the long term, even though it seems to cost more initially.

Because they can be trusted, Stage Four people usually have or can get access to more resources and information in the organization, particularly through the informal network. Generally, they are trusted with information because people know from experience they will not use it against them. This is true at all levels for Stage Fours, whether they be secretaries, managers, or directors. Even though Stage Fours are impatient with power plays and organizational games, they see politics as the way many people get things done in the organization. They don't choose to play all the organizational politics, but they are not naive. They've lived at Stage Three so they know about politics. They recognize the maneuvers, and they act according to their own best judgment. They know the rules, but if they don't choose to follow them, they also take responsibility for the results. They can say no and be unafraid of the risk it represents. They no longer have the same stakes as they did at Stage Three.

Strong

Fours are perceived as solid, trustworthy people. They take their ethics seriously and view their choices of behavior as part of their internal reflection. They are openly reaffirming and acknowledging their values and beliefs while allowing others to have different beliefs and values. They are seen as outwardly strong and consistent. People know them and trust them. Fours can afford to be forthright and honest with people because they feel little fear of reprisal and much outward confidence in handling situations. Because they've been through several stages they may understand more clearly the motivations of people at Stages One through Four. That is a distinct advantage for them in managing others if they are at all alert. The president of one company said, "There are certain people I talk to who I know will always tell me what they think I want to hear, and then there are those I can trust to tell me what they really think. Get as many of the latter working for you as possible."

Fours are still greatly aware of themselves and their role in the organization. They are a part of the system and must be aware of whom to help and in what ways, but they do it sincerely and not as a gimmick. Fours are learning to increase their influence and reputation by understanding themselves and by collaborating with others. They are still aware of the Stage Three forms of power (control, rules, and competition), but they are working on fully accommodating their emerging belief that power is infinite. A good way to describe them is that they have self-esteem, but they are not guided as closely by their egos as they were before. A phenomenon that emerges for them out of their new inner strength is the interest in leaving a legacy behind that is meaningful and not a monument. They know it takes a deeper commitment to leave a mark of purposeful living, of having made a difference. Examples of this could include a program, a redeemed social condition, a trusting friendship, a principle lived out, conscious and thoughtful treatment of others, or your writings.

This King Arthur and Sir Gawain story will illustrate the legacy of principles. You think about it. The story is very old, so we will have to overlook the female imagery to get to the broader message.

King Arthur's Dilemma

Long ago, King Arthur ruled the land. He was out riding one day and was taken by surprise by a horseman, who came out of the woods and knocked him from his horse. The enemy knight was about to behead him when he noticed it was the King. He thought for a second and offered the King a reprieve from death if he could find the answer to a riddle and return in one year with the solution. The King gladly consented to the offer and asked what the riddle was.

"I want you to find the answer to the question, 'What do women want?'" said the knight.

"Well, that shouldn't be impossible," answered the King. So he went back to the castle pondering how he could solve this riddle.

Before you read on, stop and think about that riddle. What *do* women want? What would you say is the correct answer?

King Arthur wasted no time in calling in Sir Gawain, one of his most trusted knights, to tell him of the surprising task they had to fulfill. Sir Gawain was amused and quite confident that together they could find the correct answer to the riddle. Gawain set off across the land to ask all the people he could what they thought the answer to the riddle was. He went to the wisest people, the street people, the hunters, and the priests. He searched everywhere for the answer. He searched for a whole year without ceasing and at the end of the time both he and the King had to admit that no single answer seemed adequate to answer the riddle. They were crushed.

They started off together on their journey to meet the enemy knight, thoroughly discouraged and perplexed. As they were riding slowly along, out of the woods came a strange figure. As they got closer they could see that it was a witch. And what a witch! She was so ugly she had warts on her warts. And she walked all scrunched over, carrying a big black crooked stick.

The witch stopped them and said in her scratchy voice, "I hear that you are looking all over the land for the answer to a riddle."

"Yes, we certainly have been," offered the King sadly, "but we have given up at this point."

"Well, I have great magical powers. I know right now the answer to your riddle," said the witch.

"Well, do tell us," answered the King, brightening up a bit.

"But I want the hand of Sir Gawain in marriage if the answer I give you is correct," said the witch, looking directly at the knight.

"I could never ask that of one of my most trusted knights," the King retorted. "That would be like sentencing him to life imprisonment."

"It's your choice," replied the witch.

At this point Gawain broke in and said, "King Arthur, the choice is the possibility of your life being lost in a duel or my life being altered by marriage to this witch. There is no alternative. Allow me to marry the witch in exchange for the answer to the riddle."

"This is very hard for me. I will only go along with it if it is truly your wish and you are being honest with me," responded the King.

"Yes, this is truly what I wish," stated Gawain soberly.

"All right, you get your terms." The King turned to the witch. "Now tell us the answer to the riddle."

"I would like to wait until we meet the knight," said the witch, smiling once again.

So off they rode, the three of them each pondering a different thing in their minds. They arrived at the assigned place, and very shortly the knight arrived. He looked surprised that three of them were there.

"Well, King, do you have the answer to the riddle, 'What do women want?'" asked the knight.

"Yes, we think we do," offered the King, glancing at the witch.

"The answer to your riddle," droned the witch, "is simply this: Women want sovereignty, to have independence and the ability to make choices."

"I am amazed," responded the knight. "That is exactly correct."

King Arthur and Sir Gawain were elated that the answer was correct and were anxious to start back and announce to the people that the King's life had been saved. Then they looked at the beaming face of the witch and it sank in. Now she was to be the wife of Sir Gawain.

> But, refusing to go against their honor, they put her on their horse, and they all started back to the castle.
>
> It was a glorious return. The story was told throughout the land and there was celebrating everywhere. But soon came the time to go through with the commitment that the King had made to the witch.
>
> The marriage was performed right there in the castle. And Gawain weathered the whole thing quite well. Alas, their wedding night came as it was bound to, and Gawain was about to perform his husbandly responsibilities. But just then, the witch stopped him.
>
> "Now, you know that I have supernatural powers," stated the witch. "Let me pose a dilemma for you on the eve of our first day of marriage: I will turn myself into a beautiful woman for you, one of the most beautiful women you have ever seen. But you must make a choice. Either you can have me beautiful by day and a witch by night, or you can have me beautiful by night and a witch by day. Which will you choose?"

Before you continue, what do you think Sir Gawain will choose? What do you think most men would choose?

> Sir Gawain sat back and pondered the choice for a while. He thought over what had gone on in the recent past and mused about his future briefly. Then he said, with a twinkle in his eye, "I would really like for you to choose which you would most like to be, beautiful by day or by night."
>
> The witch was obviously pleased with his response, and she, too, reflected on the events and the decisions of the last days. Then she looked sweetly at Sir Gawain and said, with the same twinkle in her eye, "Because you have given me the choice, I will choose to be beautiful both by day and by night."

This King Arthur story is a pre-wedding story passed on from one generation to the next.

Comfortable with Personal Style

Stage Fours have developed, or perhaps come to appreciate, their own personal style of doing things that may or may not fit with the most prevalent organizational norms. This may emerge in the hours they work, their management style, demeanor, or sense of humor. In fact, many Fours are respected and accepted despite their obvious differences in many areas. These would include age, sex, race, personal appearance, working habits, educational background, level of income, and length of membership. They know more who they are and are more comfortable with it. One woman remarked, "I'm so relieved to be on a team. I'm tired of making so many of the decisions. We always get better and more innovative ideas when more people are involved. And it's so much closer to my natural style."

For some Fours their style becomes part of their trademark—clothes, briefcases, demeanor, voice, hairstyle, laugh, sense of humor, and mannerisms become part of the portfolio of the person. People at other stages have a style too; they try out various styles or change them frequently, attempting to find what the organization rewards, as opposed to what suits them. But their style is frequently not as congruent as is the Stage Four style. An executive friend of mine tries new styles periodically and notices that within days, several of his managers follow suit. Fours would be unlikely to follow suit.

Fours can do at least two things better than people at stages preceding them. First, they can admit mistakes without having to be found out first. They may have to think about it for quite some time, but they can handle the loss of pride in being able to admit mistakes to others. Second, because of their style and respect, they can take more risks. Stage Four people have the confidence, reputation, and competence to be heroic. They'll take the risks in a different way than they would have before. Taking risks means feeling scared, and not knowing the outcome. And it could mean losing. Stage Fours don't have as much to gain or as much to lose as they did before. They think about the outcomes more broadly than win or lose. They think about the change that will occur either way. Stage Fours can disagree; stand alone on issues; give in, if necessary, without harboring as much resentment; and build support for others. There are more alternatives available to them and more chances for true heroism and leadership.

In order for Fours to keep taking risks and remain visible in the organization, it is important for them to maintain coalitions or networks in and outside the organization or family, because these webs of support are necessary for leadership. These networks include community, professional, social, religious, and political contacts and are most effective when they involve real issues that are of interest or importance and where solutions can be found for problems. These networks also need to be nurtured continually or they will weaken.

A strange thing can happen to Stage Four people as a result of their newfound sense of self. It happens like this: Stage Fours are seeking more meaning from their work than they get from position, promotion, and money. They want to know that what they are doing makes good sense and that it will be worth the effort. It's not enough to follow directions and have little personal investment any more. So Fours choose their priorities well, and they discipline themselves to work toward those that have the most usefulness and assurance of long-term continuity. It may take time and much patience but it's worth the effort. Then a strange thing can happen. Other people inadvertently put them on a pedestal. They begin to idolize them, emulate them, and generally attribute unreal characteristics to them. Those same people who have imagined the Four in this elevated position often grow to resent the person and begin to chisel away at his or her feet. One woman described this as being a "thermometer" for other people. When people felt good about themselves they felt good about her, and when they felt bad about themselves they resented her. She hadn't changed, but was feeling the pain of others' perceptions of her. Fours can take themselves off the pedestal by sharing more of their humanness, their foibles, and their pains with others, thus making themselves more real and approachable.

Skilled at Mentoring

Fours make very good mentors. They still have personal stakes in the organization, but they can be fairly objective with individuals, especially those at apprenticeship stages. And they are probably willing to be a mentor to a variety of people, not just those who are high achievers. Mentors are wise, objective, and gifted advisors who can look at work and life from a broad perspective. They desire the fullest development of the other person, yet they do not plan an exact path to follow. Mentors ask hard questions but do not always expect answers. One of the most rewarding experiences of a Stage Four is mentoring. It not only provides Fours with challenges and occasional successes but also a larger network of influence. People at Stage Four find they get satisfaction, as well as visibility, by mentoring both older and younger people at all levels in the organization. While Stage Threes are more generally known by the positions they hold in professional and community groups, Stage Fours are respected for the personal effects they have on individuals in these arenas. Gaining respect takes longer this way, but it is longer lasting. You can see that longevity becomes increasingly a factor for Fours—being around for a longer time and working with proven competence. It is difficult for a person who is moving from one job to another all over the country every two years to become a Stage Four person in their work.

Stage Fours may go beyond mentoring to become personal counselors for people who are going through the crises and questions of life and work. Being a good listener, a sounding board, or a catalyst for personal change is helpful, and Stage Fours are excellent listeners. Many people seek them out to toss ideas around with as well as to sort out personal issues. One thing that is always true of Fours, they will not use that confidential information against anyone.

Because Stage Four people have started taking the inner road, they may be quite misunderstood by others when they try to explain what's happening to them. It's difficult to explain in understandable terms to a person at Stage Two or Three the process of letting go, of letting go of your ego, of taking a deep inward journey. First, these are not the major motivations and values of people at Stage Two and Three, and second, trying to explain the process somehow sounds trite, easy, or even shallow. Many Fours find one or two persons to act as their mentors and then resolve to live with some loneliness for a time as a result. In fact, the loneliness becomes a friend and changes to aloneness or solitude—the feeling of being alone and feeling all right. Unfortunately, many former friends (and some spouses) are lost in the move from Stage Three to Four because of the rather dramatic shifts that are occurring inside, especially within men. All these factors make this stage the most difficult one for men.

Another reason Fours make such good mentors is that they are always open to learning in their own lives. They look for teachers because they know how much they don't know. One intriguing experience that happens in many Fours is the discovery of their hidden artistic side. It has been submerged since childhood and it wants expression. So Fours find themselves discovering art, music, dance, or writing—and wanting to express themselves.

Showing True Leadership

Stage Four is the first stage that can be labeled as true leadership as opposed to traditional *position power* leadership. The word leadership is about as misunderstood as the word power; there are several kinds of leadership just as there are several kinds of power. In order to determine which people show the characteristics of true leadership we must ask leaders whom they are promoting: themselves, others, themselves at the expense of others, both themselves and others? In this context, although some people lead others at each stage, a truly non-self promoting leadership does not begin until Stage Four. Fours have survived the integrity crisis and have emerged as more whole, honest, principled, reflective, and secure people. Stage Threes are good at being in charge or up in front, but their leadership is constructed around their own skills, their position, outcomes—and ultimately their own egos. In contrast, Fours think as much about other people as they do about themselves, therefore taking a broader approach to the issues and to leadership. They believe that no one is better than another by virtue of position, age, race, sexual preference, gender, or title.

True leaders can follow as well as take charge, but from a base of strength, not weakness. Stage Four people can see the power of turning things over to others or asking for ideas from others. They look at implications and weigh alternatives. They incite differences of opinion because they know it fosters better thinking. And they are more personally powerful because they lead from the middle. But Stage Four leaders may still feel some pressure to calculate to whom they tell what, and why. They are organization conscious and quite influential. They are trusted and respected for their judgment, not only for the hoops they have jumped through. But they are close enough to the hoops to remember the grinding pressures; therefore, they must be careful that their judgment is not unduly affected by their prior experience.

Stage Four leaders are organizational people who embrace the self-development ethic. They are more tolerant and flexible, willing to experiment with new ways of relating at work and at home. The health, learning, and development of others are important, an ethic grounded in human needs not in unquestioning loyalty to the organization. They have a strong need for meaningful relationships and productivity in the work place based on equity, respect, and cooperation.

The following anecdote regarding one of these leaders describes succinctly one of the finest characteristics of Stage Four leaders: A union official was running for head of his union against one of his close friends. After a careful scrutiny of the skills needed in the next decade for the effective managing of their union, he supported his friend for the position. He was not looking for a seat of power. He was looking for a way to continue to operate on a one-to-one basis, listening and helping to solve problems. He could do much of what he wanted to do in his present position, and he was able to teach and travel as well. He was modest, dedicated, and principled. His philosophy was to abide by the golden rule, "Do unto others as you would have them do unto you."

Many people have asked me if there are more Stage Four people in organizations now than there were in past decades. My research over the last fifteen years shows that the answer is definitely yes. And more Stage Fours are showing up in positions of power as well. But there are not enough Stage Fours yet to be a critical mass that will move whole organizations farther up the power model. My research also shows that the most prevalent stage of power in organizations in this country is still Stage Three, the home stage of most of our leaders. Crises tend to send all of us to earlier stages, no matter what our home stage is at the time. Every time we have a downturn in the economy or we enter into a war, our leaders tend to revert back to earlier stages of power or to the shadow of their home stage because of the underlying fear that comes with those events. But it is also at these vulnerable times that we have a chance to move forward and closer to Stage Four, if we do not panic. One thing I have become sure of, that those who counsel the leaders as staff people or informal mentors need to be at least Stage Four individuals and that they will be crucial to our well-being as a country in the foreseeable future. There is a whole chapter devoted to developing beyond Stage Three, Chapter 12 called "Leading from Your Soul."

Spirituality and the Spiritual Connection to Work at Stage Four

At this stage spirituality is rediscovering the Holy. This stage represents a major turning point in our spiritual lives. As a result of either a faith or life crisis, or a long flat plateau, we begin questioning and doubting what previously was clear and defined. We question the behavior or intention of a previous leader or practice. Confused, we begin an inner search for direction and meaning. Along the way we may become disenchanted, even drop out for a while. We pursue personal honesty and integrity with the Holy, letting the Holy out of the box, renewing our image of our Higher Power.

Our spiritual connection with work frequently feels meaningless. We think work is the issue, when it is just the symptom of a spiritual crisis. WE are the issue, not work or the Holy. We were running the show. Now we need inner transformation; we must live into the struggles we are having with our spiritual life, the Holy, or life itself. We may fear, or disregard work, yet we long for purpose. We spend a great deal of time wondering how our values and our work can ever be connected. We feel inconsistent, without direction. Yet somehow we continue to work. And through all this we are already being transformed personally. In our own vulnerability, we are better listeners, more compassionate, better mentors, more able to exhibit fairness. We are separating ourselves from the compulsion to "do" something. We are more able to "be."

If we get the kind of support and help we need at this stage we can begin to make the connections between our inner struggles and our work life. Spiritual direction, a relationship with a person who is trained to observe the inner spiritual process and to help one integrate one's work and spiritual life would be a wise choice for a Four. The important questions will surface. For instance, one crisis at Stage Four is the crisis of integrity. We may begin to focus on how important integrity and ethical behavior are in our work lives. We may make the connection that how we treat our peers makes a big difference in how we treat our clients; that our everyday behavior is just a part of our whole being. We might even start assisting others to see the need for a connection between the heart and the head at work and to be more conscious of the spiritual connections among us.

Here is an example of a woman making the connections her heart has longed for as a result of entering spiritual direction.

> I have been holding in Stage Four for two years now. I do want to live life from a Stage Five perspective. And yet, I am a textbook case for what holds people back. I've known for over a year why I was in a holding pattern: my ego, letting go, and lack of life purpose.
>
> Even with this knowledge I was at a loss for what to do. I was stuck. I had gone as far as I could go by myself. I needed guidance and direction. A friend suggested a spiritual director. How do you find a spiritual director? Are they listed in the yellow pages? I was told that a good starting place would be a Catholic church.
>
> I had some hesitancy. I was not Catholic and I wasn't religious. The philosophies of the East were drawing me. Could Bible verses help me uncover my path?
>
> Luckily I was willing to be open. My first session with Sister Regina was unforgettable. I did most of the talking. She listened. She heard my 'words' beneath my words. Her questions were gentle and connected to my heart. She assigned me three Bible verses to read and contemplate over the next month.
>
> I read and thought. I read and thought. Nothing was coming up to my attention. Until the twenty-eighth day. It was as though fireworks surrounded me and I got it. Sister Regina heard the small voice within me and knew where I needed to go for answers. It clicked. And it has been this way for the year we have now spent together. The Bible verses are uncovering my path.
>
> So, how am I doing with ego control, letting go, and my life purpose? I'm no longer stuck. There is forward movement.
>
> I catch glimpses of myself not leading from my ego. I smile at my own delight. Often, I am able to put the brakes on when I am ego-controlled. But, not always.
>
> Recently, I signed up for a writing class as an audit student. I didn't really want an external commentary to know how I was doing

and yet I found myself being competitive with the other students. I wanted my stories to outshine the groups'. I wanted positive feedback from the instructor. I could see myself doing this and I could laugh at what I was doing. Yet, I could not stop the need for recognition from the others and from the instructor. I couldn't let go of wanting an A. "Hello, ego."

Letting go of outcomes has gotten easier over this past year. Many times I felt I had let go. I had said the magic words for God to take over. Then days later I would find myself reeling it back in. I was holding on to a fine thread. It wasn't until I let go of my biggest desire that I felt the freedom that comes with letting go.

My biggest desire is to know my life purpose. I have been obsessed about knowing why I am here. Now, the obsession with purpose has receded. I've made friends with "What's next?" I embrace the holding pattern I feel that I am in. I am pausing for reasons that have not yet come into my awareness. I am being made ready.

There are no timetables for this disclosure. My faith in God holds me securely in the meantime. God's plans for "What's next?" are far loftier than I now have the abilities to achieve. When God knows I am ready, I will know my purpose and have the means to walk its path.

I am a Stage Five in training. Working with a spiritual advisor has put wheels on my feet. I am no longer stuck. I can be in transition to I know not where. And it is okay. There is calm in the unknowing.

This suspense is different from the suspense I felt when I let go of being a Stage Three to reach for Stage Four. The first suspense was riding a wild roller coaster. There were steep highs and lows and precipitous drops and turns that jerked me into attention.

Now I am at attention. The highs and lows are mild and not as sheer. The turns are more easily understood. This part of the path is full of joyous moments and not panic caught in my throat. I guess the difference would be that I know the direction I am going even if at a snail's pace. In the transition to Stage Four I struggled to find true north. I've made friends with the journey.

The Shadow of Stage Four

Playacting

Early in the transition from Stage Three to Stage Four, there is a strong pull towards Stage Three. Playacting behavior can occur at this point, when the transition is not yet fully made. Fours who playact subtly accumulate power for themselves, even though their external behavior may appear to be in support of others. It is alluring to use the old rules and the new respect to quietly build larger spheres of influence, resulting in more and more people who are beholden to them. They feel more assured that all will not be lost for them if this new way of being doesn't work.

Influence and coalition-building, on the one hand, are a more effective way to get things done than charisma or offering carrots, but some Fours fall into the trap of making a Stage Three-type game out of their newly emerging influence. In the end they emerge as the stars, having been seduced by their own goodness, and the power has not been spread around at all. This occurs mainly because they become fearful of going deeper; of really touching beneath the surface; of asking themselves once again who they really are, how they want to live and work, and what is important in their lives. Fours learn at this stage that one's reputation is all one has in life; it is easily damaged and not so easily repaired.

Stuck in Confusion

Some people enter the cloudiness and confusion of Stage Four and never emerge from it. It becomes so thick that they can't find their way out of it back into the light. They simply get stuck in the confusion, the never-ending-no-answer questions. They feel like they are chasing themselves in a continuous circle with no way of escape.

The issue here is the fear of facing the underlying messages, whether they are about family, values, or work. The armor has cracked and people caught in this confusion hope that by doing nothing or by running from one thing to another, the armor will somehow fix itself. The real issue has nothing to do with the armor. It is about what is inside that armor.

These Fours are particularly frustrating to others because no amount of support seems to help them. They are stuck in their stuckness, not unlike Stage Ones who are afraid of being afraid. Sometimes a crisis of higher magnitude than the crisis of confusion is what catapults them into the light side of this stage.

Mary's story might serve as an example of this shadow behavior.

Mary, the High School Math Teacher

> Mary is a multi-talented 47-year-old with an MBA and with undergraduate degrees in mathematics and music. She has worked for

> large corporations and has been a music teacher and a high school mathematics teacher. She is an avid reader and bridge player. She manifests many Stage Four behaviors including consciously choosing to mentor others, acting with integrity, speaking out when asked to do something she does not believe in. She does not show interest in typical symbols of success such as salary and title. Mary has an active spiritual life that includes daily meditation and prayer. Despite all this, she often falls apart when confronted by a challenging situation with a person in a position of authority, especially a man. For example, she had a disagreement with a medical professional over the size of the payment she owed. Instead of negotiating a mutually satisfactory resolution, she became quite defensive and withdrew after an initial difficult conversation and refused to take any further action. Her account was turned over to a collection agency.
>
> As a high school teacher she shows great creativity in her work with students and empathy for them personally. Yet, when interacting with school administrators, Mary is quick to adopt an adversarial position, which is not well received by her supervisors. Despite many Stage Four characteristics, she does not seem to be able to use masculine behaviors when they would be appropriate. Having found many Stage Three characteristics antithetical to her belief system she has not allowed herself to be in Stage Three without getting hooked by the shadows of the stage. Her regressions to victim-like stances have caused some major impediments in her life. She is cognizant of her vulnerabilities and realizes she needs to acquire more adaptive behaviors in certain areas, yet she does not know how to do this.

Mary might be stuck in Stage Four or she may be tottering at the edge of Stage Four ready to fall into the Wall as a result of not being able to deal with her fear of authority. Her behavior becomes victim-like when she does not confront her own shadows. A crisis around one of these relationships would actually be a catalyst for her movement forward.

Misunderstood

This shadow component is really more the issue with those who observe Fours than with Fours themselves, but it still needs to be noted. Most Fours are aware of this difference in their own behavior and have empathy for those who misunderstand them.

A difficulty for Fours is their mismatch with the Stage Three environment and the lack of trust that that engenders between people as a result. The people at Stage Three wonder what Fours' agenda is because they are not used to Stage Four behavior. This is not a fault of the Fours but a by-product of being different from the norm. People who manage Fours soon realize that Fours are not motivated by the same things that Threes are. They cannot be persuaded to do things by the suggestion of rewards like money or promotions. Because their motives are not traditional they are sometimes viewed suspiciously.

Another characteristic of Fours that causes discomfort is their common-sense approach to problems. They are more open, more vulnerable and invite more participation in decision-making. The Threes perceive the Fours as slowing things down, or adding roadblocks to a hasty process. It is true. Fours do slow things down at times, because they believe the decision will be a better one if more people have input. Usually the implementation is quicker this way. Fours do not demand consensus but they like people to feel they've been heard.

Here's an example of a misunderstood Stage Four person:

Riley, the Musician

> I'm a funny kind of guy, and I know other people don't understand me, nor do I fit the stereotypes of professional musicians. The only two goals I have in life are to play good music for people to enjoy and to encourage young people to participate in music. I don't stay out all night, smoke, shoot or snort drugs, nor do I yearn for the travel circuit, wait to be discovered, or long to work on a best-selling recording. What satisfies me is sitting down at the piano, knowing that the sound is mine and the quality is grand. I want to please people with my music.
>
> I have had the unfortunate experience of being discovered and being cajoled into recordings, TV shows, and the like. But the offer necessitated moving, uprooting myself without my family, and living a very stressful "successful" life. I tried it for a year. During that time the stress on my body was out-of-sight. I got sick all the time. And my family got the brunt of my tiredness. After a long hard "think" I decided that being famous right here is just enough for me. And teaching kids new jazz forms is the finest reward there can be. If people want me to record my music, that's fine, but I am not about to take on the required lifestyle of those who are aiming at the top. Life is just too short. And my music is not as good when I'm under stress, either. Now do you see why I'm considered a strange dude?

This example shows us how the stereotypes of big success can be deadly. Giving up what you've always wanted because you now know what's more important is one classic characteristic of a Stage Four person.

Let's Meet Some People at Stage Four

Lamon, the Mayor

> My job gives me a good chance to put into practice my philosophy of public administration. I feel well-prepared with two degrees in the field. I would be lying to tell you that I'm in politics for nothing but service. I have a hard time with anyone who believes that. But I like influencing people to do what is in the city's best interest. And there is a serious academic side to me that not everyone sees. I hate campaigning, for instance. If I could get out of it I would. It's not that I don't like people but you just don't get to really talk to many people on the campaign trail. I'd rather avoid big crowds where I must be dynamic for the audience, and just talk one-to-one for an hour or two so I can really hear people's opinions and reasoning.
>
> I've always felt that the finest political people have had the loneliest jobs, not the most exciting, as some people think. It can be lonely because you are aware of all the powerful special interest groups, and you also know the amount of stretch in the budget. Added to that you have the philosophy of your party, the influence of your leaders, and most important, your own reasoned judgments about what would bring the greatest good for the city as a whole. These views might all be at odds with one another, and juggling them all is a real trick. You are elected to serve the city, yet each group or organization wants you to see them as an exception. That may not be wise for the times or the city. So every time I make a decision I ask myself, "How would I decide on this if, after the decision, I would be placed in the shoes of one of the parties involved, but before the decision I wouldn't know which party's shoes I would be placed in?" I try to make decisions as if I were not going to run again although that is much easier said than done.
>
> It's hard to be an enlightened mayor without an enlightened electorate. I'm not complaining because my city has had a long history of wise decision-makers and educated voters, but I am illustrating the reality of the multiple pressures on a public decision-maker. I quickly realized that the most important thing I could do was to gather a staff around me, all of whom excelled at what they did. I couldn't afford to use only party supporters or less experienced people who would not threaten me. The way I continue to grow in

> this job is to be challenged and to continue to look at longer-term solutions to our city's problems. If I can't say of my terms in office that major development occurred, unemployment issues eased, and clean air was guaranteed, I would not feel I had done this city justice—also not without a balanced budget. So in addition to my other duties, my team has set out to form coalitions in all sectors to push forward on these three projects, providing ideas and resources but depending on the vision and leadership within the community to carry out the programs. That's what makes all this worth it to me.

Lamon represents the struggle that Stage Four people have being in public life. He is a professional public administrator, not a politician.

Jeanne, the Certified Public Accountant

> I was a classic example of an organizational success story. I went to college right out of school and joined the accounting firm with the best track record. I put in all the overtime I could in those early years, because as a woman I wanted to prove what I could do. Of course, being one of the youngest to get my CPA helped a lot. The partners noticed me and promoted me consistently along the way. I was really riding high even though I was always tired. I thought I was really making it.
>
> At a conference a few years ago I began to talk to some other women CPAs from other firms. We were just laughing and comparing notes. One woman in particular asked us some very hard questions like, where were we headed? why? and then what? What else did we have in our lives that gave us meaning? Her words and my answers started sinking in very slowly, so slowly I hardly noticed. But over the next year my subconscious noticed. I started to feel the pressure of tax time more strenuously, the promises of promotion seemed like carrots on a stick, and some of the practices of the organization that I had always accepted and taken for granted started to bother me. For instance, we had few small businesses as clients because we had to charge too much for our time, yet small businesses were my best and most interesting clients to work with. I churned and wrestled with these disconcerting thoughts and finally took a three-week trip to Nova Scotia all by myself. By the time I came back I knew I was going to leave the firm and start my own practice specializing in accounting and planning for small businesses.
>
> Well, scared as I was, I felt like a huge load had been lifted off me. And that was two years ago. Already I'm convinced that this was the right thing to do, although it was one of the most difficult decisions

of my life. Starting a business is not easy. And no one taught me how to run a business in college. It's more than numbers. I know that for sure. My banker has been invaluable in helping my company grow. I am so much happier even though I frequently work just as hard. I am helping small growing businesses, I am making a difference, I am in charge of my life. And I like myself better. I have a social life, and I build in break time. You know, I even considered building a firm out of this, but then I laughed because two years ago I left a bureaucracy. Why start another one?

Someday I might do that, but not for a while yet. I'm too busy immersed in developing new clients and in establishing a name in the field. And I want to be careful not to burn myself out even if I love what I'm doing. When it's time to grow I'll think about it.

Jeanne exhibits the confusion resulting from success that is not meaningful anymore. She experiences a crisis in her work that helps her clarify her values, experience a new way of being, and start on a different path. She may be seeing purpose as more than an extension of ego.

Don, the Procurement Manager

You know, I'm about where I'm going to be in this organization and I know it. Last year I was offered the position of department head and, after thinking long and hard, I turned it down. They brought in a younger guy from one of the other divisions. For a while I thought I had made a big mistake but the long talk I had with my boss's boss helped. The department is in need of an overhaul and plenty of energy would be required to do that. I've been gradually pulling back on extra assignments at work ever since our third baby was born. Having a blind child takes so much extra time and attention that I just can't do it all.

I know management sees me as competent because of all the awards and good appraisals I've had. But I had to accept for myself that at this point in my life I would probably not be up to this large a challenge. I've really made my own choices and they've been tough ones. It's a lot to give up and I may not have another chance. That is the harsh reality of it all. I must admit that the activity I enjoy most is developing my people, not reorganizing the department. I get the biggest kick out of seeing someone move from a lower skilled status to a more satisfying position or from a life crisis into self-confidence. I like to place my people all over the company so they can get better

> experience and they always remember to keep in touch, so I have cronies in all corners.

Don has accepted his strengths and limitations and is comfortable with the balance between his work and his personal life.

Judy, the Writer

> They told me I wasn't really going to make it, in their opinion, in the writing world. I just wasn't able to grasp the nuances of the language and provide sufficient poetic imagery to arouse my audience. I was young and naive and I believed them. And that was a big mistake. Now they were just being kind, and they were quite accurate about my skill in fiction writing. It stinks. But they never suggested that I try any other kind of writing. So I quit trying to write freelance and went to work on regular jobs with publishing firms and educational institutions.
>
> Just by accident someone asked me to do an article for a newsletter on a program at my alma mater. I said I would and started in on it. Well, that was all it took to unleash the trapped writer inside me. I devoted hours of my free time to developing my writing ability. A mentor helped me immeasurably, encouraging and challenging me along the way. Now I write nonfiction of all kinds and I am making a living at it. I just had to find my own style and quit trying to be the greatest novelist of the twentieth century. I think I've found myself through my writing too because I feel creative, relaxed, rejuvenated, and alive when I write, rarely bored and repressed like I did in my other jobs. And I am choosing to write about things that are useful to people, that help them to develop and discover their inner selves as well.

Judy had to overcome obstacles that plagued her for years. She had to discover slowly in herself the writer that was hiding inside all along.

Hank, the Corporate President

> You know I've got to admit, just between you and me, that I really used to genuinely enjoy all the perks, the applause, the admiration of my employees as a result of my position. We've been lucky to have a great management team or we never could have pulled off the continued growth in this company in the last seven years. We've exceeded all of our expectations and there seems to be little that we

> can't do if we set our minds to it. So the challenges are all there, just for the picking. But I've been suffering lately from a malaise that I don't seem to be able to cure. I know that I could move to some other very lucrative positions from where I am now and my successes could stockpile, but somehow that seems like an empty challenge. It sounds to me like more of the same.
>
> I really have been spending some long hours thinking about my life and work lately. Of course, a few days at home with the flu will do that to you; give you a forced sabbatical to think about some of the other things in life. To be very candid with you, what I came up with is that what I really lack in my life is a purpose around which all the other things revolve. Or maybe it's that the things that used to serve as purposes for me have lost their savor. I just don't want to die in my eighties with my accomplishments being only at work. That raises all kinds of other questions, of course, like what is my purpose in being? What's worth enough to me to invest time, energy, and money on? Can I find my purpose in or through my work, or is it broader than that? What do I want to be remembered for most? What do I want my kids to say about me after I'm gone? Am I passing on traits and qualities in my management team that I will be proud of in the long run or are we just following the rules? I know I'm known for being quite people-oriented, but how could I do something really significant with my company that would make a difference in individuals' lives? Can my purpose also be the company's vision? Am I ready to be a visionary leader, courageous and willing to lead into uncharted waters where few models have been attempted? What have I got to lose? Is this crisis of purpose the cause of my malaise? Whom can I talk to about this?
>
> When I read about wise people, principled people of the ages, there are certain characteristics that seem to be true of them. They all had inner crises, they found out who they really were, they knew what they wanted, they were ultimately disciplined, they suffered disappointments but kept on going, and they inspired others through their selflessness. Do I have the fortitude to follow any of their leads? Could I even take a stab at learning more about commitment and dedication to principles and purposes? Where do I start?

Hank is struggling with a deep question: "What is my purpose in life?" He thought it was work, but success in his work was not as satisfying as he thought it would be. Now what?

All these people represent some confusion between their own personal characteristics or values and the expectations of the profession or organization. They are all finding their own way of doing things, of living with themselves so as to achieve some sense of balance and continuity within themselves. Everyone chooses a different way to do this and experiences varying levels of crisis along the way. Because Stage Fours have begun to be reflective and introspective, it is more difficult to pinpoint exactly how the transitions occur for them, for they proceed on the basis of their own inner experience.

Moving to the Wall and Stage Five

The most accurate description of the movement to Stage Five is captured in the next chapter called The Wall. It is a mysterious and excruciatingly wonderful part of our power journey where our will meets another more powerful Holy will. Our job is to relinquish our ego and our will. But when we approach the wall our reaction is to kick it, or to remove one stone and put it back again. We decide to come back again later, much later. Or we pick out one or two stones and examine them. What emerges are all the things about us that the Wall hides: our wounds, our hidden addictions, our shadows, our childhood pains, our self-absorption.

We may even feel totally abandoned by the Holy for a time in the Wall. But then slowly we begin to see, to feel the pain in our core, to be embraced by the loving grace of our Higher Power in a new way. We experience the Wall through self-reflection, tough love, prayer, meditation, journaling, therapy, and spiritual direction. The personal quality most necessary in facing the Wall is courage.

You cannot go to classes to learn Stage Five behavior, nor can you buy a kit that will turn you into a Stage Five person. You can be around Stage Five people and observe how they are or read about them, but no techniques will get you there. The only way is by inner and personal experience, and it is usually done alone, though others may guide you. Anyone who assembles big groups and charges large sums of money to teach growth in these areas is usually misled, ego oriented, or just plain dishonest. You cannot learn Stage Five behavior from Stage Three people. And you cannot buy life purpose and broader vision.

In order to move to Stage Five, you must sincerely want to drop your ego and be prepared for the excruciatingly wonderful process to follow. Here is a poem by Wendy von Oech that describes the feelings one might have at this stopping place on the power model.

My Soul Seeks Stopping

I've come to the place called Stopping,
where I must go to drink.
I've come to the place called Stopping,
where I must go to think,
to pick up stones and listen
to the sounds of life below,
to rest awhile on an old tree stump
and remember what I know.

I've come to the place called Stopping,
where I must go to be
between the calls of child and man,
of home and work, of passion and plea,
to be alone and safe for a time,
to feel again the peace,
to see the wholeness of life and love,
the patterns that never cease.

To let the rhythms bubble up
within my body and mind,
to take the time to follow them
no matter what I find.
Not, for a moment, concerned about
the goal, the product, the pain,
holding true to the process,
the hills and valleys, the sun and the rain.

I've come to the place called Stopping,
where I must come to know
the well within that has no end,
that I take wherever I go.
I take with me the darkness,
the life-giving water, the unseen light.
I take with me the vision
of calm and still, of dark and bright.

When I return to Going,
to action, product, and goal,
my heart will be strong, my mind awake,
and love and light will fill my soul.
Now I can step with purpose,
with guidance, direction and grace,
for I move with the wisdom of Stopping
that time cannot erase.

What Holds People Back?

Two major factors stand in the way of Stage Fours moving to Stage Five. The first obstacle is that Fours are still struggling with ego. They run the risk of continuing to care that in the end their good deeds will be recognized, their name will be recognized, the money will flow in, or they will have others indebted to them. There are still strings attached with Fours. They cannot let go because they will lose control. And the thought of losing control to a source of power that is beyond them is frightening.

The second obstacle is when Fours have not experienced a need for a meaningful, other-oriented life purpose. They are inner-directed, but they have not sat down quietly to ask themselves why they are alive. Not just whether they are living, which was asked in Stage Four, but why? What is their reason for being, beyond themselves, in the world? This can only come out of an intense and honest inner conversation in which life's priorities are set. Buckminster Fuller spent two years without speaking following a suicide attempt before he launched into his life's mission—to serve the world through useful design.

Hagberg's Model of Personal Power

SUMMARY OF STAGE FOUR
POWER BY REFLECTION

Symbol

Key Question: What was the moment of keenest insight in your life and what happened when you acted?

Description
Influence
The sandwich stage

Characteristics
Reflective/confused
Competent in collaboration
Strong
Comfortable with personal style
Skilled at mentoring
Showing true leadership

Spirituality at Stage Four
Rediscovering the Holy

Shadow of Stage Four
Playacting
Stuck in confusion
Misunderstood

Catalyst for Movement
Letting go of one's ego, facing fear

What Holds People Back?
Not letting go of one's ego
No need for a life purpose

Ways to Move
Hit the wall, move beyond intellect, let go of control, face your shadows, go to your core, find intimacy with a higher power, take time out, and glimpse wisdom.

Chapter 5

The Wall:
A Stopping Place Between Stages Four and Five

Key Question: What one quality in you will be dangerous to other people if you are not fully conscious of it?

What Is the Wall Like?

One of the most profound transitions between stages is the move from Stage Four to Stage Five. At this point you hit the Wall. Like runners who experience the Wall, you think there is absolutely no way you can proceed. There is no way through the Wall. But by merely deciding not to stop, you move on into and through the awesome experience of the Wall.

There are things to overcome in moving from each of the stages to the next stage but the Wall is the place where the accumulation of things we have hidden from the world, or thought we had hidden, come out to haunt us. At the Wall we cannot move forward without embracing our own personal shadow behavior, behavior that we don't want to look at but can't seem to avoid any more. The Wall is the place where our shadow becomes clear and we make a decision whether or not we will deal with it.

The Wall between Stage Four and Five is not a physical wall. It is an ego wall. In the Wall we face our controlling ego. We think we are still in charge of our lives and the Wall simply invites us—compels us—to let go. At the Wall we have a choice. We can move forward into the Wall and embrace it or we can go back to a more comfortable place. People live very satisfying lives even if they never go through the Wall. But going through it and learning the wisdom it has to teach us is life-changing. However I would not describe the Wall as inviting. It looks frightening at best, to look at all the things we have swept under the rug for so long. Many of us come to the Wall over and over again and keep feeling the discomfort of its presence in our lives. The decision to move into the Wall requires courage, for in the Wall we face our darkest selves, our shadows.

Because of the pain involved in the Wall we frequently try to avoid it. Clever as we are, we devise many ways to keep it from affecting our lives. We deny its existence, dance around it, shoot holes in it, scale it, analyze it away, or label it as obsolete. We peek at it and go back to being busy. Once in a while we take out a stone, turn it over, scratch away the moss, find a little truth there, and decide that is all the truth we can handle for now. That is fine. We need to honor our own inner process. The Wall will always be there when we return. And at some point people go into the Wall and spend months or years inside it, wondering if they will ever emerge. All of these are legitimate Wall experiences.

So what happens in the Wall? It is unique to each person but there are some general experiences people share. I'll list them and then elaborate on a few. Going through the Wall is a process. It consists of letting go of your ego, giving up control, moving beyond your intellect, becoming intimate with a higher power, embracing your whole self with all your shadows, and facing your core with its darkness and light.

The Wall is a place of transformation. Once having experienced the Wall, you will never be the same again. The Wall is a place of tremendous loss and tremendous gain. It is exhilarating and it is painful. It is never easy. The Wall is the place we face our inner selves, the truth of who we are, our shame, and ultimately our heart's deepest desires. We embrace all of this and learn to accept it. People describe the process of moving through the Wall in these other ways; as a deep well, an abyss, a slow descent, a dark tunnel, a pit, a prison cell, a dark night. It is never pretty. But in it are glimpses of wisdom and light. And it is healing at a deep level, a soul level. What brings us to the Wall? Loss of meaning, desire for more depth, death, depression, abuse, a call to wholeness, failure, loss of relationship, illness, or soul searching.

What helps us through the Wall? We need to face our fear and develop courage. It is helpful to experience the Wall with the help of a trained professional who is not frightened by what you are experiencing. And these are a few of the things you can expect to experience.

Characteristics of People at the Wall

Moving Beyond Your Intellect

Most powerful people pride themselves on their minds. They can reason themselves out of most any situation. But when they come to the Wall their reasoning ability is insufficient. To become a whole person requires the involvement of the whole being: body, mind, and spirit. So the Wall experience is physical, emotional, mental, and spiritual.

You will find your body and emotions doing things that surprise you. For instance, you might start getting headaches for the first time in your life; have heart palpitations, severe stomach or backaches; or have limbs go numb for no medically related reason. It is best to check with a doctor first, but usually these are signs of a new awareness deep inside you that wants recognition. Some are even warning signals to behave differently.

One woman involved in family counseling started getting headaches when she began working on her relationship with her mother. It connected her with a memory of her mother's migraines. She slowly discovered the control her mother exercised over her with the migraines. Whenever her mother did not like one of her boyfriends, she would get regular migraines as a way to take her daughter away from him to care for her. It unlocked a big piece of a mysterious behavior pattern for the woman.

You may find your emotions erupting or changing or even appearing for the first time. These are good, but also frightening, experiences for people who are used to having control. If you let the emotions emerge, even if they are foreign to you, they will bring you new truths. In fact, this whole process may sound foreign to you and may not even seem to be in your best interest. It may go against your better judgment. That is probably a good sign you are out of your element and letting go. When you let go, the truth of your life is closer at hand and more likely to emerge.

One writer who has become a classic in this body, mind, and spirit connection is Carolyn Myss, who has written *Anatomy of the Spirit, Why People Don't Heal* and *Sacred Contracts.* She is a medical intuitive who equates what is happening through physical symptoms to levels of spiritual and emotional growth you subconsciously need. She links the eastern chakra system with the Christian sacraments and the Jewish Tree of Life. The part of the body in which the symptom occurs relates to a level of spiritual growth in these three traditions. It is very intriguing and has proven to be accurate with many people.

Another writer who is fluent in the body, mind, and spirit connection is Louise Hay. In her numerous books, including *You Can Heal Your Life,* she lists hundreds of physical symptoms and then gives the emotional/psychological connection in your life. They are often not pleasant to read; but if you are open to their truths, they can, along with astute medical treatment, dramatically assist the healing process. A third writer, perhaps the best known, is Dr. Christine Northrup. Her book, *Women's Bodies, Women's Wisdom,* is a classic text on the mind, body, and spirit connection. She regularly appears on public television and is now widely sought as a speaker. Any of these sources will make much more sense to one who is experiencing the Wall and desires to become whole in body, mind, and spirit.

Letting Go of Control: Loving Detachment

Another disconcerting experience of the Wall is giving up control of other people, especially family and co-workers, as well as control of your future. For people who pride themselves on control and planning that is a high sacrifice. And usually control is not relinquished, it is involuntarily lost as part of a crisis. We wake up as a result of a traumatic event to realize that we never really had control after all. It was only an illusion. The antidote to control is "loving detachment," letting go of trying to change the other person, but letting ourselves be free from their control of us as well.

The event that brings us to this new freedom may be losing a promotion we deserved, failing to get recognition we had counted on, getting sick no matter how much we try to avoid it, having one of our children rebel no matter what we do, finding out that we can't change our parents, or finding the old systems we took for granted do not work any more.

One executive said he reached a turning point when he realized he couldn't get his family to jump to his bidding any more. He said, "I turned the crank at work and people did what I said. I turned the crank at home and everyone just sighed and did nothing. I guess I needed to get rid of the crank."

Only when we give up control inside can we relinquish it outside, in leadership, in families, and in the world. And then the fun begins. Teamwork begins to flourish, creativity is free to flow, and friendships can move to new levels.

Ann tells her story of letting go.

I spent most of my life trying unsuccessfully to please my mother. Unconsciously she kept the umbilical cord attached to us kids and managed to manipulate and control us well into our adult lives. It seemed she was never satisfied. We always had to look better, perform better, *be* better. Her controlling behavior kept me hiding things from her that I knew she wouldn't approve of, like hiding the wine when she came to visit because she didn't approve of drinking any alcohol.

I chose to live farther away to limit contacts with her but distance didn't help. I gradually realized, through prayer and reflection, that I needed to let go—let go of trying to please her and seek her approval. I realized that what she thought of me was less important than how I viewed myself. I let go of my ego involvement—of trying to be the perfect person—and in doing so I released myself from the power she had over me. It was a time of transformation.

Now I was free to relate to my mother as an equal adult. Now I could enjoy her, not feel responsible for her well-being. I was free to talk openly, to be honest and up front with her instead of "walking on egg shells," trying not to upset her. I was free to relate to her as a person and see the good in her. I was free to laugh at her foolish expectations and martyr-like attitudes and even coax her into laughing with me because she knew that I accepted her, even her complaints, and that I loved her anyway. I respected her right to her own feelings but didn't support the ones that were dragging her down. The transformation in my own life also transformed our relationship. And that continues to be true now, many years later.

With my son, Oliver, I "hit the Wall" about the same time he cut off all contact with the family. He was the eldest child and often moody and demanding. During his adolescent years there were frequent misunderstandings between us that ended in angry, tearful confrontations. Even as a married man with children, he criticized his siblings and us, his parents, for not "being there" for him enough. For example, he thought we should be offering to baby-sit more often and bring food unsolicited, not acknowledging the many times we did baby-sit and do other favors. It was like trying to fill a bottomless pit. I could never do enough and he was never satisfied.

I began to realize that I couldn't change my son and that I was letting him control me. With much prayer and reflection, I began the process of letting go. When he argued or criticized I didn't try to defend myself but listened carefully and kept my own boundaries clear and

> firm. He must have found this frustrating because it wasn't long before he decided to have nothing more to do with us, declaring, "We have terminated our relationship with you. This goes for the entire family." Those were his exact words!
>
> During the years of estrangement from Oliver and his family, my grief was acute and intense. Although I had done all that I knew how to do to heal our relationship, including therapy, and knew that I had been a good mother to him, it was still a painful loss. I had no opportunity to see my grandchildren. Furthermore, it was difficult not to feel that somehow I must have failed.
>
> It took several years of counseling and spiritual direction before I could let go of my ego, give up trying to change my son, and stop letting him control me. I knew that I hadn't been a perfect mother. Who is? But I knew that God accepted me as I was and that I needed to do that too, for myself and for my son. What a freeing experience! I could move on and enjoy life! Now I'm able to see Oliver more objectively and feel free to love him without getting hooked emotionally. The years of estrangement were a dark time but now I look back on them as a time of inner healing that brought me through to a new place in my life.

Ann's story of lovingly detaching from both her mother and her son during difficult times is a good example of how facing the Wall can transform our lives.

Embracing Your Shadow

Embracing your shadow is another of the excruciating experiences in the Wall. Your shadow is that part of you that you have not recognized or that you stuffed away early in your childhood and is out of your perception. It is not a conscious part of what you portray to the world, yet it is very much a part of you. If you have not learned to embrace your shadow (which usually doesn't happen until you hit the Wall) then others know much more about your shadow than you do!

William Miller has written about a quick and disconcerting way to find your shadow in his book, *Your Golden Shadow*. Begin by thinking of a few people you don't like very well. On a sheet of paper draw a line down the middle from top to bottom. On the left side write all the negative qualities of these people. Then, after careful consideration, write in capital letters on the right hand side all the qualities of these people that you find despicable. Look them over carefully. These capitalized qualities are our shadow. Ouch! How could that be? Are these things really me? The things I hate in others? Yes. In me. In you.

The golden shadow resides in you too. That is the part behind the dark shadow. These are the wonderful qualities you admire in others that you have not yet claimed in yourself. You can find out what they are by thinking of people you admire. List their wonderful qualities on the left side of another sheet of paper. Then list in capital letters on the right side their qualities that you deeply admire or envy. These are your golden shadow. Unfortunately we need to start with the dark shadow, to claim those qualities first, or they will sabotage our golden shadow.

The Wall brings us in contact with our shadows and then asks us not to rid ourselves of them. In fact, we are asked to *embrace* our shadows. That does not mean we act out all those despicable characteristics, but each time shadow behavior arises within us we ask what the behavior is trying to teach us, or we take the behavior as a signal to do something. For instance, let's say you cannot stand people who talk too much yet you do not see yourself as a talker, because you try so hard to listen to others. Next time you are around people, listen to your internal monologue. Are you judging, weighing yours and others' words, criticizing people for what they say? Are you talking too much to yourself? If you judge other people, it might be a sign you are judging yourself harshly too. When you can ask, "Why am I judging myself so harshly?" you are on the way to internal freedom.

To really embrace our deepest shadows takes more work than just analyzing ourselves or watching our slips. We need to take a deeper inward journey back to the places where we acquired the need to hide the things that are in our shadows. We need to go back "home" so to speak, back to the scene of the crime that was committed against our psyches. And that is a difficult and a painstaking journey.

Paul tells his story of meeting and embracing his shadow:

> I first discovered my shadow when I was in my early thirties. I had broken up with a girlfriend and I found myself in a strange city, in a dumpy little apartment, and with no particular sense of what I should be doing next in my life. I had two careers, neither of which was going anywhere, and I was poor and heading towards bankruptcy. Out of sheer desperation I was forced to look inward and to try to make some sense of the direction my life had taken. Very quickly I discovered vast stretches of my soul that I had spent my life avoiding, and I knew that I would not be able to move forward until I had confronted them.

One thing I discovered was that I was a sex addict. Ever since my adolescence I had used sex, either with partners, or by myself, as a way to boost myself up when I was feeling down. Over the years, sex had become the way I learned to take care of all the negative feelings that lurked down in my soul. With each sexual episode, I was feeding myself small doses of "love" in a very controlled environment. In fact, it was not love at all, but something I have come to call "synthetic love." It may have felt like love in the moment, but in reality it was simply a controlled interaction that kept me from having my true feelings, and by continually feeding myself this synthetic love, I was depriving myself of the ability to have a real relationship. I didn't know it yet, but real relationships were way too scary for me. In a real relationship, I would have to surrender to my feelings without the safety of knowing how they would be received. My sexual rituals provided a sense of certainty—I knew that I would get my "fix" of love. So, while I thought I was having real relationships, I was really acting out controlled situations, where the synthetic love, in one form or another, was guaranteed. I never had to risk entering the unknown territories of a real relationship.

It became clear to me that if I was ever going to have a real relationship, I was first going to have to come to terms with my sexual addiction and my fears about relationships. One of the most frustrating aspects of this was the continual lesson that simply recognizing my addiction and my fears was not enough to help me overcome them. I had to work for many years to move past my learned behaviors. It seemed as if I was spending entire years in therapy and in groups. But over time I became more successful in embracing my shadows, and as I did, these shadows began to lose their power over me. Eventually, by embracing my addiction and my fears, I found that they no longer controlled me and I was able to move, slowly, into deeper places.

Interestingly enough, as my soul was freed up from the tensions and torments of addiction, and as I began to trust myself more with my real feelings, I also began to experience growth in other areas of my life. My professional life began to blossom on its own. I think that so much of my energy had been tied up in the circular game of need and addiction, that as I became freed of that cycle, I had vast amounts of energy to apply to other areas of my life. Simply by being true to myself, I found myself taking risks, spotting opportunities and having successes in all areas of my life.

I now believe that embracing the shadow is a skill that, once learned, needs to be applied on one level or another on a daily basis. It is the classic battle between the angel and the devil, each sitting on your

> shoulder trying to persuade you to see it their way. This is not a battle you have once in your life and you're done with it. This is a daily exercise of recognizing the shadow, embracing it, and moving past it.
>
> There was a time early on in my spiritual journey when I used to pray by sitting in a kneeling position and leaning forward with my head to the ground, Moslem-style. During one of these prayer sessions, God blessed me with this wisdom: "The more you put your head to the floor, the less the floor will come up and hit your head." Over fourteen years have passed since I first met my shadow in that dumpy little apartment. I have gotten married and I have two children. I have a successful career and I lead a normal, happy, and productive life. Still, whenever I am faced with a new challenge in life, whether it is in a relationship or at work, I find my old shadow snooping around with some proposed "solution." And then I remember—the more you put your head to the floor, the less the floor will come up and hit you on the head.

Paul's example of staring right at your shadow and embracing it shows how determination and good support can transform your life.

Going to Your Core

In the Wall experience embracing your shadow eventually and inevitably leads you to your core, your soul, if you will. It is the experience of who you are. Everything else is stripped away. It is who you are without any of the external trappings. The journey to your soul is usually a descent because your soul is the deepest part of you. In the core lie your deepest fears and wounds as well as your deepest heart's desires, and your overwhelming joy.

The paradox is that in order to find the light in our core, we must go through the darkness. It is the only way, and there is no way out but through. T. S. Eliot put it rather succinctly, the core experience, in part of his poem, East Coker, from Four Quartets.

> I said to my soul, be still, and wait without hope
> For hope would be hope for the wrong thing:
>   wait without love
> For love would be love of the wrong thing:
>   yet there is faith

But the faith and the love and the hope
    are all in the waiting
Wait without thought,
    for you are not ready for thought;
So the darkness shall be the light,
    and the stillness the dancing.

People find different things in their core but the truth they find there feels raw, unwieldy, and intensely freeing. One man went to his core and found a sexually abused child who now screams for trust and love from close people. He has a history of leaving relationships when they start getting close. Now after a lot of inner work, he can look forward to having lasting relationships.

Another man went to his core to find that his high achieving energy and drive hid a deeply insecure little boy who could never please his alcoholic father. This was excruciating to learn. But he knew he had hit pay dirt. By working with this new truth, he can be free to achieve what is in his heart and not try for the unattainable, the love of his father. Painful but at last, freeing.

An executive woman found in her core a terrified little girl who had to be perfect at everything. As an adult this perfectionist developed severe arthritis. She found out through her inner work that she needed to free her little girl from having to be perfect. In fact she had to really practice not doing everything right. Coming out of her prison helped her body too. Now her body is able to relax more than ever.

We find deep sadness and grief welling up when we come into an intimate connection with our core. But we also find incredible strength and start moving towards interior freedom when we work on our core issues. One woman described the core experience as releasing a one hundred pound backpack and watching it careen down a canyon. And this exact metaphor was the basis for one of the most dramatic scenes in the movie, *The Mission.* At a crucial juncture of the main character's ritual of forgiveness, the very people he has enslaved use a large knife to cut a heavy load from his back and let it careen down the mountain.

My personal Wall story goes deep into my core. The pain I experienced over this is indelibly marked on my soul. I had an emotionally abusive and devastating work experience with a professional colleague a while back. It left me exhausted and physically sick. I ended up having major surgery as a by-product of the experience. I knew something deeper was involved in the midst of this because of the obsessive feelings I was having in that work relationship. A supportive therapist and a spiritual director helped me begin to unravel the experience.

In the course of my counseling, I remembered back to three other work experiences and some intimate relationships in which I had been abused either physically or emotionally. Then I reached "home." I remembered for the first time how my family really was—emotionally abusive and codependent as a result of rage and the abuse of alcohol. The truth was hard to face. I had learned to be a victim. I remember my chagrin when I realized that I didn't even know what "normal" was.

In my heart I had little patience for people who let others victimize them. I wouldn't want to admit this publicly but I thought they were probably weak or ill-informed. Now I was one. *A victim*. Even the word was hard to say out loud. And I was a highly educated and sophisticated victim. It was my deepest shadow, so close to my own skin I couldn't see it without a great deal of help.

Now that I knew I was behaving like a victim, I had to face the fears it brought forth. The abyss, the darkness, and the fear were overwhelming. At one point I couldn't do anything but sit in the dark and listen and cry. In my desperation I pleaded to God for help. Pleading with God became problematic because I had the same issues with God that I had with men. I experienced God just like I experienced my father; big, scary, stern, unloving, and demanding. I found out I had to heal my image of God before I could tackle the issues I had in relationships.

As I worked through my difficult childhood issues and started to trust myself, one of my writer friends called me to see if I was interested in working on a project to raise awareness of abuse in the community. I said yes. I got involved in putting together a memorial exhibit for the women who have been murdered as a result of domestic violence. Our small group of artists and writers created red life-sized wooden figures representing all the women who were murdered in acts of domestic violence in our state in one year. We called them the Silent Witnesses.

Early the morning of the first public appearance of the exhibit, a statewide march I had helped to plan, I tried to get out of bed and I couldn't move. I could not even roll over in bed. My husband got me to the emergency room but no one could figure out for sure what was wrong. They said it might be gall bladder or perhaps a muscle spasm. I recovered after several hours and attended the march but I was weak and shaken. I never found out exactly what had caused this. The second time I was to appear publicly with the exhibit a similar but less severe pain occurred. No coincidence this time. There was a pattern forming.

I slowly figured out that my body was reacting to my speaking out against abuse. I came to see that my body was trying to protect me from breaking one of our family rules, which was "do not speak publicly about our secrets." I decided to work with my body instead of curtailing my appearances. So I talked to my body gently before each speech, let it know it was safe, and took some Advil to help relax my muscles. That, along with good counseling and support from friends, worked and I felt more confident about speaking publicly about domestic violence.

Then I had a dream that would change me forever. I dreamed I was inside of a locked boxcar that was on fire and moving slowly on a track shaped like a figure eight—the symbol for infinity. On the outside of the boxcar there was a sign with my mother's name on it. I woke up shaking and feeling horrified. It seemed clear to me I would live out my mother's legacy of an early death if I did not break out of the pattern I was in. The inner work I have done since then became the bedrock of my life.

I will always be a "survivor," in the sense that I survived abuse in childhood, in the workplace, and in intimate relationships. That is part of my make-up, but when my "little girl" inside begins to feel victimized by someone else or myself, I can love and soothe her and immediately go to work nurturing myself and defusing the harmful behavior. This does not mean that I take responsibility for the abuse, or that I do not hold the other person responsible for their behavior. But I can only control myself. I am responsible to not let myself be abused. I can set boundaries, ask for things I need, say no to behavior, get out of the room if necessary, and leave abusive relationships. I know how to act and I know in my heart what is harmful to me. My shadow, which is victim behavior, has been my finest teacher and my experience allows me to be more compassionate with other people who have been victimized. I am less judgmental of others now because I know what it means to be a survivor and I know how hard it is to embrace that truth. I will know that I have healed profoundly when I can have as deep an understanding and compassion for those who abuse me as I have of the victim place within me, while keeping myself safe and holding others responsible for their behavior.

I believe that once we embrace our core, which for me was the victim experiences I had as a child and had repeated in adulthood, then we are free to let go of that behavior and move forward. In the case of victims, I believe that if they keep embracing that part of themselves that is prone to being a victim, they become survivors and then they move on to becoming victors. If they continue to do more inner work they become healers and then they can move on to helping others become healers.

Finding Intimacy with a Higher Power

A critical insight about the Wall and Stage Five is this. It is the juncture where psychology and spirituality meet. Psychology can take us successfully into the Wall but adding spirituality to that takes us through it and out the other side. Our society slows this process by being so divisive about what is right and wrong in spiritual practices.

In the transition between Stage Four and Five the spirituality I am talking about is not about dogma, or liturgical practices, belief systems or organizations. The spirituality that takes us to Stage Five is the development of an intimate relationship with God, our Higher Power, the Holy, Great Spirit, Ultimate Reality, Allah, or Sophia. Only this personal vulnerable trusting intimacy will allow us to face the fears and develop the courage of Stage Five. I have suggested ways in which each stage of power experiences spirituality in this book; however, my book, *The Critical Journey* (co-authored with Robert Guelich) chronicles the stages of spirituality in our lives, and especially the Wall, in more depth and explains in detail the phases we all experience on our spiritual journeys.

One woman says, "I didn't realize when I took my sexual harassment complaint to my boss that I wouldn't have the inner strength to stay with it. He began telling me my behavior was too provocative. Thank God I got back into a spiritual relationship with Elohim, my feminine name for God. She gave me the courage to not only stand up to my boss but to go to the next level in the organization. I was scared but had so much peace inside. Now we have a sexual harassment policy due to my actions."

A man adds his perception, "I couldn't face the stress in my customer service job without knowing I am unconditionally loved and accepted by my Higher Power. I know I make mistakes but my Higher Power teaches me to be vulnerable and open with people and to stay with the issues until they are resolved. It is a lot less stressful on my body and on my mind. Knowing I am loved is the bottom line now."

For some people the real crisis at the Wall is facing their need for an intimate spirituality, or relinquishing their need to play God, or relinquishing their religiosity. What a threatening place, this Wall.

Glimpsing Wisdom

As you proceed deeply into the Wall and begin to experience the journey that takes you to your core, you will start to recognize sparks of wisdom. They are many-faceted. You may get insights you never had before; experience a peace you never dreamed was possible; discover that while hating the pain you also have a deep sense that this work is absolutely the right thing to be doing; experience the love of a friend for the first time; speak out on something important to you. Every miracle of wisdom comes in a different package.

Be on the alert. These bursts of wisdom mean that the light is beginning to shine. There is a new world you are opening into. Your soul is sensing freedom at last. You are going into the valley but you will also view the mountaintop. Hold onto these images in your heart. Savor them. And keep asking for more.

The Worth of the Wall

People at Stage Four need to give themselves time and support in approaching the Wall. It does not come naturally, although there is within each of us a craving for wholeness, I believe. This transition on the power model is, as I said, one of the hardest but it has the most to offer, if we are willing to give up what we don't think we can afford to lose. We give up our vision for ourselves since at Stage Five we will receive a different vision, both for ourselves and for the world. At the Wall, Stage Fours come out of the self-reflective cocoon. They see beyond the self, the department, even the organization to a broader view of the world. They ask hard questions and don't know the answers but they don't seem upset about not knowing either.

Fours who experience the Wall are less and less dependent on the external rewards and more oriented toward internal rewards that are not ego-oriented. If no one ever found out what they have accomplished, they can still feel good about it. They start to fit their work in the organization into the larger framework of their personal calling. They begin acting consistently at home, in the community, and at work. They can drop even more of their roles and accept themselves as "servants." They are beginning to grasp the idea of leading from behind.

The characteristics that begin to show up as a result of moving through the Wall are the Stage Five qualities; courage, fearlessness, creativity, inner depth, self-acceptance, interior freedom, and passion. Life takes on ultimate meaning. Curiously, the world begins to notice that they are different, but by the time they reach Stage Five it doesn't matter to them whether the world notices or not.

Spirituality and the Connection to Work at the Wall

At the Wall our work is to develop or renew or transform our spirituality into an intimate relationship with our Higher Power, the Holy. So in a sense, at the Wall spirituality and healing *is* our work. And slowly we begin to see glimpses of how this inner movement will work itself out in our lives. But during the depths of our Wall experiences, we have a hard time connecting our spirituality with our day-to-day work.

The most wonderful aspect of our spiritual journey in the Wall is that there is a spark of grace—or love—even in the darkness. We are never alone, even if it seems to us that we are. A short example here says it all. A minister in his late forties who hit the Wall was in deep angst about his life and even his role as a minister. While he was in therapy in the depth of his struggle he preached other people's sermons for two years.

Shadow of the Wall

Each of the stages of power has shadow behavior within it, so why do we speak of embracing shadow as one of the major characteristics of the Wall and how is that different from the shadow of the other stages? At each of the other stages one can either get stuck by staying in the shadow of that stage or move through the stage and on to the next one without coming to terms with the shadow of that stage. The shadow describes the dark side of that stage. So at Stage Two a person could get stuck being a chameleon and never find the confidence to search out a true self. Or at Stage Three one could avoid the shadow by finding competence and success without getting caught up in the egocentric part of that stage.

But at the Wall we cannot move forward without embracing our own personal shadow behavior, behavior that we might have been shoving under the rug for years as we moved through the other stages. The Wall is the place our shadow becomes clear and we make a decision whether or not we will deal with it. The major thing that gets people stuck at the Wall, and usually catapults them back to a safer, more comfortable place, is their conclusion (either consciously or unconsciously) that they have too much to lose by moving further into this Wall, this darkness.

Two things can happen as a result of avoiding the darkness of the Wall. One is that the person gets caught in the darkness and can't seem to get away from it; for instance, their addiction flares up worse than ever and, rather than seeing this as a sign they've hit pay dirt, they see it as a reason they need to back off and not go through the Wall.

The second thing that happens, especially if they do not seek spiritual direction or psychological help, is that they get so frightened by this inner work, they hasten back to an earlier stage and stay there in safety for quite some time.

Now, the Wall is not easy. None of us walks into it and straight through it. The stories you've read in this chapter describe years of inner work with personal demons at the Wall in order to quiet their voices. So it is like walking up the Wall and taking a stone or two out at a time, looking it over, and taking it with us to eventually build something creative with it, making it our own. It's not fun but it doesn't have to destroy us. It can free us. But when it is too intense we go back to Stage Three or Four and stay there for a while, and then when we are ready we pry one more stone from the Wall. We need support and sustenance while we are doing this work for it may take several years and isn't ever fully completed.

Catalyst for Movement

The major catalyst for growth within the Wall is the adoption of the belief that pain is truly an opportunity for growth. This goes against our grain as individuals, as organizations, and as a country. But it is the truth. Look at your own life and see if pain, well-attended, did not yield new growth, new ideas, and new life.

Those who spend their lives warding off pain may be safe but they will not become wise.

What Holds People Back?

It is simple to describe what holds people back. It is their will. We simply do not want to let go, to lose our control. It is too scary, too unpredictable. And at the base of that, for some, is the belief that they are not loved or lovable. There is no power beyond them who, they believe, cares enough to help bring about their deepest heart's desire.

We can still have experiences of Stages Five and Six without fully embracing our shadows at the Wall. But to live in Stages Five or Six as our home stage presumes we have learned to embrace our own personal shadows.

Ways to Move to Stage Five

- Stay accountable to someone who knows your story.

  Spend time regularly with a professional who cares about you and is willing to hold your feet to the fire. A list of spiritual directors in your area is available at the web site of Spiritual Director's International. You can find a reputable counselor by calling your insurance company or by asking friends, ministers, or priests for a referral.

- Be willing to explore your passion.

  Let yourself imagine that what your heart most desires, even though it seems strange or out of reach, is at least imaginable. Read biographies of others in history who have lived out their heart's desire. Take a pilgrimage to a site where someone else has lived out his/her dreams.

- Believe in healing before it happens.

  Ask for such an increase in faith that you will cease to be afraid, insecure, angry, or anxious.

Hagberg's Model of Personal Power

Summary of the Wall

Key Question: What one thing about you will be dangerous to others if you are not fully conscious of it?

Description
Transformation
The courageous ones

Characteristics
Moving beyond your intellect
Letting go of control
Embracing your shadow
Going to your core
Finding intimacy with your Higher Power
Glimpsing wisdom

Spirituality and Spiritual Connection to Work
Grace in the darkness

Shadow of the Wall
Too much to lose

Catalyst for Movement
See pain as an opportunity for growth

What Holds People Back?
Will

Ways to Move
Stay accountable to someone who knows your story. Be willing to explore your passion. Believe in healing before it happens.

Ask yourself these questions about Stage Five:

Yes	No	
____	____	1. Do you care more about other people's development than you do about your own?
____	____	2. Are you comfortable with yourself enough that other people's opinions of you do not affect you?
____	____	3. Do you have a life purpose that reaches beyond yourself and your organization?
____	____	4. Do you have a deep inner core of spirituality?
____	____	5. Do you genuinely enjoy being alone?
____	____	6. Do you operate out of a quiet, inner sense of calm?
____	____	7. Is your ego getting smaller and less significant all the time?
____	____	8. Have you lost track of the organizational ladder?
____	____	9. Do you consciously give power away by empowering others?
____	____	10. Do you feel your work and your life are becoming more integrated, less splintered?
____	____	11. Do you believe power is infinite?
____	____	12. Do you often laugh at your own foibles?
____	____	13. Are your weaknesses more meaningful to you than your strengths?
____	____	14. Do you act courageously, despite the consequences?
____	____	15. Do you have a sense of "calling" about your life and work?

Yes answers indicate that you identify with this stage.

Chapter 6
Stage Five: Power by Purpose

Inner Vision

Key Question: What is your deepest heart's desire?

What Is Stage Five Like?

Stage Five is unlike all of the preceding stages. Its uniqueness lies in the strength of the inner person relative to the strength of the organizational hold on that person. The guide for behavior in Fives is their inner voice. They trust it more than they trust the rules. Stage Five people are different internally *and* externally now. They are more congruent because they no longer have to live two separate lives as Stage Fours do. And it is even harder to spot Fives because they don't care if they're ever spotted. In fact, they may even hide a bit.

Fives have a life "calling" that extends beyond them. This has resulted from a deep, inner churning; a long, slow, or painful evolution in which the old rules have dropped away temporarily and old allegiances, ideas, and people have been reevaluated. These people have encountered themselves head on. They have hit the wall. They have engaged intimately with their Higher Power. They are letting go. They have glimpsed wisdom. And they are finding their inner truth, a life calling, and a moral imperative that goes beyond them. As the button-maker says to Peer Gynt in the play of the same name, "To be yourself is to demolish yourself."

Stage Five people are courageous. They have faced, and continue to face, their fears so they can act in spite of fear. They take risks, tell the truth to the organization, seek compassion, and love mercy. They do this despite the consequences. To be at home at Stage Five means giving away power and leading from behind, as a servant of the group. It is letting go of the written or organizational rules and living with a sense of inner compassion and order. It is learning to strive for others or more often for principles. *Above all it is not ego oriented.* That is why Stage Fives are called the irregulars in organizations. This is the reason they are so easily misunderstood. No one knows what their agenda is because they don't have an agenda.

The symbol for Stage Five is one person passing power to another. Stage Five people believe that power multiplies infinitely. The more power you can give away, the better. Power is like love: You can't have it truly until you give it away or let it go, and the more of it you give unselfishly, the more it multiplies. Fives know that love or power given away comes back full circle but not in the same form in which it was given. They do not attempt to gain or accumulate power because they find the other forms in which it reappears, like caring, appreciation, and friendship, more rewarding.

An example of this unselfish behavior in a community might be this: Joe decides to nominate Charlene for a community service award because she is truly a significant contributor and highly deserves the recognition. He has no motives other than wanting her good work to be rewarded. He writes a very well-documented, concise, and engaging application for her, remaining anonymous himself. Charlene never finds out who nominated her but she is very touched by the nomination. Years later, when she and Joe are on a task force together, she asks him if he nominated her. He smiles and only says that he knows the person who did. A Stage Five person does the thing precisely because there will be no personal return.

The definition of power at Stage Five is inner vision, which has many connotations and elicits marvelous images. Stage Fives have keen vision. They can see beyond the obvious and look with an inner eye. (The eye is an ancient symbol for inner vision and wisdom.) And this vision includes, and goes beyond, the self and even the organization. Although Fives may be involved in organizations their self-image is beginning to extend to the larger world. They have compassion for others in the world because they know pain and have come to befriend it. They are not islands unto themselves but members of the human family.

What emerges for Stage Fives is a sense of calling in their lives and work. Vocation comes from the Latin word vocare, meaning to call. Fives feel their life is a vocation, a spiritual calling. Frederich Buechner defines vocation as "the place where your deep gladness and the world's deep hunger meet." Fives have a deeper meaning to their "work" whether it is in the community, in the family, or on the job. Their concept of work has changed and expanded.

Since Stage Five people are now emerging from their long inner struggle of definition and self-acceptance—which takes years for some and a lifetime for most—they can concentrate on essentials, the things that give meaning to them and to the lives of others. They can take on the task of helping just one person or they can make changes in the world, or both simultaneously, because both are equally important to them and require the same dedication. A Stage Five person made this telling remark about his work: "I used to think I was helping others by my community service at the soup kitchen. Now I know we are brothers and sisters in pain."

No particular jobs or positions necessarily lend themselves to Stage Five behavior. To have one's home stage in Stage Five means that some symbols of the external stages have been achieved and, more important, that much inner work has been accomplished. In fact, Fives and Twos may sometimes look alike and thus confuse observers. They both may appear unassuming or non-ego driven. The difference is that Fives consciously give away power, influence, and information they have accumulated, while Twos have not yet tasted power. You can't give away something you don't own. Letting other people manage you without knowing first how to manage yourself, which is more typical at Stage Two, usually occurs as a result of newness or insecurity.

People who feel the Stage Two/Stage Five split express another confusion that arises. They are experiencing a deep inner journey in one part of their lives (Stage Five), but in areas like work or relationships, they are at Stage Two. So they feel pulled in two directions, with their home stage generally at Stage Two. I usually recommend that they apply the same process they used to get to Stage Five in one area of their life to the other areas; i.e., if you've learned to be honest with yourself and to let go of control in your family situation, why not try to do the same thing at work? Or if you have learned to take leadership in the community, why not take a little more leadership in the family? It does give hope to people to have experienced Stage Five, if even briefly in their lives, to know that when they are operating in other stages there are other options ahead.

Stage Five people have experienced the inner struggle and evolution as a totally individual experience and do not feel that others must have the same set of experiences they did in order to find inner peace. Also people need not reach a certain level in the organization to experience Stage Five, as long as they have received some of the recognition of Stage Three and have then looked inward to learn the meaning of themselves at Stage Four. Many people who hold positions of external power or prestige in organizations are firmly entrenched in Stage Three. They may lead exciting lives with lots of activity and challenge, but at the same time they are caught in the web of unending expectations with no larger vision beyond their own ultimate success. They do not have peace of mind and inner calm.

The kind of power that is emerging in Fives, that of power from the inside out, is described by Rollo May in his classic book, *Power and Innocence,* as "nutrient power;" that is, power for the other. It shows caring and giving with respect, not manipulation. As examples he cites teaching at its best, healthy parenting, political statesmanship, and diplomacy. Nutrient power wishes other people well and does what is within its influence to develop or provide for them.

You may be thinking that Stage Fives sound too good to be true. In some respects they are. But they are not beyond being human and they are not arrogant about their experiences. They are disciplined in their inner life, and their detachment from the things that run most people's lives sets them apart, but not by design. They live from the inside out, not from the outside in. And that may be very frustrating to those around them who want them to be different.

I have probably never experienced Stage Five as my home stage but I do think there are occasions in which I tap into its unusual inner power. Two experiences come to mind. One is the profound sense of peace and spiritual grounding I feel each time I consciously name abuse in my own life or in the world and then do something to heal it. As I mentioned in the wall section, I work on a project called the Silent Witness Initiative, a worldwide organization that started as a result of seven artists and writers getting involved with domestic violence. We created 27 life-sized wooden figures representing the Minnesota women who were murdered in acts of domestic violence in one year.

The intent of Silent Witness is not only to honor the women who were murdered and to raise awareness but also to heal this country of domestic violence. Our goal is to reduce domestic homicides of women to zero by 2010. As of this writing the homicide rates have dropped 40% in the last several years. Over the years I have come to see that unless we heal all those involved in domestic violence we will keep repeating it. So when we found projects that actually healed people, both perpetrators and survivors, it changed my understanding of what our organization was all about. When I realized that this healing work was my calling in life, my whole life took on new significance.

It has been exhilarating and difficult work. The exhilaration comes from seeing the passion and positive work of our activists, people whose lives have been changed, and who in turn change the way in which their communities react to domestic violence. It has been difficult to see well-meaning people actually prefer revenge and punishment to healing. At times we have been attacked and even threatened for our public stance on healing. But I believe the healing models will prevail and I will spend the rest of my life working towards that healing. I feel my role is not only to be a healer of domestic violence but also to support and encourage other healers within this movement around the world.

The other profound experience of this stage for me is my fifteen-year volunteer experience of relationships with women in prison, especially women who are convicted of murder. I am moved beyond words by their lives. They teach me the true meaning of survival. They taught me about abuse, rejection, candor, and generosity. I have developed a woman-to-woman connection with several women as a result of sharing their pain and their healing. And it moves me deeply to discover the pain we have in common. I learned early on not to try to do anything special but just to show up regularly and listen to them. They were very patient with me and trusted me with their stories. For that I am forever changed and forever grateful.

Characteristics of Stage Five People

It is more difficult to describe the behavior of Stage Five people because so much of what goes on in their lives is totally hidden from view. Also Stage Fives do not seek the limelight, and they share their inner processes only with a few as an illustration or an empathetic gesture. Therefore, you may know them more for what they don't do than for what they do.

Self-Accepting

Stage Fives are perhaps the most genuine and human of all because of their near total self-acceptance and their tight grasp of reality. Stage Sixes for some seem out of reach or too advanced to be understood. People at Stage Five know their strengths and limitations. They have embraced their shadows and are embracing their weaknesses as well, knowing that these are signs of a need for self-care. Fives are good at self-nurturing, especially in tense times. For instance, let's look at people who were severely wounded emotionally in childhood and their tendency is to take this pain out on others. They know this about themselves and whenever they feel their blaming and judgmental feelings rise, they know it represents childhood wounds opening. They can now choose new behavior, self-nurturing behavior, instead of the blaming behavior. They may take a walk, take a break, go to a movie, eat a special food, or just humor themselves. They are befriending the wounded child within and also taking care of their grown-up needs for nurture. Their weakness has become strength. They are not afraid of their feelings and that is their power.

Stage Fives can be outstanding managers and leaders because of this self-acceptance. As a result they are more accepting of others and can encourage others to be fully functioning. Stage Five people will remove themselves from situations in which their weaknesses get in the way or will simply laugh at those situations in which their ineptness is shown. I know several people who are the most assured, competent people professionally in their work, and can speak comfortably to large groups of influential people but who are totally inept with twenty people at an informal social gathering. They laugh about sitting in the corner or hiding gracefully behind the nearest plant, pretending to be invisible. People at Stage Five can laugh at themselves; in fact, they get quite a kick out of their incapacities. And it is wonderfully comforting to others who have not yet learned to admit publicly to any weaknesses. Stage Fives are frustrating to others, though, who feel one should always be working on perfection. To hear Stage Fives say they will probably always be critical, or messy, or depressed distresses self-developers.

Courageous

Outer courage comes from facing inner fear. Stage Five people are naturally more courageous because they are not afraid of being afraid. Following their calling is more important, more central to their core, than yielding to their familiar sabotaging fears. Courageous people face the fears of loss, failure, death, abandonment, woundedness, and lack of love. They faced them headlong in the wall. Now they continue to face them. They use the energy and wisdom gained from facing the pain of the wall to fuel their inner vision.

Courage is a conscious reflective decision to act on life-giving principles, despite the consequences. It must grow from within, from facing ourselves. It is a decision and it requires action. We do not simply contemplate courage. We are courageous. The principles we act on are life giving. That leaves out Hitler and Jim Jones and Osama bin Laden. The hardest part of being courageous is acting in spite of the consequences. Courageous people are aware of consequences. But they act in spite of the consequences. That is what amazes other people. For many of us, courage simply requires too much. The potential loss is too frightening.

Courage comes in many forms. We see glimpses of it all around us. In the movie, "Fried Green Tomatoes," the woman restaurant owner illustrated courage by refusing to let the community hang a black man for a murder he did not commit. Instead she went to trial herself, knowing she was innocent but expecting to be convicted.

In a family a courageous husband of an alcoholic wife goes into therapy and subsequently confronts his wife. He faces his fears and says he will not leave her but he also will not support the alcoholic behavior any more. Two painful years ensue while the wife hits bottom and finally faces her denial. The family begins the long painful journey to emotional health.

A woman manager refuses to find subtle reasons to let her competent older employees go and puts her job on the line. Her boss gives her a poor performance review and finds reasons for letting the employees go. She supports them in an age-discrimination suit. They win. Her boss leaves. She has great difficulty finding bosses who want her to work for them because she has now become "dangerous."

An act of courage inspires us, even though it may haunt us. It touches us deeply in a place that longs for that kind of fortitude. The more time we spend cultivating the behavior of the stages beyond Stage Three the more we will tap into that place of inner freedom.

We cannot expect society to reward us for courageous behavior. Others may even be threatened by courageous behavior. We may only experience the rewards of courageous behavior internally, or spiritually.

Calm

Along with self-acceptance and courage comes a contagious kind of calm that is a mark of Stage Five people. They're usually not in a hurry to get places because they are content with their situation and life. In fact, their internal calm can be sensed even when they are in tense and frightening situations. They are not blocking the feelings but their reservoir of serenity is deeper. Their calm is like a faint perfume that scents the air; it is emitted non-verbally to the surrounding environment.

This calm content behavior is not to be confused with that of shy or quiet people who may indeed be tense inside or afraid to speak. This calm is also not the same as that shown by judicious types who are quietly analyzing the situation to appraise it. Calm people can be outgoing or quiet. What they emit from the inside makes the difference.

The sense of peace inside comes from knowing and accepting themselves, knowing they are loved and accepted for who they are by their Divine source, and trusting that they will be continually led to "right action." Their presence is calming to others.

A wonderful story illustrates the source of that calm. Barbara Brown Taylor, in *The Preaching Life,* says that faith can best be illustrated by contemplating going across a beautiful but deep gorge by way of a swinging bridge. You know that this is the only and the best way across the gorge and that others have crossed ahead of you. It finally boils down to believing in the bridge more than you believe in the gorge. That's where you get that deep calm, from believing in the bridge!

Conscience of the Organization

If Stage Five people are valued in an organization they must be nurtured and protected, usually from people who are living in the shadowy regions of Stage Three. Fives are not only beyond the traditional rules and norms, they do not always fit well into the accepted culture of the organization. Most organizations do not have many Fives in traditional positions of power because they are not motivated by the rewards that accompany those jobs. And what's worse, they really don't care a whole lot. Since the symbols no longer persuade or motivate them, other forms of motivation must be considered if they are to be kept in the organization as useful contributors. Why then would anyone want to keep Fives around, if they don't fit? For precisely that reason. They can be a conscience of the organization and thus a visionary for it as well. They are not afraid to ask difficult questions, to present preposterous arguments, to be creative, to suggest alternatives that go against the rules. And they are deliberately non-self-serving. They give away ideas, find ways to promote others, and do not usually bid for more responsibility. They tend to be more naturally creative in a form that fits their style and background. They have the necessary risk-taking ability to be leaders in power positions and yet they frequently want nothing to do with being at the helm. They would rather lead from behind. Wouldn't it be amazing to see an organization headed up by a Stage Five person?

Stage Five people, though different from the norm, are still in touch with reality in the organization. Fives provide a different model or basis upon which to operate that is useful but not easily tolerable to Stage Threes. Threes want to control all the variables. Stage Fives are not predictable, they ignore politics, and can be counted on to disagree if they think it is justified. But they are not troublemakers or rabble-rousers. Most people can't figure them out, can't find their vulnerable spot or motivate them with money or threats. They usually can't be "had." As a result, most organizations can tolerate only a limited number of Fives but in reality they need more of them.

Some officers of progressive organizations say they can specifically identify their Stage Five people because they give wise counsel and respond reflectively on almost any issue. The employers admit to having to protect these people at times, or at least explain to others why they continue to keep them around. In one organization, the presence of a Stage Five person was described by a fellow employee like this: "I'm not at all sure what Al does on his job any more. All I know is that long before any major decision is about to be announced in this place, there is a steady stream of important people to his office."

Stage Five people do have vision but it goes beyond money, profits, and position, to asking and answering questions like: What is the best long-range strategy for this organization? What is our role in the community and in the world? What are the most important issues we will face in five years? How do we trust our people to be self-motivated and productive? How do we tolerate differences in our leadership? How can the workplace be more humane and provide more equality? Where do we fit into the emerging world community? What kind of a say do employees have in our future? Are we in the wrong business for the wrong reasons? Fives are the conscience of the organization. They call the organization to do what is right, even though it may be uncomfortable. For example, they will call attention to any discrepancy between the organization's publicly stated goals and the way those goals are actually pursued.

Humble

Probably the most critical variable affecting Stage Five people is the lessening of their egos. This one characteristic distinguishes them in an astonishing way from other people. Diminished ego, however, does not mean loss of self-esteem. On the contrary, persons with less ego, who have consciously given it up, often exhibit more self-esteem than others. Fives make a conscious decision to transfer the energy expended in struggling with themselves to other arenas—people, ideas, or organizations.

Their reduced ego sometimes makes Fives hard to understand. This is because they are not generally motivated by the usual things and therefore can't be as easily figured out or manipulated. The more consistent and integrated Stage Five persons are, the more profound is their influence on others. Some people have said they have been influenced by Fives simply by observing them or being around them. Their operating style appears and is expressed in the way they process information, the kinds of questions they ask, the breadth of their knowledge, and the depth of their self-awareness.

Since this ego reduction is one of the distinguishing characteristics of Fives, it would be nice to describe how one goes about obtaining such a trait. Unfortunately, there is no course or credo that offers a magic way to achieve this. It is a development that occurs deep within the person and is often not even shared with those closest to them. In fact, the more that is spoken, the less authentic may be the experience. It may be just one more strategy for building up the ego. And ego reduction may, in fact, be a byproduct of other things Fives do or experience, not a goal unto itself. It may be like happiness in that respect. One does not seek it for its own sake, but enjoys it as a result of an experience, thought, or event.

Practical Mystics

To Stage Five people, spirituality is the spark that allows their inner fires of purpose to burn freely. Hildegard of Bingen, an activist of the twelfth century says, "Humanity is the spark of God, but not the fire itself." So to Stage Fives spirituality is an intimate relationship with the Holy, an intimacy that was made real to them in the wall. It allows them to commit to vulnerability over dogma, to truth over rules, and to inclusiveness over separateness. They may be religious but they are not caught up in religiosity. They believe deeply that their spirituality is their call to courage. It is their call to sacrifice.

I like to think of Stage Five people as practical mystics. Mystics are those people who have experienced the love of the Holy, not from afar, but by direct and prolonged personal experience. Every spiritual tradition describes them, so the experience is nothing new. They are everywhere in our world and not hidden away as some might think. I have met urban mystics, rural mystics, social justice mystics, corporate mystics, educator mystics, parent mystics, banker mystics, and writer mystics. They are engaged in the everyday work of the world, bringing to it new levels of healing and forgiveness, elegance and grace. The kind of work they do is no longer the issue. They can be bringing beauty to the world, healing social ills, raising healthy families, or running corporations. Whatever they do in the work world, they usually think of their calling as something much simpler. Their calling may even sound odd, like "to be available" or "to reach out" or "travel light." What matters now is how they relate and treat other people and how they live out their inner faith. Their associates can feel the depth of their commitments and can sense their integrity without even having to discuss it. They are the healers in the world.

We all have within us the seeds of spiritual mysticism. And mystics are just like the rest of us except for one main factor. They desire intimacy with the Holy with their whole heart and soul and mind and they live their lives as prayer. Mystics do not have to be saints or special people set aside to be holy. And we don't have to be a saint to experience a spark of God as Hildegard mentions. Frederick Buechner speaks cogently to all of us potential mystics about taking this journey with the Holy seriously, in *Summons to Pilgrimage.*

> We are all of us more mystics than we believe or choose to believe... We have seen more than we let on, even to ourselves. Through some moment of beauty or pain, some sudden turning of our lives, we catch glimmers at least of what the saints are blinded by, only then, unlike the saints, we tend to go on as though nothing has happened. To go on as though something has happened, even though we are not sure what it was or just where we are supposed to go with it, is to enter the dimension of life that religion is a word for.

John Powers, author of *Holy Human*, and a student of mysticism, says that mystics were not comfortable with labels or any uniqueness. They were often "dragged screaming through the illusions of life, finding greater sanity, serenity, and sanctity in the acceptance of God."

He goes on to say "they were ordinary men and women, extra-ordinarily alive to the aliveness of God...God-seers wide-eyed to the color of divinity in every human interaction...filled with the wondrous intuition that every coincidence seeps with the eternal mystery of God, and sages of the imagination..."

People will describe their path to their spiritual source differently. The place to focus is not on how one arrives there, but what one believes about the source and how one behaves based on the inner core of spirituality that underlies and pervades their lives. They trust the inner messages they get from their Divine source because they are no longer grounded in their egos, but fueled by love. They do not talk much about their spiritual practice; they just live differently in the world. Since their egos are diminished and they are secure, they can participate in a wide range of activities or events and feel a consistency and calling.

For those who read this and are interested in ways to move into more intimacy with the Holy, I will briefly list a few suggestions for ways to get started. These are from an unpublished book I wrote with Rev. Dr. Gary Klingsporn, called *Who Are You, God?*

Ask the Holy to come closer to you (but be careful what you ask for, you might get it)

Look for the Holy in the ordinary

Be honest and real with the Divine

Talk to the Holy and listen for the Holy

Let the Divine stimulate your creativity

Journey with supportive people

Share someone else's pain

Trust the Holy to bring you your deepest heart's desire

The results in your life will include an increase of trust in the Holy; a sense of contentment, peace, and humor; a reduction of fear; and a sense that you are having a compelling effect on others without trying.

There is a story told by Meister Eckhart, a German Dominican mystic of the thirteenth century, which illustrates the philosophy by which a mystic lives. It is cited in John Powers' book, *Holy Human.* It seems a learned man searched for many years for a teacher to give him the truth. Once, during a time of great emptiness, he heard the voice of God say to him, "Go to the church and there you will find a man who shall show you the way to union with God." Off the man went only to find a poor man whose feet were torn, who was covered with dust and dirt, and whose clothes were rags. The educated man greeted the poor man:

> "I hope you have a good day!"
> The poor man answered, "I have never had a bad day!"
> "God gives you good luck then," said the learned man.
> "I have never had bad luck," said the beggar.
> Frustrated at the poor man's answers the learned man said, "Well, may you be happy!"
> Quietly and without fluster the poor man answered, "I have never been unhappy."

"How can this be?" exclaimed the learned fellow. "Please, explain it to me," he asked the poor man. The beggar fellow answered willingly, '"You wished me to have a good day. I have never really had a bad day for if I am hungry I praise God. If it freezes, hails, rains, if the weather is fair or stormy, I praise God. If I am despised and looked down upon, I praise God, and so I never have an evil day. You wished that God would send me a bit of luck. But I never had bad luck, for I know how to live with God. I know what God has done is best for me, for what God ordains for me, whether good or ill by my estimate, I take cheerfully as the best that can be, so I have never had bad luck. You wished that God would make me happy. I was never unhappy, for I only desire to live in the will of God. What God wills, I will."

The learned man then realized that humble abandonment is the surest way to God. He talked to the man further and then asked, "How did you achieve such a summit?"

"Through silence, good thoughts, and through union with God," answered the poor fellow. "I could never rest in anything that is less than God. Now, however, I have found God and have eternal peace."

Elusive Qualities

Several other qualities seem to develop either along with or because of the loss of ego and practical mysticism. I hesitate to even describe them lest they be misunderstood. Just because people acquire one or all of these qualities does not necessarily mean their egos will be diminished, only that I have noticed them in people whose egos are reduced. The first of these qualities is a tremendous *need for solitude*, for time alone to respond to the power within and beyond and let it wash over oneself. The solitude refreshes, awakens, and clarifies. The ability to be totally quiet without reading, writing, or thinking is a gift and one to be savored in this frantic world. Fives seem to be able to do that even in the middle of a day strangely enough, in a group or on the go. They carry solitude with them, like a cloak, yet they can be easily with people.

The second quality is an increased willingness to listen to their inner voices and to distinguish between their own voice and the voice of the Divine. This gets tricky because so often we try to make the voice of the Holy conform to our will. The ability to distinguish the two is called discernment. Stage Five people are *discerning*. They know that what their Higher Power tells them to do will not always agree with their will or their reason. They receive intuitive messages through the small inner voice which only whispers and is never wrong.

The third quality that develops in Fives along with a lessened ego is a *different kind of humor*. They have no need to put others down, make them look stupid, or use sexual connotations to demean them. Whereas Fours are just finding their own style of humor, Fives find their humor by laughing gently at their own foibles and by observing the silly, ordinary things of life, like children's antics and lowly puns. Their humor is fresh and honest, not sarcastic or angry. They have little need to elevate themselves by putting others in an inferior place. In fact, some people don't even develop a true sense of their own humor until Stage Five. They're either stern or serious or they adopt the humor of the marketplace to fit in. Their own humor has been buried for years, only to resurface at these later stages. It's a joy to be around people who can laugh at themselves and mean it.

Yet another quality of Fives resulting from a lessened ego is their *apparent innocence*. Rollo May, in *Power and Innocence,* once again sheds light on Stage Five behavior by describing this quality of innocence in personally powerful people. It is "a way to confront powerlessness by making it a virtue. A conscious divesting of his/her power . . . not in a harmful way but free from guilt . . . and with no evil intention." He describes the quality in some artists and poets as a quality of the imagination that gives a childlike clarity in adulthood, a freshness, newness, or color. These people reflect the awe and wonder of spring that leads one toward spirituality. They preserve their childlike attitudes into maturity without sacrificing the realism of their perception of evil, nor their complicity with evil. They are authentic.

Generous in Empowering Others

Stage Five people cannot help but affect others. Since they know this, they have consciously chosen as a way of life the empowering of others. Not only is it a healthy discipline in reducing ego but in the long run it's always the right and just thing to do. Empowering others gives them dignity and does not diminish the giver. So everyone wins.

The ultimate objective of most Fives, whether stated or not, is to empower others: to raise them up, love them, give them responsibility, trust them, learn from them, and be led by them. In fact, Fives exhibit leadership by empowering others. They feel they are merely a conduit of ideas, energy, and power to be given out or passed along. This comes through in their lives and their work. Alexander Graham Bell was heard to say, "I feel like my discoveries come through me, that I am a channel for forces greater than myself."

Fives do not need to be in charge. More often now they choose to be behind the scenes. They would rather participate as good team members or individual contributors in an organization and develop others' leadership. Frequently they are encouraged to assume leadership positions, but if those positions do not specifically fit their life calling they will usually decline. There are some basic reasons why Fives are such good behind-the-scene leaders. First, they are not afraid of change. In fact, they welcome warranted change and see it as a way to learn. They often find ways for the change to help each individual person or they help each person to see the change as an opportunity. Second, they have vision. They will look longer range and see the bigger picture. And third, they are less fearful. Since they have less at stake in the organization, they are not continually covering their tracks or worrying that people will use them or their information.

Herman Hesse wrote a book, *Journey to the East,* which illustrates the kind of leadership with which Fives are most comfortable. In this book a group of people are on a journey accompanied by a servant who ministers to their needs in the most unobtrusive ways. They did not realize until he was away from the group for a time that he, indeed, held the group together and was, in fact, their leader. Only when they arrived at their destination did they realize that he was the acclaimed leader they were journeying to see. Hence the idea of servant leadership.

To empower others Fives usually choose the least obvious and public ways. For instance, when a Five becomes a mentor for another person, it is usually inconspicuous. More often, they simply sense a need for mentoring and respond to it. And being mentored by a Five does not mean being told what to do or given their model to follow. In fact, getting information from Fives about their lives and career strategies is difficult. They'd rather tell wonderful stories or metaphors for you to figure out. So the best way to learn from a Five is to be in a more casual relationship or setting with them, learning from their style and listening to their conversations, rather than asking for procedures or posing questions on technique. Then later, perhaps years later, you'll hear yourself make their kind of response to a question or situation. They're wonderful in that long-term mentoring capacity. You can feel their presence long after they're gone.

Another important way in which Stage Five people empower others is to give everything away: ideas, titles, responsibility, leads, solutions. They have no strong inclination to hold on to these ego-building things. This trait is confusing to others, however, who wonder how someone can freely give up the things that are supposed to mean so much. But this gets progressively easier for Fives because they find great satisfaction in selfless giving. They've discovered that to diminish oneself is to know oneself. Their deeper, true-to-nature traits emerge more authentically when they remove the armor. And all their fears—fear of reprisal, of failure, of loss, of being alone—are taking a less central place in the whole life of Fives.

Yet another way Fives empower others is to use them as teachers. Fives are intuitively curious people. They have a depth of knowledge or expertise in some area but have also developed a breadth of interest in addition to that. They are not afraid to wade into experiences that are foreign to them and just be there. For instance, Stage Fives are least afraid of engaging with Aids patients, homeless people, or battered women. They not only engage them, they learn from them. And they notice how alike we all are. The persons teaching them also gain—self-respect and satisfaction through sharing their experience.

Stage Five characteristics can be viewed from the perspective of another culture very different from our own. The following are nine principles for learning the way to highly develop oneself, according to Miyamoto Musashi in his Ichi School of Oriental Training from his book, *A Book of Five Rings*. The characteristics of highly complex people in our two cultures are amazingly similar.

1. Do not think dishonestly
2. The way is in training
3. Become acquainted with every art
4. Know the ways of all professions
5. Distinguish between gain and loss in worldly matters
6. Develop intuitive judgment and understanding for everything
7. Perceive those things which cannot be seen
8. Pay attention even to trifles
9. Do nothing which is of no use

Confident of Life Calling

Stage Five people know what their life's calling is, where their deep gladness and the world's deep hunger meet. And they are able to wed this to their lifestyle and their work. From a deep spiritual place inside they have naturally evolved what has always been waiting to be recognized. They now have a sense of mission or vocation for their lives. It can be their volunteer commitment or a paid job. It can be almost anything. But they receive their calling from their Higher Power, the Holy. It is not the same as life goals. In fact it may be a surprise when it emerges. You can set life goals at any stage but at Stage Five you live out of what you are called to do or to be more fully. Usually our life calling can be stated in very simple and straightforward terms; e.g., to be available, to love, to be vulnerable, to obtain peace, to heal, or to wisely lead. The exact thing or idea we are given really doesn't matter, except that it comes from the Holy, resides within, and is the reason we get up every morning. We may not think about this purpose every day but ultimately it is our underlying reason for living. We may devote time, money, ideas, work, or a lifetime to our calling once it can be articulated, for it brings internal rewards that cannot be measured in tangible ways.

Fives are not likely to burn out from working on their calling for the simple reason that they are aware of their limitations at this stage. If you were to ask them what their calling is, they might be embarrassed to talk about it or may tell you something very acceptable. It is not important to them that others know, only that they themselves know that their calling is worthwhile, respectful of others, and egoless. Reinhold Niebuhr said in one of his most quotable observations, "Nothing that is worth doing can be achieved in a lifetime; therefore we must be saved by hope. Nothing which is true or beautiful or good makes complete sense in any immediate context of history; therefore we must be saved by faith. Nothing we do, however virtuous, can be accomplished alone; therefore we are saved by love" (from *Tomorrow Is Now* by Eleanor Roosevelt).

Here is an interesting story about a man's life calling, which affected others around him in varying ways.

Tales the Silent Watcher Tells

> Once upon a time, in the Village of Man, one of the many began to dream of his homeland and became full of longing.
>
> In time, the others became concerned and, thinking it would be a kindness, called on him to tell of his dreams.
>
> The one was at once pleased by their interest and readily told them, in glowing terms, of such a place as they had never seen and could not imagine.
>
> The more he told them, the more uneasy and confused they became until suddenly they broke in upon him declaring, "There is no such place as you describe. You are ill and raving! Return to your work and dream and say no more." They then turned from him and thereafter avoided him.
>
> In time he withered and died and they said it was a strange disease—one that first maddened and then killed him.

Later, by a clear stream that passed near the Village, the Silent Watcher heard two of the water carriers saying,

"I wonder how the one could describe so vividly a place we say does not exist?"

and

"How could he know about such a place if, as we say, he could never have been there?"

Still later, a shepherd was heard to ask of his sheep,

"What made us turn from the one?"

and

"Did he not die of loneliness and not madness?"

One evening a fire-tender was heard to ask of the fire,

"If the one had denied or kept silent about his homeland, would he yet live among us?"

A star-watcher was heard to wonder of his star,

"What if we are the ones who are mad and this ever-the-same life of ours is our death?"

and

"Did not the one in dying return to his homeland?"

After the Silent Watcher had carefully recorded this tale in The Journal of Man, he noted:

A man died—others had turned from him and avoided him.
A man withered and died—his difference was not welcome among others.
A man died; others became thoughtful.
Thus Man learns.

Spirituality and the Spiritual Connection to Work at Stage Five

Spirituality at this stage is surrendering to the Sacred, to the Holy. Our life's meaning comes from discerning our purpose, as supplied by the Holy. We embrace our shadows as a basis for our spiritual calling. Out of a calm, grounded place, we focus on our passion—even to the point of giving up important things or people in our lives.

Our work connection is simple. Our crucial work is prayer, discernment, self-care, listening, obedience, and wholeness. Out of those practices our *real* work in the world emerges, no matter what work we do for a living. Our focus changes. We gravitate slowly and personally to the most simple things of this world; beauty, nature, love, gratitude, forgiveness. And sometimes we even apply these simple things to the toughest issues of the world that are largely "unsolvable," like love, healing, peace, poverty, violence, homelessness, bigotry, economic inequality, abuse, disease. Our role is not primarily to solve the problems but to be a powerful presence in the midst of the unsolvable situation and to work in our own way in easing pain. Success is not as important as faithfulness.

Stuart is an example of this selfless love. Here is his story, told by his friend, Lois.

> "I know Stuart would be embarrassed to have himself cited, but I really feel he is an example of someone who has found his true self and his spiritual calling in life. Stuart was in Korea during the war and never forgot the look on the faces of the children who had lost their parents or who were hurt in other ways. He really had a hard time adjusting to civilian life after he returned. He went to business school on the GI bill and worked for several years at a large company. From what I know he did fine but he says he wasn't happy most of the time. He just couldn't get those faces out of his mind. As I recall he said he just dropped out for a while and starting searching for himself spiritually.
>
> Along the way he needed money, so he worked part-time as a teacher's aide in his local school. Slowly he recognized in those children's faces some of the same sadness behind the eyes, the same searching in the stances, the same joy in a response. He decided to start over, to pool his money, and open a candy store in a poor neighborhood. He knew it was the right decision no matter what it would cost him. And he was finding out more about himself through the children every day. Now he's been a candy store owner for twenty years and he's stayed in the same neighborhood. Every fifth year he takes off three months so he can refresh himself. But while he's working he serves as a friend and father figure for many of the kids in his neighborhood. He makes sure they have shoes for dances, suits for graduation, contacts for jobs. They bring their spouses and kids back to see "Pops," which is their nickname for him. He has such a large amount of love and energy for them that some people are curious if he's on some wonder drug or something. Oh, he has his bad days, but he tells me that he's found the purpose of his life in the changes he sees in those faces when they are cared for and loved by another person. He says that all he wants is to touch the lives of children and I believe him."

The Shadow of Stage Five

Pseudo-Innocence

Fives come across as innocent to many people. In the shadow of Stage Five there is a danger to that quality of innocence. Rollo May describes it as "pseudo-innocence." Stage Five people can be vulnerable to danger if they fail to protect themselves adequately. May says pseudo-innocence is a defense against having to confront the realities of power, including status, prestige, and the war machine. It can become a shield from responsibility and growth. It protects us from new awareness and from identifying with the sufferings and joys of people. In reality, this behavior in Stage Five people suggests they have actually reverted to Stage Two shadow behavior.

Pseudo-innocence means capitalizing on naiveté, says May. It is childhood never outgrown, fixation on the past; childishness not childlikeness; it is utopianism, closing our eyes to reality and persuading ourselves we've escaped it; it makes things simple and easy; it means not coming to terms with the destructiveness in ourselves or others; it cannot include the demonic and therefore becomes evil; it is a Garden of Eden mentality. It lacks the dialectic movement between yes and no, good and evil. It is the denial of and absence of good power. Pseudo-innocence hopes there are no enemies, which is to deny history.

Stage Five people who are not in the shadow are acutely aware of the darker side of themselves, of all people, and of organizations. Living with it daily, they know people can be evil, good, greedy, and warm. Yet Fives are especially able to walk the tightrope, adjusting continually to the necessary balance not with naiveté but with innocence renewed—a suffering innocence. This innocence is born not out of fear or lack of responsibility but out of a new sense of accountability. Their self-acceptance is not a declaration that evil is good but that it must be recognized and confronted. Fives understand deeply the concept of tough love. So Fives understand others and feel a connection with them through their suffering and their joy.

Perceived by Others to Be Impractical

Stage Five people are not the ones to call on if you want to get things done quickly or in a tough-minded way. To workaholics they appear to even slow things down by the questions they ask or the process they engage in. While this is technically not a shadow quality of Stage Five, it is something that can get in the way when they are working with others, especially if those they work with do not perceive the Five's role to be useful in the larger scheme of things.

In most organizations Stage Fives are informal counselors or mentors to others, but not the hard-driving leaders of others. Their motivations are not for financial rewards or personal recognition. They are motivated to live out their life's calling, pure and simple. They are usually peaceful and competent but they can frustrate the people who want to get things done the quickest and most efficient way or who think that the Fives are not being helpful to them. Fives do not respond well to pressure for quarterly results on issues that require years in order to effect lasting change.

Perceived by Others to Be Undeveloped

Since Stage Five people have spent arduous hours in the Wall, meeting and embracing their own personal shadows, they are not very interested in trying to further develop their strengths and weaknesses. They would rather be accepting of their faults and learn what these faults have to teach them. They are not interested in going to many personal development seminars. So they look hopeless to many go-getters. Fives can even laugh at themselves, while others (usually the ardent Threes) are trying to change them. It's not the fear of change; it's the fact that they already have made the inner change necessary at their *core*. Now they are living in the strength one gets from an intimate understanding of one's weaknesses. At times they can be so self-revealing as to be challenging to an individual or an organization and that might make others uncomfortable.

They are seen by some as particularly undeveloped as leaders. Although they may have been in positions of power previously, they are frequently less interested in the career climbing they strived for earlier. People in power positions know there is something different about them and they know that many people see them as influential, wise, creative, knowledgeable, or visionary in the organization but they certainly do not consider their model of servant leadership very rewarding or something to strive for.

In conclusion, there is a general rule of thumb regarding shadow behavior: as one moves through the stages of power, one's shadow gets smaller and smaller.

Let's Meet Some People at Stage Five

Stage Five people are not likely to describe themselves so we will let others do it for them.

Ruby, Describing Sally and Ken, Parents

I am very close to Sally and Ken and lived through with them the experience I am about to relate. Although it did not happen to me I will try to do justice to the effect it had on them. Ten years ago Sally and Ken's lives appeared to be over. Sally gave birth to a child who had cerebral palsy. She was so scared and disappointed, so despondent that she thought of ending her life right there and then; yet somewhere deep inside, a small flame of love for this infant of theirs caused her to go on for just one more day. They sought counseling and support from parents of cerebral palsied children and slowly, I mean inch by excruciating inch, they moved along. Ken was very busy with his work at the time, being a new supervisor in an electronics-manufacturing firm, so he felt pulled in all directions at once.

They had a four-year-old as well so Sally was kept busy without trying. The first thing they learned from the group meetings with other parents was to try to talk openly together about their fears and frustrations as well as their joys. Some parents just needed to let off steam or feel sorry for themselves and others talked about how much they were learning about themselves through their child. At that point all Sally and Ken could see was that they were learning survival. After one frustrating evening at the group meeting, another couple asked if they wanted to have coffee with them. That evening was the beginning of a long and deep friendship that they consider one of the most special things in their lives. The couple shared their struggle with Sally and Ken in such a realistic way, yet all the while sharing the joys and the growth that occurred in each of them and in their family. Sally and Ken now know exactly what they meant. Their lives are different. They care about Bobby's welfare and Susan's too, but it calls them both to search out the deeper meaning in their lives. They're grappling with questions such as, what really makes us human—success or suffering? When all is said and done, aren't our friendships one of the most lasting things we have? How could we go on without faith in a higher power who understands the complexity of our lives? Their calling now is to share their life journey stories with other couples in similar circumstances and to be close and available to their friends.

This example reflects the effects that a disabled child can have on the lives of its parents, enabling them to deepen spiritually in the process.

Carl, Describing June, the Banker

I know June won't talk to you openly about what she's up to, so all I can do is describe her for you since I think she is rather exemplary. June was shocked into adulthood at age thirty due to the sudden death of her parents in a plane crash. She was left with the family bank and a lot of grief. She had been educating herself to move into management in three or four years but at the time she was a loan officer for a major bank. Needless to say, she had a dilemma on her hands because she was in no mood to even work. The stress was enormous. She hasn't told me the details of that part of her life but I know something very important happened inside. Over time she emerged from that experience a different person, and it shows in the way she runs the bank.

She did decide to take on the management of the bank with help from several mentors. And there were some rough times. June believes that her community bank is there to serve the community. She spends as much time out in the community as she does in the bank. She delegates responsibility to bright and competent people whom she encourages to challenge her; and she has opened the board to a broader cross section of people who can bring her fresh views and more educated opinions. She is willing to learn but is also willing to take responsibility. She is particularly strong in her beliefs about people and work. She shares the profits and losses with the employees, encouraging each of them to feel part of the entire bank image and success. In fact, she is helping us all to redefine what success is, beyond financial growth. She is honest and rewards others who are. The honest bearer of bad tidings does not get punished in this bank but encouraged. She wants to be informed, even if the news is bad. "How can you work to change if you're not aware of the need?" she would say.

She feels she, as an individual, is expendable, but the group is not. She relies on all of us and expects us to run the show. In fact, she gives the impression, with her quiet self-confidence, that she's really the invisible leader who is only there to remind us of principles we've agreed on or to ask questions we've overlooked. And she gets right to the heart of the matter without leaving us shattered or embarrassed. She always wants to know if our customers benefit from our plans as well as the bank, not just whether the plan helps us compete with other banks. In fact, she has a community advisory

> council to raise issues in the bank and the community that need to be addressed. She spends most of her time out in the community so we don't see her as much. We just keep things running and she's happy.
>
> You just get the feeling that she is secure enough not to be threatened by much at all. And that makes her very powerful in the bank and in the community. Not powerful in a negative sort of way but in the sense of being able to free other people to do their best for themselves, the bank, and the community because they don't have to be afraid of her or fight her. It's hard to describe her without making her sound perfect, which she's not. But when she feels a mood coming on or is not in a good frame of mind to talk she will postpone the meeting, turn it over to someone else, or remove herself from the discussion. She regularly takes time to reflect and think. You really ought to meet her to see what you think. I've been working for her for eight years and am content to stay another eight because of all I've learned.

This example shows the way in which an employee views the behavior of a Stage Five bank president.

Jed, Describing Sam, the Conscience of the Organization

> There is this guy at our church whom many people would like to ignore but whom I consider one of the most important people around. Now, I can't say what makes this guy tick, because he appears to be pretty weird, but I do know that he acts as our social conscience. He's been through about every experience imaginable in life, and he isn't shy in telling about it. If I had been able to survive half of what he has and remain sane I'd be happy. Nevertheless, he's a weird duck. He dresses strangely, he looks strange, and he acts strangely. And people don't know quite what to do with him. But he has unselfishly dedicated his life to working with the street people through whatever means necessary. That's why I call him the conscience of the church.
>
> Here are some of the things he does that make us squirm. Almost every week he brings people with him to church who just happen to be living with him until they move on to permanent quarters. Regularly he manages to entice a few members to get involved in some prison project or a support group of some kind. Of course, we always get more out of it ourselves than we feel we give to others. Another thing he does is to arrive at church meetings ready to challenge us on the way we spend our money or the ways in which we measure success. He even needles the minister, suggesting that he

encourages the status quo or caters to the wealthy. He is relentless, but he and the minister are still dear friends.

The very sight of Sam reminds me that there is more to life than my own and my family's comfort. Sam stands for dedication to simple principles and a clear purpose. He is not sophisticated or suave. He is love personified. He has been around the block several times but he has been plucked out of the mainstream to lead a different kind of life. He raises the hackles of people but in the end his style confronts us sincerely and allows us to think about the critical things in life.

This example shows how a person's role in an organization can serve as a symbol of Stage Five—a conscience. In this case, the person may not need to be at Stage Five himself to have this effect.

Peter, Who Is Working on Gratitude and Amends

Peter is in his fifties and has done a great deal of counseling and inner work to find out who he wants to be in his career. Even though he is a consultant, he is really a healer and he exudes healing in his relationships with his clients. He just can't help it. The major way he broke through as a healer in corporate life was to work diligently on gratitude and forgiveness with his spiritual director and it was difficult work. You see, Peter had a lot of amends to make. He had had more than one sexual affair as a younger man while married, and these weighed heavily on him as he grew older. He had learned a lot about himself and had processed why he had the affairs, and he had been relieved of the shame that was attached to them, even felt forgiven by the Holy, but he still felt something was missing.

He still felt there was something else he could do to heal at a deeper level and be free of the burden he felt. After a lot of conversation and prayer, he decided to write a letter of gratitude and amends to the women he had had affairs with. First he had to find them and in the process he had to be honest with himself that he was not trying to re-ignite these relationships. Then he wrote a letter starting with the gratitude that he felt for the good things they had given him and the gift they were in his life. Second he told them what he was sorry about and what he wanted to be forgiven for, in this case, for letting the relationship go beyond a personal or professional one. And lastly he said he was not fanning a flame or even looking for a response but he was merely admitting what he had done and asking for forgiveness. Some letters he sent and some he didn't. He expected nothing. The feelings it brought forth in him though, were

> miraculous. It was so freeing. And for those who did answer, it was a healing experience even after several years had passed.

This is an excellent example of the deep healing that comes from forgiving oneself and others.

Bill, Describing Martha, the Problem Solver

> I think Martha's been around here since this place opened. And she's probably had most of the jobs as well. But when a company grows as fast as we have in the last fifteen years, you need people who can wear all sorts of hats. Martha started in manufacturing and soon became a supervisor. She's been in accounting (learned it on the job), procurement, personnel (she started that office), and a few others. She just learns so quickly and accomplishes things so well we kept giving her different assignments. A few years ago she'd covered most of the new territory and we were at a loss as to the next direction for her. We thought seriously about making her the manager of a group of departments but she was absolutely against that. She said that managing others was not the skill that she wanted to use.
>
> Martha came up with her own solution. She wanted to be the "Problem Person," she said. That meant to me that people anywhere in the company could come to her with problems and, with her background, her ability to gain people's trust, her wonderful contacts, and a great mind, she could help solve them. Well, let me tell you, it was the greatest idea by far. She has no title because she wants none. She just goes to her office or wanders around the company until she finds a problem or until a problem finds her. Then she goes to work. She doesn't threaten anyone because she's not their boss and she gives them all the credit. She's the most dearly thought of person in the entire company. I found out by chance that she has instructed the compensation people to hold her raises. She doesn't want to move to her next tax bracket and she's having too much fun to have to start managing more money at her age. Amazing.

The role of a Stage Five person in an organization may be to remain titleless but to be available to do the things one does best and the things the company needs most at the time.

Brian, the Counselor

Brian was a 32-year-old, high-powered sales manager for a national firm when he had a heart attack. His doctor told him his job was killing him and he needed to make a drastic change in his life. Brian responded by moving his family from a major urban area to a small rural community where the pace of life was much slower.

After relocating he spent several months deciding what gifts he had and how they might be used in a less stressful career. Being a very warm and empathetic person, he decided to return to school to become certified as a personal counselor. After graduation he opened a counseling practice and soon gained a reputation for his excellence. His heart attack was the physical crisis that got him to move beyond his Stage Three life. Relocating geographically and reorienting his career to one in a helping profession elicited many Stage Four behaviors in him.

As he continued to grow, he discovered a spiritual dimension within himself. He began meditating and reading spiritual writers from a variety of religious perspectives including Christian, Buddhist, Hindu, and Native American. Brian surprises people who go to him for counseling. About ten minutes into a first session, he might look at the person and ask, "Who are you when you're not playing some social role?" Hardly anyone ever asks that of a person and usually not within ten minutes of meeting him or her. Brian has a way of teaching a lot in relatively few visits!! One of Brian's favorite sayings is "Heaven is a state of mind. It's out there waiting for you. Go embrace it." Thoughts like these are characteristic of Stage Five.

Brian is an example of how a physical crisis can impel one into moving beyond Stage Four.

Cal, Describing Maya, Community Activist

I'm not even sure what Maya does for a living, although I know she leaves work early sometimes to come to meetings. All I know is how much she does for this community very quietly and with determination but with no interest in thanks or recognition. She decided about five or six years ago, after a TV report on the high incidence of drug use and the increasing number of broken homes, that our community was not looking after the welfare of all of its members adequately and she feared it would get worse in the future.

> She decided to see what the energy of one little person—with the help of lots of others—could do to rally the community. She went personally to the mayor to get a task force set up on family solidarity. She chose not to chair it but instead got a prominent citizen who was respected by all. The task force represented all partners in the issue including parents, school officials, teenagers, business people, and youth agencies. They came up with a multi-year plan to work on the top three issues they had identified, which would involve all the groups represented. The plan was not limited to drug information sessions but evolved into family retreats, employment training programs, emergency counseling and referral, and community pride campaigns. The entire community was touched in some way or another by the program because of its pervasiveness. And in every part of the program Maya worked she pulled strings but moved into the background. She told me laughingly that it had nothing to do with humility; it just wouldn't have worked any other way. I haven't seen her for a while, but I assume she's resting up for the next challenge in meeting unmet needs.

Acting as a catalyst but not as a ringleader is often the mark of a Stage Five person. In this example Maya clearly put the good of the community ahead of her own good.

Moving to Stage Six

The crisis that people experience in moving from Stage Five to Stage Six is that of understanding the universe. No longer does the individual matter in the larger scheme of things and yet the individual is all that matters. That paradox, once understood, accepted, and humbly loved, moves one toward wisdom. In fact, coming to understand paradox as a guiding force in life is one of the clues that a Five is moving to Stage Six.

A paradox in the move itself is that Fives do not seek to move anywhere; they just live and may or may not emerge as Sixes. It doesn't really matter. And that may be why they become Sixes.

Life becomes a true mystery as people evolve beyond Stage Five, for just understanding their place in the universe is in itself mind-boggling. But increasingly their knowledge combines with their spirituality to create wisdom. Wisdom goes beyond knowledge or intuition and adds an extra dimension that comes from deep within. People who are moving from Stage Five are content to wait for wisdom, for they know it is gained through a deep understanding of life and of suffering.

Beyond Stage Five, people begin to see the role of death in the scheme of life and they become friends with death because they have seen beyond it. They have faced their own physical, emotional, intellectual, or spiritual death. Again, this is a mystery to be lived and perhaps not totally understood but it allows them to see the world in different ways and to live more calmly and genuinely. How this occurs is impossible to explain because it is unique to the individual, but once it occurs, one can never again live as if one didn't know it. They feel intimately connected to all people, to all things, to life. Yet they are lovingly detached as well.

Stage Five people in transition are connecting with several dimensions that go beyond the ordinary ways of perceiving, knowing, and being. In our culture they risk being considered crazy or too far out. So, for support and acceptance, they must look to something beyond ordinary reality. Once they have learned this and experienced it regularly they cease to need cultural inclusion. They can be committed but detached. The energy and inner power they have is almost totally fueled by a holy source.

This life stance allows Sixes to give up anything and everything to be about a larger universal purpose. Fives in transition sometimes find their lives taking slow but strange turns so that their way of life begins to merge with their calling. If Fives put their jobs on the line, Sixes put their careers and lives on the line for a life-giving purpose. Many of us can imagine that but not operate from there on a daily basis.

Fives generally do not move beyond that stage by themsleves. They feel a slow, inner drawing toward Stage Six wisdom and they discover teachers along the way who they least expected could lead them. But they are content to let themselves go and to learn another way of approaching life. We all know Stage Six people; we just haven't classified them in this way. And we all have a spark of Stage Six in us, just as we do the other five stages.

What Have People Done in Moving to Stage Six?

It would not be wise to try to describe how to obtain wisdom. As the old saying goes, "He that breaks a thing to find out what it is has left the path of wisdom" (J. R. R. Tolkien). The move has to do with peace amidst suffering, commitment to the journey, obedience to one's spiritual calling, and sacrifice.

What Holds People Back?

Most people will never know why more Fives don't move to Stage Six because people rarely talk of experiences at these levels. If they do, it's usually for the sake of instructing others. In fact, when people freely offer the information that they are Stage Five or Six people, they probably aren't. It's another one of those paradoxes. One woman told me with a broad smile that she had moved from Stage One to Stage Six in one year. I responded that I was simply amazed and that I hoped she would not stop there.

The main reason people won't move to the most complex stage of personal power is usually a lack of faith. They just can't let go of assurances in order to get to the final step of living with no fear, deep spirituality, and true paradox. It is too ambiguous, or it is too frightening or unpredictable. Another reason people won't move to Stage Six is that most have too much to give up. We've lived for varying lengths of time accumulating reputations, possessions, knowledge, and know-how. Stage Six people have to be willing to sacrifice all of that if they are truly to live the integrated life. They must even consider giving up their lives in some cases. Can you imagine Sister Teresa asking what kind of return she will get on her investment? Can you imagine Nelson Mandala saying that if he had to risk going to prison for 27 years, he didn't want to work to end Apartheid? Usually the very things that we hold most dear are those things we are asked to give up in moving to Stage Six. We cannot be attached to (get our life's meaning from) things or people and still operate fully in Stage Six.

Hagberg's Model of Personal Power

SUMMARY OF STAGE FIVE
POWER BY PURPOSE

Symbol

Key Question: What is your deepest heart's desire?

Description
Inner vision

Characteristics
Self-accepting
Courageous
Calm
Conscience of the organization
Humble
Practical mystics
Elusive qualities
Generous in empowering others
Confident of life calling

Spirituality at Stage Five
Spirituality is surrendering to the Holy

Ways to Move
In individual ways

Shadow of Stage Five
Pseudo-innocence
Perceived by others to be impractical
Perceived by others to be undeveloped

Catalyst for Movement
Understanding the universe

What Holds People Back?
Not understanding the universe
Lack of faith
Too much to lose

Please refer to note on page 305 before copying.

Ask yourself these questions about Stage Six:

Yes	No	
____	____	1. Do you see all of life as a paradox?
____	____	2. Do you understand the interrelationship of all things?
____	____	3. Is service to the world of individuals your "work"?
____	____	4. Do you operate on an inner set of ethical principles that pervade your life?
____	____	5. Are you committed yet detached?
____	____	6. Are you unafraid of death?
____	____	7. Do you frequently ask unanswerable questions?
____	____	8. Do you have a life calling for which you would die?
____	____	9. Do you feel deep peace of mind during times of suffering?
____	____	10. Are you considered a sage?
____	____	11. Do you enjoy long periods of solitude and silence?
____	____	12. Are you complete?
____	____	13. Do you honor your life as a sacrifice to a higher calling?
____	____	14. Do you feel powerless?
____	____	15. Do you feel compassion for the whole world?

Caution: This is a trick quiz. Yes answers to these questions do not necessarily mean you identify with Stage Six.

Chapter 7
Stage Six: Power by Wisdom

Sacrifice

Key Question: In the deeper spiritual life, our lives are consumed by the fire of the Holy Spirit. How close are you willing to come to the flame?

What Is Stage Six Like?

Being at Stage Six is like acting in a play and being in the audience watching it at the same time. Stage Six people are very involved with life yet detached from their involvement. They see from a different eye, hear with an unusual ear, and feel with a new heart. They are a paradox, even an oxymoron. For instance, they are content with themselves and with life; yet, at the same time, they are deeply moved by the pain and stress in themselves and in the rest of the world. They work on issues that will bring more mercy or peace to the world yet they accept their own pain peacefully without a hint of martyrdom. This unusual behavior results from living their lives on a different spiritual plane than they ever have before.

Stage Six is an extension of Stage Five, in that the spiritual behavior at Stage Six is more deeply embedded than it was at Stage Five. It is impossible to search for Sixes in organizational structures. They are there but they prefer to be invisible. And they don't enjoy being singled out. Any Stage Six who, inadvertently, becomes known, usually as a result of their life passions or calling, does so by the truth of what they are about, not because of the force of their personality, their achievements, or their egos. Frequently they are going against the tide, not perpetuating the status quo.

Mother Teresa's mission was to help people DIE—with dignity. Her work had a zero percentage chance of saving lives, which is the exact opposite of what the world would deem successful. Her work called on the conscience of the whole world. She was not aiming for success. She was practicing faithfulness. A story I heard about her illustrates her inner strength. A well-meaning man visited her in Calcutta and was impressed enough with her work to send her ten thousand dollars to build a small hospital. She sent the money back saying that she was sorry that she had misinterpreted her ministry to him. She said she was not there to help people live, but to help people die—with dignity.

Stage Six people are sometimes thought to be different, maybe even strange. Many times Stage Six people are perceived as being out on a jaunt, alone with their world. But when they are available, they are warm, inviting, and nurturing. It's just that they live in domains that are not totally accessible to others. Their habits generally include periods of solitude, silence, and reflective thought. They need to do this because they are so oriented to giving, to being available, to listening intently that they can become depleted without being aware of it. The energy they possess comes from a spiritual source beyond them, so being continually open to that source is part of the way they live their lives.

Sixes are sages. They may be well-known or unknown. They may be persons who touch only one life profoundly, or they may be internationally known heroes and heroines of centuries past and present, like the Dalai Lama. They are godlike without being gods in the flesh. They can be one's grandmother, the owner of the local candy store, a philosopher, a day-care administrator, a boss, or a writer. All of us have a bit of Stage Six in us, just as we have a bit of the other stages, but fewer people live congruently with this as their home stage.

The theme of this stage is wisdom. Part of the mystique of Stage Six people is that they may not fit all of our preconceived notions of how wise people ought to be. We may have an image of what wisdom is and we may indeed have had a relationship with a person we considered truly wise but we saw them in a subjective way. In other words, a person who appears wise when you are in Stage Two may look very different to you when you are in Stage Four. It doesn't mean the person wasn't really wise; it means your understanding of wisdom has changed. Stage Six wisdom comes from deep within the person as a result of embracing their whole self, experiencing suffering without yielding to victim-hood, having compassion for others, grasping unutterable joy, and feeling intimacy with their supreme being. No wisdom figure I know would admit to being one—and that's part of the paradox. They would laugh at taking a quiz to find out whether they are wise. They might, in fact, answer all the questions "no" because they are so humble. So if you answered the questions "yes," you are probably *not* at Stage Six yet. (That's why it's a trick quiz.)

The description of power at Stage Six is self-sacrifice. Sixes are fearless, especially when it comes to death. This is because they believe their life's work is so important that sacrificing their life would only further that work. In order to operate at Stage Six, this basic human fear must be met head on. Sixes are no longer tenaciously avoiding pain or suffering. Nor do they unconsciously fear deep joy and peace. Both are keys to their calling in life. Inner peace even accompanies their pain and that is remarkable to observe. Sometimes having a near-death experience introduces people to Stage Six. Sometimes experiencing the death of another gives us a new wisdom. Stage Six people are thankful for whatever life experiences they have, and they have accepted the fact of their own death. They are no longer trying to defy or ignore it as most of us do. Sixes frequently experience a glaring weakness in their lives that haunts them even when it is embraced. It is that "thorn in the flesh" that ensures their humility. It is the clay that they recognize in their own feet.

Sixes see the whole picture. They see the gestalt of life. Gestalt means more than the sum of the parts. The whole has a dimension that transcends the total, and Stage Six people see this. Thus, they can ask questions that seem to be on a higher or broader level or that call into question some underlying assumptions. But Sixes do not try to one-up others or embarrass them. They merely share the insight or vision that comes to them, if appropriate. Sixes exude power of an inner origin.

The symbol for this stage depicts a person whose personal power pervades the surrounding space. They have some indefinable quality about them, which may vary from person to person, that permeates the space they occupy or touches the people they are with. Their presence comes from an inner well of calm, of quiet strength, in which they live. And it may be disconcerting to some who are not used to it or are anxious themselves. One wise person I've observed is very quiet while people are talking to her; in fact, at times she will close her eyes to be able to listen more acutely. I watched her do this with a highly verbal person, who became very disturbed by it, since eye contact was an important part of the conversation to him. The scene became almost humorous as it continued. The speed and the intensity of the one-sided conversation increased until the wise person said, "Let's continue this chat over a lemonade." Her peacefulness and attention made the other person nervous.

Although disconcerting at times, the wisdom of Sixes affects people positively. These people want to know more. They are intrigued. I am told of a well-known actor who exudes personal power and wisdom when he walks quietly into a room. He consistently and genuinely cares about serving others instead of himself and his career. He purposely takes himself out of the limelight and supports and trains others to go beyond him. People around him say that he is a wonder to behold. The more selfless he is the more people admire him—though that is not his aim—and it makes him very uncomfortable. In fields in which stardom is the primary goal (which could be almost any field), it is sometimes more difficult for the brightest shining stars to move beyond that role. They have too much to give up, too much to lose. The nagging fear of being forgotten or dismissed haunts them, so most of them never get past Stage Three.

Power by Wisdom also leads to the concept of transcendence, meaning "beyond the limits of human experience or knowledge." The Stage Six person can tap a source of power and insight that is holy, infinite and all-knowing. Their source becomes a way of life, a part of their being, a peace of mind, not a technique or a costume. Some Stage Six people may not obviously exude personal power or affect us right away but after a while they astound us with their presence in our lives. We hear their voices when we least expect them.

Rabbi Harold Kushner, in his book, *When All You've Wanted Isn't Enough*, describes Stage Six people well, as mensches.

> To be a mensch is to be the kind of person God had in mind when he arranged for human beings to evolve, someone who is honest, reliable, wise enough to be no longer naïve but not yet cynical, a person you can trust to give you advice for your benefit rather than his or her own...A mensch acts not out of fear or out of desire to make a good impression but out of a strong inner conviction of who he or she is and what he or she stands for. A mensch is not a saint or a perfect person but a person from whom all falsehood, all selfishness, and all vindictiveness has been burned away so that only a pure self remains. A mensch is whole and is one with his or her God.

I suggest to you that Stage Sixes are not only menshes and modern mystics but that their role in the world is to teach, develop, inspire, and support others to become mystics and menshes as well. They do this in some ways that we can document, like talking deeply with people, challenging them on a personal level, writing timely notes to others that they as the writer do not know are timely, giving people inspiring things without knowing that the things were inspiring. They also do more subtle things, like use spiritual practices to influence others, pray, heal without touching, influence without being noticed. However they spread their wisdom, those who are ready to pick up on it are deeply affected. People are drawn to Stage Sixes partly because of their exquisitely strange ways of being in the world.

Stage Six people are not hermits. They don't hide in caves or cloisters. They are out among people. That is not to say they do not spend time in solitude. Activity and wisdom pervade their outer and inner life whether they are managing people, playing baseball, or parenting. They know their life passion and do it faithfully. This can involve them in large visionary programs like programs to end poverty or revitalize the corporate world. It can also emerge in simple images, like bringing beauty to the world or living simply and serenely. Whatever they do, they are intimately connected to their holy source. Gandhi prayed for a whole day a week and he helped free India from British rule. Just think if he had prayed two days a week!!

The model I am presenting presupposes that Stage Six people are in relationships with others. Stage Six people, involved and active in the world, get their energy from a different source now and their activities serve others almost entirely. Their level of compassion is high because they can identify with the pain of others without burning out. They know how to be in chaos and still take care of themselves. Their motivation comes from their vocation, and that emerges from their souls.

Sixes are not limited to any one setting, type of work, or way of life. So one does not become a Stage Six by engaging in a certain type of work like political activism, social service, health, business, or the ministry. And there are fewer Sixes around than other stages, no matter where we look. They may be the very people we least expect to see as wisdom figures, so how can we recognize them? One man related the experience of "meeting wisdom," as he describes it. He was on an airplane flight a few years ago and happened to sit next to a frumpy looking older woman. He hesitated to engage in conversation with her but when he finally did he was astonished. In her gentle way she gave him wonderful new insights about himself and the world. "She tapped into my soul," was his conclusion. He has never seen her since but he will never forget her.

We might all identify with this man's experience in some way. When we are around wisdom figures they touch a part of us that has experienced wisdom, that, at least momentarily, feels as if everything fits, that all is interrelated, and that there is a larger plan for us. All of this may be slightly unsettling or it may give us peace of mind and a reason for being. This Stage Six part of us peeks out occasionally and surprises us or makes us yearn for more contact: but we are not able to hold on to it for more than brief periods of time, nor are we even sure that we want to. Most of us have never thought about it. So when we are around Stage Six persons, this unfamiliar, neglected part of us is touched and uplifted without our full awareness—until later, perhaps. Because this part of us is so strange, it may frighten us when it emerges, and the Stage Six persons who have caused it to surface may frighten us as well. Picking up the phone and calling someone only to find out that they were just thinking strongly about you and were just planning to call you is an example of experiencing our Stage Six self. This is routine for some people.

Stage Six people operate at a level of power Rollo May, in his book *Power and Innocence,* calls integrative power or power with other people. They certainly do not need, nor do they want, the limelight. It is the kind of power that invites criticism and feedback because ideas develop best when they are digested and reworked. It inspires hope but it is not naïve. A prime example of this simple and mystical kind of power is the nonviolent resistance of Gandhi and Martin Luther King, Jr. The nonviolent method has a way of disarming its opponents by exposing moral defenses. It works on the conscience and on the memory. The opponent has to live with himself or herself after injuring a nonviolent person. So working with Sixes may draw criticism or even hatred because they are not playing by the rules. Being with them requires a real commitment. They will never manipulate others to join them.

Sixes see life as a paradox, as opposites balanced in tension with one another. And they themselves are seen as paradoxes to others: They are calm yet passionate, patient yet vexed, and complex yet simple. But somehow they still seem integrated as a whole. Life is a wonder to behold, a mystery to be lived, and a miracle to be appreciated.

To reiterate, wisdom is a complex concept and open to several interpretations; however, to me it is a quality of being that goes beyond information and even beyond knowledge or intuition. It is a quality of sageness that is so deeply embedded within each person that it takes on the nuances of that person's total integrated style. Wisdom is akin to this definition of love from John Dunne in *The House of Wisdom*. He describes "...an encompassing peace that defines love as seeing with God's eyes, feeling with God's heart, and when I come back again to myself, I find it subsists as a direction in my own life, seeing with my own eyes, feeling with my own heart." Stage Six people live their lives seeing with God's eyes, hearing with God's ears, and feeling with God's heart.

My personal experience of Stage Six is limited but I will cite a few examples. In my prison volunteer work I've made personal connections with many women who have been my life teachers. Several have remained friends after they left prison. One woman comes to mind. Her tragic life story of abuse helped start a transformation in my own life so I have a special "soul" affinity for her even though we see each other rarely.

Part of my life's calling is the simple act of writing notes to people as I get an internal signal to do so. Whenever I think of this woman three times in one day I write her a note. Once, after not seeing her for two years, I bumped into her. She said to me, "I just want you to know something you said in your note last year saved my life." I didn't ask her what it was but I got chills all through my body. And I didn't even remember writing to her.

I have experienced much grief in my life and have learned to face it instead of flee from it. For that reason I am able to be with other people in their grief in almost uncanny ways. They say my presence calms them somehow. I think it might have something to do with facing fear. Because I have faced fear I can be open to their pain and tears as well as to the deep and wondrous experiences of grieving. One of those experiences is the special contact that grievers have temporarily with the spirit of the deceased person. I believe these experiences are spiritual gifts, to be honored and seen as sacred. Overwhelming coincidences, as well as experiences with angels, are also Stage Six phenomenon I have personally witnessed. These are all deeply spiritual experiences and need to be handled with utmost awe and respect. To misuse any of these experiences is to severely diminish it and reduce its holiness.

Characteristics of Stage Six People

Integrating Shadow

Through most of the power stages we struggle to find the answers, to separate the right from the wrong way. And we may come to some conclusions only to find they don't necessarily work for all circumstances. Then we go through a period in which there seem to be no answers at all, just lots of confusing questions. Slowly, we find that there are lots of answers to every question depending on our view, and then we decide which view we want to take. Stage Six people aren't concerned about answering questions at all. Asking questions is more interesting and they do not need answers. Things can be amorphous, ambiguous, and abstract. And almost everything seems to be a paradox, a combination of opposites or contradictions.

Some of the paradoxes that Stage Six people live with might be:

The more we know, the less we know.
Continuity is change.
The question is the answer.
Humility requires deep self-love.
Commitment means detachment.
Evil and good are siblings.
Our strength is our weakness, our weakness our strength.
Everything is interrelated; everything is separate.
We are all significant; we are all insignificant.
Everything is simple and complex.
The transcendent is the real.
Active is reflective; reflective is active.
Everything matters; nothing matters.

Sixes are not perfect by any stretch of the imagination. In fact, they accept their humanness and are more aware of it even than Stage Fives. The main difference is that they have gone beyond the acceptance of their qualities (strengths and weaknesses) to the point of integrating and, in fact, appreciating their quirks and their shadows, as we described our negative qualities in Stage Five and the Wall. Some folks fight with or run from their shadow all their lives, fearing that it will take them over. If we can accept and then befriend our shadows, they can become useful companions, keeping us in balance and our life in perspective.

Weaknesses are now gifts to appreciate. Some of our best work comes from being able to use our weaknesses. We then need to be more reliant on our Higher Power to work through us. For instance, in dealing with the aftermath of Apartheid, Bishop Tutu showed us that in order to fully heal we needed to practice forgiveness in the face of evil, a practice that turned the old revenge motive upside down. Most of us have a weakness when it comes to people we think have wronged us. We think they deserve our resentment and revenge. Our weakness is offering forgiveness appropriately. That is what is required of us at Stage Six.

Befriending our shadow sounds easy yet it may require a lifetime of reflection, work, and pain to accomplish, often with professional help. One reason this is such a task is that we must become vulnerable and honest with ourselves, admitting to lies that we and others have perpetuated, before we can move on to more authentic living. The paradox of our shadow is that frequently it is disguised as our strongest positive trait and we can't believe that it would "do us in." Take, for example, the strong, emotionally stable people whose strength isolates them from feeling or experiencing personal human tragedy; or the beautiful people whose beauty becomes a defense against understanding the ugliness in themselves; or the perfect people whose compulsion leads them to the height of anxiety. Because Sixes have learned to incorporate their shadow and even have a sense of humor about it, they can disarm and even intimidate others, but with no pretense. Sixes may appear to be idiosyncratic or individualistic, but this usually reflects who they really are rather than a need to become unique. And there is a big difference between the two. Threes and Fours strive to become unique, while Sixes are content to be who they really are. An anonymous author said, "Maturity consists in no longer being taken in by yourself."

Not only have Sixes integrated the shadow behavior, they have also come to a new realization of their mind-body-spirit relationships. There is a heightened perception in Stage Six people of the unity, the gestalt of the mind-body-spirit dichotomies. They think of themselves as more of a process than a person; they have combined their being with a much larger universal wisdom that puts all things and events into a larger perspective. It is as if they can step back from their linear life lines and observe the whole cinema—past, present, and future.

For instance, Stage Six people may experience an illness or some emotional stress. Instead of fighting it or overanalyzing it or blaming themselves, they recognize that they may also see some meaning in the event from a broader perspective, or they may take the time to do some reassessment. When a loved one dies they do not deny the anguish and the pain, but, at the same time, they realize that this is the beginning of a new relationship with the person on a somewhat different plane. This event has been an abrupt break in the continuity of the relationship but they believe it may resume, after a time, in a different way.

Unafraid of Death

Possibly the characteristic most comforting to Sixes and most baffling to others is their lack of fear of their own and others' deaths. Sixes have experienced, sometime in life, a dress rehearsal of their own death or have in some other way deeply prepared for it. It could have been physical, mental, or emotional but it was real to them. The event changed the way they view life. They see themselves as part of a longer continuum. Elisabeth Kubler-Ross and others have conducted extensive research on the subject of death. Their conclusions suggest that in most cases death is not a frightening but a calm experience. Most people reporting the observation of their own death or near-death experience have said it was not scary or evil or awful. Instead they claim that it is hard to come back to reality because it is so much calmer and lighter on the other side.

A woman relates her experience regarding her physical death. "There I lay on the hospital surgical table all broken apart and bleeding. That was one part of me. The other part of me, the spirit, I guess, was floating above the table watching the goings on. I was calm and rather amused at all the effort they were going to when I knew that I had already died and gone to the other side. I had been broad-sided in a terrible car accident. I was rushed to the hospital but I knew it was too late because I had already left my body and was greeted by a wonderful person on the other side with a shining light. Then as I watched I began to feel tugs pulling me toward the table. I didn't want to go back but the tugs were stronger all the time. Finally I gave in when I could no longer resist and the next thing I knew I was recovering in the intensive care ward. I have never been the same since. I now have very little fear of death. In fact, I am almost looking forward to it. But apparently, I have some other things to do."

Having met death, Sixes find it's their constant companion and helps them put life into perspective. Their values change now because of what they have learned about values on the other side. No wonder material possessions—status, jobs, titles, control, fame, or money—cease to matter. What matters now may be very different for each Six but it is usually the intangibles: caring, love, service, giving, peace of mind, wisdom, integrity, beauty, friendship, and fairness.

This acquaintance with death and with people who have died is one way to account for transcendent qualities or a sense of the mystical in Sixes. They have a source of contact beyond human experience. Another explanation is their strong spiritual tie to a supreme being. There is indeed a contact point or a bridge between these people and another plane of existence. They draw frequently or continuously from that plane for their energy and insight, claiming none of these insights originate within themselves. In a sense they have given up both their external and their internal power to draw from their higher power. Their goal, if any, is to avoid being an obstacle in the path of that power.

This spiritual sense of other-world contact is not to be confused with popular trends and quasi-self-actualizing experiences in the psychic realm. After the encounter group era of the '60s and the narcissistic era of the '70s, the spiritual and psychic era of the '80s, and the free-for-all '90s, people are getting digital super power now in the way they were getting sandals and long hair in the '60s. There are classes in every kind of edge you can define. Nothing is off limits any more. I mention these things not because they are particularly bad in themselves but only because they can be substituted for the real and difficult work of deep self-exploration. In fact, most of these experiences can distract the person, if only temporarily, from the central work, that of knowing one's real self and one's connection to the central pervasive force of life. If these experiences do less, then they are distractions. In fact, some of these psychic or even religious experiences can be dangerous for individuals who are vulnerable or emotionally unprotected.

Any experience that promises powers that sound too good to be true or that requires strict discipleship to another person should be suspect. The guide I use to determine whether an experience will be helpful is to ask these questions of myself: "Why am I doing this? How am I going to use it?" If I am not careful, I can be drawn to these bigger-than-life experiences because I want to remain in control of my life or I want to avoid the Wall.

A useful analogy for me is likening my life to the climbing of a tree. I may want to experience the exhilaration of creeping out on some limbs and even swinging from the branches, but I do not want to go so far out on weak branches that I fall and risk injury. And in my more vulnerable times staying in near the trunk and the large, sturdy branches is the best course of action for the time.

Powerless

In an ironic way Stage Six people have come full circle to the point of needing very little tangible power. The external power no longer matters, and the internal power has been transformed. Like Stage One people, Sixes seldom strive to get ahead; instead, they appear apathetic about improving their own lot. There are some major differences to be sure but, on the surface, Sixes sometimes appear to be uninterested in doing many things they should be doing for themselves. They are more interested in moving other people forward or in furthering principles in life.

When asked about their life purpose Sixes would probably reply that life is purpose. Just living from day to day brings purpose. Each day reveals new people to serve, new roads to travel, old friendships to nurture. They make no lists of things to do or career goals to meet. Living, for them, is giving and the rest works itself out. This can mean that Sixes are terribly committed to living out certain ideas, philosophies, or causes, but they live them from day to day without talking about them.

From this perspective it is easy to see why the lives of Sixes seem to become simpler rather than more complex. They can reduce their possessions and their lifestyles to the simplest of essentials because the richness of life emerges from within. They know that life can be such a game anyway. For many, the game proceeds in this manner: The more you earn the more you want. The more you have, the harder it is to manage it and the more concerned you are about losing it. The more worried you are, the more stress you have and the more you cling to the external symbols. Think about this scenario: Suppose you were able to pay off your home mortgage and invest enough money to live frugally on the interest, which would rise with inflation. Would you be satisfied with that secure but small income that offers you the choice of working or not working or changing your type of work? Not many would, I'm afraid.

One wonderful person comes to mind as an example of a deliberately chosen lifestyle of simplicity. During all his years as a college teacher, Cal gave of his time and most of the money he earned from teaching to students or causes or traveling experiences with others. He had a habit of keeping money available in certain drawers in his desk so students he knew well and who were poor could help themselves without having to ask him. He financed trips for students to see special games, he bought new suits for their graduation, and so on. He never asked for or expected any of the money to be returned. In addition he simply befriended students whom he liked or who needed befriending. He talked with them, played games, taught them, laughed with them, traveled with them, and gave generously of himself. At the age of fifty he started having what was to be a series of heart attacks and had to retire early from teaching at age fifty-seven. His pension and social security are hardly enough to sustain him, even though his needs are minimal. His friends to whom he had been so generous sustain him now. One provides him with two round trips to the east coast, another brings him to the Midwest. One family orders the New York Times for him. Another makes sure his clothes are in good repair. Some just send checks. What does he say to all this? "Oh, my gracious, my goodness! How could an old man be so lucky?"

Quiet in Service

Sixes may be found in any occupation. Their work for pay is usually secondary to their primary work, which is some form of serving or helping others to achieve a purpose, whether it be running a co-op, harvesting a crop, nursing a neighbor, listening to a person in pain, or visiting a child. Their paid work could also be their service, if it works out that way. Their service may even be to remain alert to every person they meet to make sure they are available for whatever needs to be said or done with each one. They tend to operate on a day-to-day basis, without much care or worry for tomorrow. That ability to put aside worry and anxiety is an unusual characteristic in anyone. Because Sixes have come to terms with their fears (for the most part) and because they understand their life mission or calling, they find very little to be anxious about. And it gives them much more energy to use on other things. One Stage Six person I met has lived with cancer for six years and has a philosophy of life that goes something like this: "I live each day and each event as it comes, knowing that in each situation I have something to give and something to learn. When I got cancer I looked back over my life and decided I liked most of it, hated some of it. I resolved to live out my remaining years doing the things that have the most meaning for me. I changed my area of nursing from surgical to working in a hospice, and I lead grief groups in our church in the evenings. It's ironic, but in facing death, I feel alive again."

Since Sixes are not motivated by the regular things and want to find meaning through their service, they tend to operate independently and live quite simply and well, blending their work with their lives. And that could be doing just about anything. It's not the exact work they do that counts, but the kind of effect it allows them to have on others. The distinguishing characteristic is that their work does not feed them or build their egos, nor do they have much attachment to it. Their real energy and stamina comes from a transcendent source and flows through them to others, no matter what the setting.

This chapter is strange to write. I feel at times that I should have left it out, because to talk about Stage Six almost demeans or destroys it. In fact, one of the reasons it is so difficult to describe Sixes in detail is that they don't talk about themselves or name themselves as such. For, as I said earlier, anyone who tells you he or she is a guru, a master, a wisdom figure, or a spiritual guide, isn't. The very nature of self-enhancing roles or relationships is anathema to Sixes. They may know very clearly inside that they are in the role of spiritual guide or counselor to others but it is a nonverbal acknowledgment. They may even warn others to be careful in describing the relationship to others for a following could develop that may force them to be the center of attention.

Readers might think they would find many Stage Sixes in religious or spiritual roles (clergy, spiritual leaders, gurus). This is not necessarily true although we are most expectant of our spiritual leaders being role models and we are extraordinarily disappointed when our spiritual leaders exhibit shadow behavior. They, too, have to go beyond their roles, hit the Wall, and give up their wills. All organizations reward Stage Three behavior, even religious organizations. Religious professionals may strive to be a Stage Six person, yet many of them will have a hard time of it because they are afraid to accept their own humanness. And one of the hazards of their profession is allowing themselves to inadvertently be put on pedestals by others. Sixes may or may not be involved with organized religion but certainly they associate with a supportive community of spiritual people.

Sixes can be unknown or well-known, as with every other stage, but they are more difficult to spot. This is because there are so few of them and also because of their quietness about their activities. If you think about the Six part of you, it is the part that fewest people see, that comes forth in the brief moments when you feel connected to the universe: experiencing a miracle; watching a flower open; healing a friend; following the inner voice; experiencing deep, empowering love; or creating a poem. During those moments nothing else is really of consequence. Sixes live a large part of their lives in that state of mind. So even though they might confuse us some part of us can relate to their behavior because we have experienced it, if only for brief moments.

In fact, to be at Stage Six means to be often misunderstood and even unappreciated by others. But Sixes are not trying to impress or change others, so they just accept these things with grace and a sense of aloneness yet connectedness. One of the main reasons there is no danger of the world becoming overrun with these "strange" Sixes is that it takes too much commitment to move to Stage Six. It requires giving up a great many of the things that are most valuable to most of us. It reminds me of the rich young ruler who asked Jesus what he must do to be saved. "Give everything you have to the poor and follow me," replied Jesus. The wealthy man went away very disappointed. We all seem to want more yet we are not willing to give up in order to receive more on a different plane. We're too afraid of the void that occurs once we give up something. What if the void is not filled? We are afraid to risk the chance of nothingness, so we go on searching for an easier route. A life of service sounds boring to some because they assume it must lack excitement, challenge, and recognition. Peace of mind even sounds dull. A life of service can be very exciting or very quiet—usually both. But excitement does not motivate Sixes. They would live a life of service no matter what it brought. So you see, Stage Six is not for everyone.

Conscience of the Community and the World

Another distinguishing characteristic of Sixes is their code of ethics. They understand, and even incorporate, the inevitable evils of the world into their vision because they are realistic, but they abhor acts and events that deliberately harm other people. On many occasions they must say or do things that may bring sadness or anger temporarily, but they always trust the long-term effects of their actions or at least are aware of them. They cannot participate in events or situations in which people are plotted against or deliberately sacrificed for the greed or ego of another. On the other hand, they would die for a just cause. That's why they are sometimes so unpopular. They simply call it the way they see it. Their sense of right does not mean doing what will benefit them but what will be best in the long run for all people involved. They have integrity and a sense of moral justice that goes beyond the law at times.

Ethical behavior is a quality that comes from an intention to be just, not from an intention to legislate another's values or morals. Sixes do not expect people to believe as they do, but to have thought through the issues and come to their own conclusions. Sixes generally make decisions or recommendations because they are the just things to do. At times this may even mean a loss for them or an admission of being wrong or uninformed. They can admit mistakes and do not usually let false pride get in the way of the truth—even if it is painful. Since they see the larger picture they can make decisions based on long-term justice and mercy rather than on the expedient action.

For example, let's say a Stage Six person is asked to consult on a situation in which two groups in an organization obviously need to merge. The leaders of both groups would be very appropriate leaders overall, but one of the candidates is overly confident, while the other is more insecure. It seems pretty clear to most people that the confident person will get the job. The consultant to the situation knows both of the people quite well and thinks through the situation carefully. Then she suggests that the more insecure-appearing of the two be selected because he would learn more about himself in the new job than the one who is overly confident. Since long-term development of people is a key objective of hers (and of the department), it follows that the confident candidate would learn more about himself and life by having the experience of being passed over once. The Stage Six consultant simply takes an intuitive, commonsense, and morally sound approach in the situation and she is confident that it will turn out well in the long run. And she does not need to talk about the recommendation to other colleagues. The mystique of morality grows too when it is not always explained. Moral people have fewer regrets in life because they do not need to hash over or become defensive for their actions. They ask questions before making choices, like, whom will it hurt? How could it turn out to everyone's advantage? How will this decision affect the more important things in life, in the world?

Sixes are the kind of people whose advice rings in the back of our minds over the years. We can always count on them to be fair, not to always agree with us. And their advice may seem unusual, like telling us to forgive our enemies or to not defend ourselves or to let go or to give others what they've stolen from us. It is hard advice which we usually find a way to avoid following. We recall their voice when difficult times arise and then our choice is whether to heed it or not. Gandhi gave advice to a raging Hindu man whose son had been killed by a Muslim. When the man asked how he could be set free from the hatred, Gandhi answered, "Find a Muslim boy your son's age whose family has been killed. Raise the boy to be a man, and raise him to be a Muslim."

Stage Six people make us think about ourselves differently simply by their presence among us. They do not do this deliberately. It just happens because of who they are. They act consistently on their principles and that is disturbing or enriching but fairly unique. For instance, if they are passionate about love and acceptance, they do not limit that to people who are like them, or even people who believe in the same things they do. Love goes beyond judgments. They can truly love their enemies without condoning their behavior. Compassion arising out of mutual pain seems to be a foundational principle underlying their behavior. You do not find moral or spiritual arrogance among the Stage Fives or Sixes.

When you are around a Stage Six whose life calling and principles are clear, something inside calls you to act more seriously on your own principles. You feel compelled to think about what you would do in a similar situation. You ask what is really important to you. Sixes do not demand respect but they elicit it because of the nature of their principles and nonself-serving behavior. They are not out to get anyone. They are answering their call.

Frequently, being around a community conscience type Six is distressing because we realize how deeply fearful or insecure we are. Most of us ward off fear as a full-time occupation. So when Sixes go about their vocations without fear it inspires us and scares us. We want to be like them and at the same time wish they would go away. It is part of the paradox we feel being around them. It calls us to a different place within ourselves which we are not yet comfortable exploring.

Take, for example, the work of battered women shelters and activist organizations across the country. They are naming our nation's horrendous family secret and it touches all of us in some disturbing way. One of their mottos is "when even one of us is oppressed, none of us is free." When we hear the high statistics on domestic violence we are sobered, angered, and hopefully moved to inner conviction to stop and heal the violence inside us and around us.

Compassion for the World

Stage Six people are children of the universe. They have a larger understanding of the world and the universe than most people. The pain and joy of the entire world is like that of their family. It's easy to see why they are mostly against war, since there is no enemy who is different from us. Some of the Vietnam veterans speak profoundly of the difficulty of facing the enemy in Vietnam, who turned out to be villagers—men, women, and children. It was much more complicated, they said, than tanks fighting tanks, and rows of soldiers attacking each other head on. Sixes understand that war will never cease because humans will always be competing for power, but their understanding transcends the use of force to feel superior over another, to revenge past deeds, or to compete for world power positions.

Sixes also understand the depths of pain and even feel others' pain acutely, though not always directly. A story describes this idea.

> A very old man lived in a small town in the mountains of Austria. One day he got a message from a friend in the next town, ten miles away, requesting that he come see him right away for he was in terrible shock over the illness of his son. The old man hobbled through the mountains to his friend's home only to be astonished by his friend's response. "I am so glad you're here, but how did you know that I was in such a terrible state?"
>
> "Something inside told me that I should come see you and I got here as soon as I could," the old man said to his friend.
>
> "It is amazing to me that you are here, but I don't understand how you knew. Let's go and talk over a good, long meal."
>
> The old man stayed three days with his old friend until his son was over the worst of the illness. Then he trudged back over the mountains to his home.
>
> A year later, the old man once again received a message from his friend, this time with the urgent words, "I'm dying, please come." The old man hurried over the long road to his friend's home only to find him in the local hospital with a heart attack.
>
> "How wonderful to see you, my friend. I am very ill and I thought I would never see you again. But how did you know that I was ill?"
>
> "I got another message from inside like the last one. It seemed urgent so I hurried right over to see how I could be useful to you."
>
> "This is indeed confusing to me because I don't know how you knew I was ill when I didn't tell you. Anyway, I'm glad you're here again. You do know the times I need you most, my friend."
>
> Years later, when the old man died, his family and friends were going through his meager belongings and they came upon a very interesting journal that the old man had kept for the last forty years

> of his life. His friend's son happened to be among the company as they were lovingly reading excerpts from the journal of this wise old man. One of the entries stated at the beginning of the day, "Deep prayer, voice of Peter, son is ill, I need you, come." The friend's son was overwhelmed by the message. He asked to read the excerpt from the next year, around the time of his father's heart attack. The same sort of entry appeared. "Morning meditation, voice of Peter, I'm dying. Come soon." He wept with joy over the sensitivity of the wise old man for his friend. No wonder there were no letters or calls!

It's better not to ask Sixes how things happen; it's better to just trust them that things happen. They understand it all on a plane different from the one on which we operate daily. And most of us haven't even scratched the surface of the other levels in which we could operate. To penetrate that surface takes a deep connection with the spiritual universe and requires long periods of discipline and quiet listening.

Wisdom figures find themselves alone in many different ways. They are not part of the establishment or the tradition of orthodoxy. Wise people speak and live the truths we all wish we were capable of living. They are at the margin of life but in its center. They are the question-askers, who explore larger visions with no thought of its effect on their position or power. They can function persistently in the presence of power, but their role is to challenge, to enlarge the vision, to give wisdom, to provide a basis for good choices in others. They are the souls of the universe. They have made peace with themselves and can function peacefully with the world.

Spirituality and the Spiritual Connection to Work at Stage Six

At this stage spirituality is reflecting the Holy. The intimate connection that Sixes have had with pain and shadow allows them a new freedom and wisdom without having to suffer. They live in obedience to the Holy and are models of compassion. They are the master teachers of others in the spiritual realm, mostly by the way in which they live. This whole chapter describes their spiritual behavior.

Their connection to work is this. Their best work comes out of their weakness; then they are dependent on the Holy. They are servants of the divine, living out of that spiritual energy. And the Holy does things through them that they never knew they were capable of, using skills that they didn't know they had. Their spiritual egos are diminished so they can practice tough love and take risks others might consider unthinkable. And their creativity, in whatever form, soars. It doesn't matter what their occupation is as long as they can live out their calling through it.

The Perception of Shadow of Stage Six

Appear to Be Out of Touch with Danger

Ironically Stage Sixes are willing to sacrifice their emotional, physical, or mental lives for a principle greater than themselves. They know when they are in danger but they don't care. That is not the most important thing for them to keep track of. Their calling is. So to others they seem dense, naive, or very impractical. How can they continue to do their work if they are dead? For some, that is the best way to insure that their work will go on, to die for it. Since their fear is gone, there is nothing to fear in death. It is seen as a transition, not an end.

Appear to Be Too Sacrificial

Like the previous shadow quality, this one bothers others who observe Sixes much more than it bothers Sixes. They can't be too sacrificial. It is their calling. But it can look like they have given up their influence prematurely by giving up too much. Since their motivation is so internal and spiritual, to them self-sacrifice is not even perceived as sacrifice. That is mind boggling to the rest of us. The book, *The Plague,* by Camus comes to mind, in which a doctor stays with victims of the plague even though he knows he too will succumb to the disease eventually.

A toxic chemical spill occurred in a large metropolitan area in the Midwest some years back. The whole area was evacuated because of a poisonous cloud hanging over the city, threatening everyone. The local press caught the story of a man who made the decision to stay in the city instead of driving to safety. He brought his van around to a nursing home and transported frightened and confused seniors to a safer place, all the while comforting them and playing music tapes of the 30s and 40s for them to enjoy.

Let's Meet Some People at Stage Six

I will illustrate Stage Six people in two different ways. The first is to tell the story of the movie *Resurrection* in my own words. You could also read about Gandhi, Hannah, or Elijah. The second way of illustrating Stage Six is to give brief quotes from others whose lives have been affected by Stage Six people. It would be difficult to describe them in case examples because they are easily misunderstood. They appear so simple that their complexity is lost. Also Sixes prefer not to have their stories written.

The movie *Resurrection* illustrates how one woman moved through the six stages of power. It is obviously over-simplified but also very revealing. Let it soak into your soul. Ellen Bursten, the female star, had just surprised her new husband with the birthday gift of a lifetime. It was a new red convertible. He was ecstatic. They took it for a spin on an ocean-side drive right after work on his birthday. Out of the driveway of a home on the drive came a teenage boy on a skateboard, heading right into the path of their car. The car swerved, went out of control, and plunged over the edge of the cliff. Ellen's husband was killed on impact and she lived, although she lost complete use of both legs with no chance of ever walking again.

Her father came all the way to California to get her and bring her back to live with him on their farm in the Midwest. Her father had always been abusive but she had no other choice. She stayed in a separate house at the back of the lot, a house that hired help usually stayed in. Here alone, afraid, and depressed she tried to repair the broken pieces of her life. Everyone gave her advice. And she tried many things. Some helped. Some didn't. And she did start seeing a man from the area she had known before she left. He liked her tenacity.

At a neighborhood picnic she was chatting with an old friend when the daughter of one of their neighbors got a nosebleed. This was dangerous because she was a hemophiliac. The girl's mother got hysterical and Ellen instinctively took the girl in her lap, soothed her by massaging her nose and speaking quietly to her. The bleeding stopped. The mother was astounded. Her daughter had never before stopped bleeding without medication and hospitalization. She looked at Ellen and said, "This is a miracle." Ellen knew it was too. And she thought maybe she should go and ponder what had happened.

Over the next several months Ellen practiced her newfound healing gift on herself, going through much frustration and pain in the process. But after long hours of massage and muscle work, she was able to get her legs working again. And she learned to walk, haltingly at first, but definitely walking.

Ellen began healing people from the surrounding area at public healing meetings. She even healed a wound of her boyfriend. As a result he thought that perhaps she was Jesus and her boyfriend's fundamentalist preacher father condemned her as the devil. A team of university researchers asked her to do her healing in the presence of scientists so they could learn more about how she healed. She reluctantly agreed to participate and performed a miraculous healing on a woman who had been crippled for years. Now the researchers were astounded. So was she.

But things started to turn bad for her. The more she healed the more she frightened some of the people around her. Her boyfriend now began believing that if she wasn't Jesus she must be the devil, for only those two could do these things. Although she was deeply spiritual she honestly didn't know where her healing power came from and she did not attribute it to anyone. So one hot August afternoon while she was healing in a small group out on a hillside outside of town, her boyfriend rode by the group on his motorcycle and shot at her from close range. He hit her in the shoulder. Immediately he was surrounded and tackled to the ground. She begged the men not to hurt him. But she knew she had to take some action on her own behalf quickly. Things were getting out of hand. She realized she had to leave home.

The last scene of the movie shows her many years older, living alone and running a gas station on the edge of a desert a long way from her home. She had remembered stopping at this station on her way home to the farm from California after her accident. She had connected instantly with the proprietor, an eccentric and spiritual old man who had a live two-headed snake to show her and wise old tales to tell her. Now she was running the place and the two-headed snake was preserved in a large jar. She has also added a large terrarium to the back of the station, with plants from the desert growing abundantly there.

A family van came rolling in one day, needing gas to cross the desert. Ellen noticed the seven-year-old boy's scalp and asked the mother quietly if her son had cancer. "Yes, and I'm afraid this is his last trip with the family. It's liver cancer," the mother explained. Ellen asked the parents and sister to go visit her terrarium while she spent some time with Tommy. She showed him her two-headed snake and told him stories from the desert. He was thrilled. Then she offered him the puppy that he had been petting throughout their conversation. "No," he said. "I won't be around long and it would make my parents very sad to have him after I die." Ellen nodded and said, "Well, in this case I think that it's all right." "Really?" he said, looking straight at her. "Yes," she said.

His parents came back and he told them about the puppy. They were very touched that Ellen would give him this gift so they allowed him to keep it. Then as the family was about to leave, Ellen said, "The only pay I want from you, Tommy, is a big hug." While Tommy was hugging her she silently took the cancer out of his body and sent the family on their way. That was the end of the movie.

What astounds me about the story is that her gift of healing remained the same. Only the way in which she used it changed, but in so doing, she experienced a profound transformation. Each of us has a gift. And we all can use it in a wide variety of ways. The stage of power that we occupy at the time determines how we will use it. What is your gift and at what stage are you using it?

Now for some quotes from people who have observed the behavior of Stage Sixes.

> "I've never known anyone who cares so much or so genuinely for other people. She is always seeing to it that others' needs are met, sometimes at the expense of her own. It seems she carries this deep, exuding love with her all the time, and she is not a martyr."

> "I know my mom and dad respect him a great deal and go to him for advice, but I think he's wacko."

> "He is the deepest, wisest person I know. I always go to him for his judgment and he never fails to amaze me. He makes me reason and struggle through my questions so I come out with an acceptable answer, yet he only listens and asks a few questions."

> "I think this guy is just washed up. He got passed over several years ago and now he's rationalized it so he can live with himself. He says he loves what he's doing now more than ever but I don't understand how he can. He's not moving. I can't figure out why he's so darn calm all the time."

> "I can't comprehend what makes her tick. She's just very closely connected with a deep well within her out of which perceptive wisdom swells. She provides vision for my life, gentle, unassuming, powerful."

> "She is so committed to this cause, she lives and breathes it, yet I don't think of her as the leader. She moves the cause along with invisible forces."

"For his sake, I'm glad he's off on his own now. He should have left this organization long ago. He's too real, too perceptive, too threatening to the others. He doesn't try to be at all, it's just that he's so right on, it scares people. He asks questions that stymie us all."

"I'm totally confused by her. She has her own wavelength in life, and it's not the one society lives on. So I tell her what I want from my career and she smiles, saying something to the effect that this is indeed where I'm headed but not the final destination. Now how can she know that? But she's usually been right."

"Every time I'm around him I get nervous. He's so deliberate, so quiet, so intensely interested in me. I just feel like squirming, or I talk a lot more or faster. After about a half hour, though, his presence seems to calm me and I relax. I wonder what it would be like to live that way?"

"You know I'm positive the reason he was assaulted was that he was getting too close to the powers that had a lot to lose if his redistricting plan went through. If his plan went through people of color would be a majority. It's going through for sure now. And he would say it was worth it."

Hagberg's Model of Personal Power

SUMMARY OF STAGE SIX
POWER BY WISDOM

Symbol

Key Question: In the deeper spiritual life, our lives are consumed by the fire of the Holy Spirit. How close are you willing to come to the flame?

Description
Self-sacrifice
Souls of the earth

Characteristics
Integrating shadow
Unafraid of death
Powerless
Quiet in service
Conscience of the community/world
Compassion for the world

Spirituality and Stage Six
Spirituality is reflecting the Holy

Shadow of Stage Six
Appear to be out of touch with danger
Appear too sacrificial

Catalyst for Movement
Humanness

What Holds People Back?
Human constraints

Chapter 8
Leadership and Power

True Leadership

One of the two premises of this chapter is this: ***People can be leaders at any stage of personal power, but they cannot be TRUE leaders until they reach Stage Four—Power by Reflection.*** Leadership is always tied closely to the idea of followership and people can motivate and guide followers at any stage of power, but true leadership is a term reserved for those who have experienced the crisis of integrity—people in Stages Four, Five, or Six.

What is integrity and the crisis of integrity? It is interesting to note that integrity and integrate (the latter meaning "make whole, complete; to unify") are from the Latin adjective, *integer*, which means "whole, complete in itself." Integrity, a noun, has two similar meanings, each one beginning with "the quality of being." That alone suggests that integrity is not a momentary feeling, an act to play. It is a way of being. Integrity is "a quality or state of being of sound moral principle, honest, sincere, upright"; it is also "a quality of being complete, whole, sound, unimpaired." This does not mean totally perfect to me but rather that we care and ask about the difference between right and wrong in dealings with people and organizations and take stands on issues that have been worked out inside. It means not lying, even if we may be well served as a result. It means saying what we genuinely feel and think, not what others want us to feel and think. It means not always having our own way but being able to compromise when appropriate. It means accepting our whole self and feeling all right about the parts that are not so sterling, accepting being human and imperfect, which may be what it really means to be complete. It means being worthy of trust and respect even from people who disagree with us.

The requirement of an integrity crisis for true leadership does not mean that people in Stages One through Three lack integrity. It simply means that as they resolve crises in their work and lives the issue of integrity is not the major one they face. And they have not had a battle over the integrity issue yet. They think of their decisions in other ways, more linked to the structure or the norms of the organization. For example, each might say, "The norm around here is so strong that I would be ostracized if I didn't conform," or "I'm only doing what the stockholders demand," or "Those who have the gold make the rules," or "Once I get to a higher position of power, I'll change the way things are done," or "I can't be myself here but those are the breaks." People at Stage Three will undoubtedly bristle to hear that you cannot be a true leader if your goal is simply to hold positions of authority. I'm not saying that people in positions of authority cannot be true leaders but only that the position or status is no guarantee of true leadership. The quality of the person is what determines true leadership, not whether he or she is in a position of authority. In fact, at times true leaders need to get away from power positions in order to lead more effectively.

One other question may arise as true leadership is discussed: If it takes getting to Stage Four to be a true leader, are all Stage Four, Five, and Six people potential leaders? Probably not, or at least not in the ways we currently think of people as leaders, i.e., those in positions of power in organizations and elected officials. Fours, Fives, and Sixes do not actively pursue positions of power for their own sake and may even shy away from them if the norm of the position is Stage Three behavior. They tend to lead by moving with, through, or behind others and do not gravitate toward the glory. Some of them would flatly decline the offer to lead because it is not part of their life purpose, or they would agree to be in a position of power reluctantly, only because they see the long-term changes that are possible.

The question of whether elected officials can be true leaders is especially interesting. I heard a group of emerging community leaders discussing this very issue with a group of elected officials. Someone noted that it is especially hard for elected officials at any level to be true leaders because there are so many pressures on them from constituents who threaten to defeat them if they do not support their point of view. Also elected officials feel they are principally reactors to crises, the needs of people, and to issues that already have support, rather than originators of new, creative, or venturesome ideas. The group concluded that leaders, in fact, might operate best from outside the political establishment, influencing and advising those in elected positions.

The question has also been raised as to whether managers are leaders. Dr. Robert Terry, director of a leadership program, makes the distinction between management and leadership: Management makes the system hum, attends to facts, motivates others, completes projects in a timely fashion, controls budgets, connects systems, sets goals, and builds teams. Leadership, on the other hand, sees the larger context, looks for quality relationships with followers, holds dialogues, and thinks of ethical considerations. These are useful distinctions. And it would be interesting to add that management tasks may not necessarily lend themselves to leadership but that the quality of the person in the management role makes all the difference. Managers can be leaders depending on how they view themselves, others, and the world, and at which stage of personal power they reside.

James M. Burns' seminal book called *Leadership* cites two types of leaders: transactional and transforming. Transactional leadership means one person contacting others to exchange valued things, whether economic, political, or psychological. Examples are votes, goods, money, or hospitality. No enduring purpose holds the parties together beyond the transaction. Transforming leadership means one or more persons engaging with others to raise one another to higher levels of motivation and morality. Transforming leadership is moral in that it raises both the leader and the led to new levels of human conduct through inspiring, uplifting, exhorting, or preaching. Transforming leaders are involved with the led. Their purposes fuse and they feel a mutual support. Burns says the crucial variable is purpose. Leaders inspire followers to act for certain goals that represent values and motivations, wants and needs, the aspirations and expectations of both leaders and followers. Comparing Burns' description with the stages of personal power, leaders at Stages Two and Three would be transactional leaders, and leaders at Stages Four, Five, and Six would be transforming types. People have asked the question why leaders like Hitler and Osama bin Laden would not be considered transforming leaders since they have a purpose they share with their followers and they are inspirational leaders. The main characteristics that separate them from *true* leaders or transforming leaders are integrity and morality (not to mention ruthlessness).

To reiterate, true leadership is a term reserved for those who, as leaders, understand and consistently operate with integrity and thereby acquire the respect of others. I strongly advocate that we redefine leadership in broader terms and that we each think more seriously about what it means to lead in our own lives. We need to redefine those qualities we are expecting from our leaders, both in organizations and in elected office. Perhaps instead of choosing from among the candidates who run for office, we should collect our Stage Four, Five, and Six people (thoughtful, egoless, wise) and choose among them for our leaders. Those who want it the least could be our first choice! Perhaps in organizations we could work harder to develop our people more personally and deeply rather than rewarding them for short-term skill-oriented performance.

Leadership and Our World

Some of you reading this may be asking yourselves at this point, "So what? What difference does it make to have Stage Four or Five leaders as opposed to having good Stage Twos and Threes who are really motivated to get out there and achieve? Haven't we gotten along all right with the range of people we've had in the past? Look at how successful we've been. We're the most powerful nation in the world!" People who ask these kinds of questions illustrate clearly what part of the problem with our "leadership" has been. A majority of our leaders, both in elected and organizational positions of power, are not true leaders who operate consistently with integrity. They are more likely to be Stage Three leaders whose major goal is their own success. Since the stages of power are cumulative, if we develop leadership behavior at Stages Four and Five, we can also use our Stage Two and Three qualities when necessary. And all the stages are useful at different times and for different reasons. We add tremendous value though by the inclusion of Stages Four and Five. So, even if we do not have a President, for instance, who operates at Stages Four and Five, we need people in appointed positions around the President who operate at those stages and have influence on the President's decisions.

Thus, my second premise: ***In order to survive in this new century, we must go beyond our traditional definitions of power and leadership (Stage Three–Achievement) and develop or encourage leaders who operate at higher stages (Stages Four and Five–Reflection and Purpose).*** We tend to think of ourselves as against others in the world, as the most this or the least that. We gauge our success by whether we are the biggest, strongest, or best. These are all Stage Three concepts and a Stage Three way of thinking in a world that is rapidly becoming an international and interdependent neighborhood. Buckminster Fuller has said that nations are obsolete. He meant we are already inextricably linked to the global community and we can't think of ourselves as separate any more. Just as in the time of the thirteen colonies when we had to become the United States, we are now over one hundred countries that must become a whole nation in order to thrive or even survive over the long term on our planet. And that won't be easy. Already we see that oil prices in the Middle East profoundly affect us, that war or natural disaster elsewhere often affects us, that our elections and economy affect others, and that terrorism and nuclear war will affect us all. With those threats of destruction so close to our consciousness now, we will have a far greater chance of survival if we have people representing us on all fronts—

business, education, religion, politics, athletics, arts—who are Stage Four or beyond. Let me list for you the major characteristics of *TRUE* leaders.

True leaders:

follow a calling, a purpose, an ideal,
allow for win–win, not just win–lose,
embrace their own shadows,
empower others, not themselves,
have balance in life, between work, community, and family,
can be vulnerable and reflective,
treat women, men, and people of color as equals,
ask why, not how,
have a spiritual connection to a power within and beyond themselves,
see the bottom line as a means to a larger organizational purpose, not an end in itself,
live with integrity as their hallmark.

We are at a turning point in our nation's development and in the world's development, and it will take wise and visionary leaders to keep us from moral and financial bankruptcy. We need leaders in this century who will look at power and beyond and who can make a careful, long-range guess at our collective future without solely considering the good of one country or group of countries and their success; who will find it more important to serve than to win; who will not subscribe to the premise that anything goes as long as you don't get caught. Where are the lone, prophetic voices? Where are the people whose lives operate on the basis of principles, on thoughtful and clear values that uphold justice and mercy? Why do we find it so difficult to elect and live with unglamorous candidates who speak their conscience rather than what is expedient? How can we truly be of service to people in the world if we are solely intent upon winning the worldwide race for power? Now is the time for understanding, not naiveté or fear tactics. Now is the time for humility. Now is the time for building bridges. Now is the time for diplomacy.

We are full of material possessions but impoverished in leadership. Inner poverty produces a drive to have and to get that is not satisfying. *The real hunger in the U.S. is for integrity and intimacy*. We must go beyond the competitive view, experience our own crisis of integrity as a country and begin being a true leader in the world. We must take the risk to operate at Stage Four, being more honest and less self-serving, less greedy, and thereby encourage others to operate on higher principles as well—again, not naively, but with foresight. We may have to think differently about our role in the world. We may even have to give up a few of our symbols. I cannot prescribe exact actions because that subject is far too complex, but only reiterate that integrity is a quality of being based on moral principles. It can be developed and it can make the difference. In fact, it may be the only thing that makes any difference.

Suppose we hypothesize that the traditional forms and definitions of leadership are not sufficient for our coming age and that we need to re-conceptualize leadership. Suppose we think of leaders as those who would empower other people, create and give away things and ideas long-term and short-term, collaborate on solutions to problems, put integrity before expediency, develop others' capabilities, be self-aware and self-accepting, non-judgmental, and wise. Then grandmothers, artists, writers, poets, musicians, ministers, teachers, counselors, and secretaries could be more influential leaders. We would see different forms of leadership such as idea leadership, servant leadership, mentor leadership, moral leadership, aesthetic leadership, and caring leadership as opposed to leadership based on ego, political, material, and financial criteria.

Suppose leadership really means striving for wisdom, as described in our ancient books and ideals. Suppose we really could depend on others to make decisions that were not self-serving but just. How would our management systems be different? How would we plan and implement ideas? How would we serve our customers and clients?

Suppose we viewed the world as our neighborhood and all people as our brothers and sisters. How would we make decisions and work out conflicts? Suppose that the good of all was our chief basis for deliberation on worldwide policy, not just the good of the governed. Wouldn't our pettiness decrease?

What would happen if we all thought seriously about our life purpose and acted in congruence with it? What if we could remove our egos from the middle of our daily discourse and act on the basis of broader ideas? What if we had leaders who really knew and accepted their shadows, who would be comfortable with the ramifications? What if all people had a connection with their own source of spirituality and lived accordingly? What if we were not afraid of death?

What if a condition of our emerging leadership consisted of having to choose two people who were younger than we to mentor along the way and to school in the arts of true leadership, as we would be learning from our mentors? What if we had a cultural tradition of true leadership that we could pass down verbally and behaviorally from generation to generation like our Native American friends? What if we really cared about the future of our world and our leadership?

What if we rewarded people for being innovative, for taking risks, for empowering others, for trusting themselves, for encouraging the continuing personal search, for instituting alternatives for dead-ended people, for working out differences? *What if inner power were just as important as outer power?*

What if females and males were acknowledged for their own personal gifts and not as sex roles? What if people of color were acknowledged for their own capabilities and not as ethnic group members? What if people could go openly to each other to express their fears, concerns, and desires with no fear of reprisal? What if females and males could be free to use both their feminine and masculine traits when appropriate? What if age were revered?

Fritjof Capra, the eminent physicist, wrote years ago in his book, *The Turning Point,* about the qualities and characteristics of what he called the rising culture in our world. He described the types of principles and beliefs upon which we have operated for the last several hundred years and argued convincingly that we were at a turning point. The rising culture he described would require a new type of leadership, one that accepted a systems (everything is interrelated and integrated) view of life that is self-organizing and self-renewing. It would require leaders who look at the world in terms of relationships and integration, not splintered pieces. Economic supremacy would no longer reign as the predominant goal of national policy. His views are still relevant today, aren't they?

Leadership at Each Stage of Personal Power

Let's look more carefully at each stage's primary way of guiding or leading people. These differences show why there are varying levels of effectiveness among the different styles. Basically, leaders at each of the stages develop followers who are or want to be like them. The stage of the person comes out in his or her leadership behavior.

Stage One Leadership:
Guiding others by domination or force
Inspires fear

At Stage One people who lead generally use domination or force of some kind to get people to obey. They threaten others verbally or use physical force to produce results. They operate on the basis of inspiring fear in others largely because they feel powerless and insecure themselves. They know of no other way and they are so afraid themselves that they cover it with authoritarian or even tyrannical behavior. Many times the motivation of the leader is bitterness or revenge due to having been treated in the way they are now treating others. This is especially true for people who have been physically or emotionally abused as children. People respond to this form of leadership only because they are fearful, unorganized, and powerless as well. Their only goals are to survive and to escape more physical or emotional abuse.

In organizations, this kind of leader requires blind obedience from followers. There can be few questions raised because this form of leadership is easily threatened and will punish whoever does not obey. The authoritarian dictator and the terrorist organization leader are perhaps the most obvious examples of this form of leadership. There must be obedience and subservience of one's will to the leader. This is to ensure that all directions are followed in times of danger.

One of the most obvious reasons why this authoritarian form of leadership does not work effectively in the long run is that people rebel under such strict control. Many people do not like to be so closely governed and they resent the use of force to maintain order. Military coups led by young army officers are good examples of what happens when leaders are excessively authoritarian.

Here are some examples of the ways in which Stage One leaders think:

> "I can't afford to let everyone do what they want to do. The whole place would be in chaos. People basically need to have structure and order. They are more secure that way."
>
> "I don't care what you think and I don't care how you feel, boy, just *do* what I say."
>
> "If you don't improve, you'll have to find someplace else to work."
>
> "I don't pay you to come up with alternatives. I pay you to get the job done, and done right."

Stage Two Leadership:
Guiding others by sticking to the rules
Inspires dependency

Stage Two leaders are eager, genuinely wanting to do a good job in their leadership positions. They lead by finding out what rules and guidelines

Hagberg's Model of Leadership and Power

Leads by force.
Inspires fear.
1
Leads by the rules.
Inspires dependency.
2
3
Leads by personal persuasion.
Inspires a winning attitude.
4
Leads by modeling integrity.
Inspires hope.
5
Leads by empowering others.
Inspires love and service.
6
Leads by being . . . wise.
Inspires inner peace.
Leadership
and
Personal
Power

senior management has formulated and sticking to them faithfully. Twos are learning to be loyal to the organizational norms. Being good at collecting data and gathering information, they make good resources for their people. They are answer-finders and they encourage people to come to them with questions. It reinforces their competence in the eyes of employees.

The Stage Two leaders look to the Threes for their inspiration and authority. They are willing to learn what it takes to do the job right. And they can be exceptionally well-organized, having read, watched, and learned the rules of the organization. Efficiency and thoroughness are their hallmarks.

Twos have difficulty making decisions because they are just insecure enough to second-guess a decision. So they efficiently gather more data and wait, which makes them less effective. Basically they love to learn and follow the Threes' lead but they are reluctant to take risks themselves. Their most important learning is learning about themselves in order to gain confidence. Having a mentor would be exceptionally helpful to them.

The reason they inspire dependency is that Twos do not want their followers to go around or beyond them. They think it will make them look bad. So they are extra helpful and competent with their people. What they fear is rocking the boat or having to defend an unpopular decision.

Here are some examples of Stage Two leaders' thinking:

> "Say, I'm really feeling pressure from my boss to get this project done. Could you make this project a priority for the next two months? If you get any grief from anyone else, send them to me."

> "I can't give you a decision on that issue yet. I need more information."

> "If you have any questions at all just come to my office. I'm sure I can find the answer for you."

> "Why don't we go out for a long, quiet lunch somewhere, just you and me, to talk it all over in a more relaxed atmosphere?"

> "If you have any questions on that procedure we discussed just check the policy manual."

Stage Three Leadership:
Guiding others by personal persuasion and charisma
Inspires a winning attitude

Leadership at Stage Three is focused on success strategies. The goals must be clear and the means spelled out. Goals usually revolve around more clients, higher market share, shareholder return, new products or more profits. The leader may be a technical expert, a great teacher, an issue spokesperson, or a charismatic personality. Each different style of Stage Three leader has his/her own way to convince others to support and work with them. Usually their track record is one most people will identify with so the effort has good odds of succeeding.

Being part of the team or organization of a Stage Three leader captivates the energy of the followers. They want to be part of the action, and to share in the recognition and rewards. They are inspired to work hard in order to be part of that winning and competent team. In many instances, especially in corporations, the words the leader uses suggest sports competition or war; tactics, penetration, counter offenses, punting, or tackling.

Threes have an insatiable need to get consistently better. They restructure, try new approaches or development programs, survey the competition, and look for new and innovative ways to accomplish results. Because so much is on the line for them personally they can get very upset when results are not forthcoming. Either they shame themselves unmercifully or they project the blame on to others. They do not tolerate mistakes very well even though they may verbalize to followers that risk-taking is great. They just have a lot of their personal values, competence, and ego on the line and therefore take failure very personally.

In return for all the success they are willing to share, Stage Threes ask for loyalty. Sticking with the team, no matter what the circumstances, is expected. When the going gets rough and the risks are great, Stage Three leaders need to know that the team will go on despite injuries or setbacks. Those who sign on make a real commitment.

Stage Three is the most prominent form of leadership in organizations. Stage Three leaders are the most driven and outwardly successful of all of the stages. The major reason for a Stage Three leader failing is when the need to succeed causes that leader to do things that are illegal, immoral, or something that disagrees with the stockholders. Usually Stage Three leaders can inspire most everyone if they can talk to them and share their goals with them. But not everyone shares the idea of success that these leaders adhere to and soon some begin to ask deeper questions.

Examples of Stage Three leaders' thinking:

> "We have so much talent in this team, there is no way we can fail. I'll see to that."
>
> "I am absolutely sold on this idea. We are all going to look so good when it's over, they'll be asking us to run the whole company."
>
> "Give me three reasons why it can't be done, and I'll give you twenty reasons why it can."
>
> "The only trouble with us is we need a bigger challenge. Give us a chance and we'll show you what we can do."

Stage Four Leadership:
Guiding others by modeling integrity and generating trust
Inspires hope

Stage Four leaders are mostly concerned with doing the "right" thing, the fair or just thing in the long run. They do not depend only on immediate results but on maintaining quality and effectiveness. They lead with integrity. They lead because they have become deserving of the trust that followers have in them and they are honest with their followers, even if it is painful for them all. They not only share their leadership, they share in the joys and pain of their followers. Above all, their sense of rightness evolves out of the deepening inner resources of their souls, and they take care to be among the people—not separate or apart. Stage Four leaders are not afraid to learn from others and they don't have to be in front. Fours nourish an environment that encourages others to flourish, innovate, take risks, and learn about themselves without shame. They genuinely care about other people.

Fours lead by inspiring hope in others and helping them see what qualities are evolving out of them and out of the group. They may help the group change direction because they can sense the necessity before the group can. They're not afraid to talk about the things people usually try to hide. The sense of direction in a Stage Four leader comes less from the established plan and more from the ongoing life of the total group. They truly let the group decide, rather than merely talking about it and then making the decisions themselves anyway. They are beginning to trust themselves and their inner resources more and that is why they are appearing more quietly confident. They can take ups and downs in stride more easily because their self-esteem is not so tied to their success. They can listen more effectively and do not have to take strong stands on every issue. They do not hop on bandwagons but are known to be innovative by their style.

Fours think more deeply about how they lead people; for instance, those who are truly effective may lead people who are at different stages in slightly different ways even though their overall style will predominate. For example, a reflective leader might give a Stage One person choices among a few options, and give a Stage Three more discretion.

In return for insightful leadership, Fours ask for consistency and honesty from their followers. They would rather have the truth now and think of ways to solve the problems together, than have to deal with a series of cover-ups later that only exacerbate the problem. Fours, in fact, can usually tell when someone is lying and they often have to confront the behavior and try to help the person who has a fear of honesty.

There are no obvious or easily recognized examples of Stage Four leaders. They can be almost anywhere and are not identified by their positions or status. The quality of the person is the distinguishing characteristic. Stage Fours are those people you meet on boards, in meetings, in social settings who inspire people to listen to them because they are not self-serving, but thoughtful, sensible, and honest. Stage Four and Five leaders are the most effective in the long run because they think more broadly and begin to take themselves out of the equation. They may not be rewarded for this behavior, however.

If Stage Four leaders are not effective, a reason may be that the organization highly values the norms of Stages Two and Three. Stage Four leadership will not be nurtured if all that matters is the achievement of success at the expense of less tangible rewards.

Examples of Stage Four leaders' ways of thinking are as follows:

> "I happen to have a number of people reporting to me, and I am finding, through too many years of experience, that the best way to teach people how to lead others humanely and with respect is to treat them humanely and with respect. The big decisions we make around here are far less critical than the ways in which we treat people every day. All those days of treatment add up to the morale issues as much as the business decisions do. For example, when times are tough, as they are from time to time, it is much easier to share the dilemma with people and talk about alternatives that will usually cost them something if, all along the way, management has shown care and respect for them as individuals. What do I mean by humane and respectful treatment? I mean talking to them frequently, keeping in touch with their issues, helping them find ways to solve problems, giving them ongoing, honest feedback about their performance and

behavior, listening when they need me, giving them as much authority and responsibility as possible, resolving conflicts between us, recognizing their achievements, thanking them for good work, sharing their joys and sorrows, being open and vulnerable. Whatever comes up I try to remember to ask myself what is really the right thing to do. Not how will I look better, or how can I punish them, or how can I get rid of them so I won't have to deal with them. Some days it is extremely difficult to model the right thing to do because I'm tired, bored, or frustrated. So I may just say that and deal with what I can, waiting until a later time to complete the rest. But they usually understand and let me have my bad days too."

"Each and every morning I remind myself why I am continuing to remain in public office; not for my ego, which is always a battle given the attention I get; not for only one issue or interest group; not for reelection. I have to continually remind myself that there need to be voices of reason, less partisan views of issues that must be dealt with wisely in order for us to reach any fruitful future. Some days I wonder whether I wouldn't be more successful as a voice of reason outside of elected office. Practically the only thing that keeps me going sometimes is my trusted friends and colleagues who also can see beyond the daily political rat race to a broader picture. I spend a great deal of time reflecting, reading, thinking, musing so I can't get caught up totally in details. This means I have to have a superb staff whose competence and judgment I trust. They are really extensions of me and I could never handle public life without them."

"I guess you could say I am a powerful person—or at least that I am in a powerful position. I'm not sure exactly how I got here considering my strong views against our usual leadership. Perhaps they thought I'd keep my mouth shut if I were one of them. At any rate, my sole basis for taking this position was to influence positively the climate for personal risk-taking and creativity and to get as many other people of thoughtful, realistic persuasions involved as possible. I'm very clear if we are not secure enough to be creative and take risks none of the other things we do really matter. Our organization depends on it. Someone has to speak up even if it's not necessarily the best timing. I don't want to be removed from office before I have time to act, but on the other hand I'll influence from wherever I am. It has become my passion."

Stage Five Leadership:
Guiding others by empowering them
Inspires love and service

Stage Five leaders can best be described as servant leaders. They see their main goal as empowering others to be more fully human and more fully satisfied. To accomplish this, Fives strive to be of service to others, to provide ideas, support, encouragement, and love so as to draw out the best in people. Stage Five leaders have vision that goes way beyond the individual and the organization. It is of larger significance, like love or justice, or peace for all. They share their calling through their behavior without talking about it because how they live out their vision matters to them—not how they can enhance their own egos. Stage Five leaders are convinced that the good of all followers is more important than the good of leaders and they behave accordingly. They give and give and give selflessly, not begrudgingly. They do not expect rewards in return except those inner, intangible ones that result from seeing others more satisfied and human. They have faced themselves, they have hit the Wall, and they are connected to a supreme being as their source of strength. They can take risks most of us would shy away from and therefore they are an asset to any organization. In fact they are a necessity, even though they may not be comfortable in organizations any more.

As with Stage Four leaders, it is hard to identify obvious examples of Stage Five leadership. One way is to identify how you feel when you're around them. After you've been around a Stage Five leader you feel lifted up, encouraged, affirmed, not cajoled, threatened, or sold a bill of goods. You have more courage and more dignity. You feel more self-acceptance and even a sense of a calling yourself. For these are the qualities that Stage Five leaders seem to draw out of followers. Often it is really hard to explain but they get a sense from a Stage Five person of a non-critical, accepting nature. It frees followers to expose their fears and insecurities and then to slowly rise above them. A Stage Five leader inspires followers eventually to find love for others and a service of their own, no matter how insignificant it may appear to be. Service makes us feel worthwhile, as if we matter to someone else and thus to ourselves.

If Stage Five leaders are not effective, a reason may be that so many people are caught up in Stage Three and they cannot consider or understand the simple principles of Stage Five leaders. They do not understand and thus they fear Stage Fives.

Here are a few examples of the thinking of Stage Five leaders:

"I don't think of myself as a leader any more. I hate applying for positions, running for office, or being in charge of groups. I like to sit back and reflect on what is being said, then offer perspectives on the issues that perhaps haven't been considered yet. Often, to my surprise, the naive-sounding questions I ask turn out to jog the thinking of the group and they get into a pretty fruitful discussion. I have to be careful though that I don't call attention to myself too much or people start looking to me for the answers too. That's the worst thing that could happen. For one thing, it's better for the group to find the answers and for another thing, I don't know the answers anyway."

"I have chosen or perhaps been given a mission to accomplish in my lifetime. I think about this mission as the guiding force for my life and, no matter what I'm doing, it seems to permeate my consciousness. Therefore my work has really slowly molded itself around my mission, which involves being of specific service to people in the world. I know it may sound far-fetched but it is my guiding light. It evolved out of a really deep crisis in my life in which I realized I had nothing to live for. Slowly I have evolved and I have written and followed a set of principles for five years now, a credo, for my life and work. Everything I do must meet the conditions of my credo or I know it is not consistent with my mission. It took me five years to think about and write my mission and credo and I now have great peace as a result."

"The most important thing I do in my life is to find ways to help other people develop. In my job I see people come and go every day because I am in such a busy, public place; my goal is to get to know those whom I encourage so that I can support, encourage, brighten up, challenge, or touch them in some way. I can ask questions that allow people to open up with me quite easily, so I just ask questions that will make them think or will challenge their negative thinking. I've heard some people say, after they've known me just casually for three years, that they really look forward to seeing me because I seem to know where they're at and I tend to say something helpful. I know it may seem trivial but I believe that's how people change and get healthier.

Stage Six Leadership:
Guiding others by one's depth of wisdom
Inspires inner peace

Stage Six leaders are rarely found because most Stage Six people have no aspirations to leadership of any kind. They are so truly selfless that if they were to emerge as leaders it would be simply as a result of genuinely living their life purposes and acting on the wisdom that dwells so deeply within. Their way of leading then emerges out of their deep wisdom and insight into the issues of the entire universe. For that reason our world, which is run with much narrower visions, rarely can appreciate or truly encourage the emergence of Stage Six leadership.

This kind of leadership inspires in others that which comes from deep within, namely inner peace. Stage Sixes leave people feeling that there is no reason to fear or even to strive for things. Things just are and will be. Survival is not even the major goal but living consistently with moral principles and a connection to deep spiritual sources. Stage Sixes lead in strange ways, perhaps through their art, their touch, their writing, their eyes, their music, their visions.

Though full of inner peace, Stage Six leaders are somewhat uncomfortable for others to be around because of their total dedication to that which their wisdom guides. Their model behavior asks the same of others and calls them silently to look inward and find out what their real calling is. They ask others to be unafraid of losing anything or everything along the way. This makes many people uncomfortable so they choose instead to remain in awe or fear of Stage Sixes. If Stage Sixes are not effective, it's probably that they are not interested or that they are not acknowledged as leaders. Stage Sixes don't lead, they just live.

Here are a few examples of Stage Six leadership thinking:

> "My art is a way for me to express the churning feelings I have about the present stage of our culture. I want people to see, to think, to feel the destiny that we are creating. I try to make the message loud and clear as well as subtle so that people will stop and think. I experience our culture in a certain way and this I create. I can only create from the experiences that have been given to me, yet all of our experiences are deeply rooted in the same underground universal stream. So if I touch inside myself deeply, I can touch others deeply as well. And I want to create a lasting idea, a creation that can speak after I move along, a chronicle of my own and perhaps the culture's transitions."

> "I listen, I speak, I wait for messages. I'm on a day-to-day adventure with life. If I'm tuned in, I have an unusual ability to understand the

inner workings of other people, not analytically but intuitively. For instance, I'll be given a message from some source within to call a person, say a certain thing, give someone a book, or ask a question. Almost invariably, for a reason unknown to me, the action on my part hits some chord, and I often get very quizzical or relieved looks from others. I've been part of some miraculous changes in people's lives. I've given up trying to figure it out, take any credit for it, or even be surprised. Now I'm just careful to listen for the messages."

The table on the following page is a summary of how leaders lead at each stage of power.

Summary of Leadership and Power at Each Stage of Power

Stage	They lead by	They inspire	They require
Stage 1	Domination, force	Fear of being hurt	Blind obedience
Stage 2	Sticking to the rules	Dependence	Followers to need them
Stage 3	Charisma, personal persuasion	A winning attitude	Loyalty
Stage 4	Modeling integrity, generating trust	Hope for self and organization	Consistency, honesty
Stage 5	Empowering others, service to others	Love and service	Self-acceptance, calling
Stage 6	Wisdom, a way of being	Inner peace	Anything/everything/nothing

Developing Leadership in Myself and Others

Has reading this book inspired you to experience leadership beyond Stage Three? Are you ready to do that? If so, read the last chapter, "Leading from Your Soul." It shows you an in-depth process for developing into a leader who operates beyond Stage Three. If you are not ready to begin this process don't force it. Be where you are and let yourself develop to the next level, whatever that is. The best way to stimulate behavior beyond where you are is to think deeply about it and talk it over with someone else. Don't let the feelings pass and become deadened, or it may be a long time before they will resurface. These are the fertile moments in your life.

One thing I know for sure: You cannot become a leader in the sense I describe without being keenly aware of yourself and willing to give up many of the traditional beliefs about power and leadership. You must at some point take a "leap of faith" toward the emerging model of what it means to truly lead and away from the need to be successful, famous, rich, in control, or powerful. The kind of leadership I am advocating arises out of the understanding of pain, the loss of innocence, the love of others, the larger purpose, the pursuit of wisdom, and the humor of life. Ask yourself if you are willing to take the risk.

True leadership begins with the willingness to be someone other than who the world wants you to be.

Chapter 9
Managing People at Various Stages

One of the most difficult tasks in the world is to manage people well. Long-time managers tell me that the business side of management, the part they thought would be ninety-five percent of the job when they first took on the challenge, is a piece of cake now and takes up a far smaller percentage of the time than it did before. The human side of management, which is still an art and upon which almost all of the business side ultimately depends, is the more difficult of the two, taking far more time and energy and, of course, constant attention. And most of the seasoned managers say that only a certain amount of the human side can be taught. The rest must be gleaned from experience on the job. Some get very good at it by learning with each experience, while other managers never do learn the art, no matter how much they study or how much experience they have.

Why is it so difficult a task for some to manage people and not for others? Or what are the characteristics of successful managers that make them different from poor managers? The latter question is much easier to answer and has been answered to varying degrees by many management theories and consultants. Some of the theories agree; others contradict each other. Describing each of the various approaches is not the goal of this book but it is useful to have an understanding of management theory and practice as a starting point when analyzing a good manager's style.

The first assumption in this chapter is that all organizations are made up of people at various stages of development or power and that no one management theory will accommodate them all equally well. People at different stages of power need to be motivated and managed in different ways. A manager who relies on one theory only will surely not meet the needs of a wide variety of people. Here is a case in which treating everyone the same is clearly not useful or productive. This does not mean giving special treatment to certain people or giving up on others because they don't fit. It means learning eventually, as a manager, how to read employees and choose, in addition to the most comfortable managing style, one or two other available styles with which to manage them. For instance, a highly participatory decision-making style with Stage One people is premature because they lack necessary information about the organization to give input on decisions outside their own job. Structure and direction with encouragement and support are more appropriate until their confidence is strengthened. Too open a style may breed insecurity, confusion, or resentment at this stage. A manager's own most comfortable style may be participatory but with Ones it would not be the most effective style. Eventually these insights come intuitively but, at first, they may seem difficult.

The second assumption is mentioned less often in management circles: that managing bosses may be just as important, if not more important, than managing employees, and the dynamics are different because of the power relationship. Understanding the people they work for—at any power stage—can teach managers more about themselves and their inner dynamics than most other work experiences. Most people's complaints about their work have more to do with their bosses than with their co-workers or employees, yet most people are never taught the fine art of being managed. Before we get too much further into this topic, let's look at the ways in which managers proceed through the stages of power as they learn the steps in managing people effectively.

Stage One—Powerlessness
Motivated by fear
Manages others by muscling

This stage corresponds to the feeling employees get down in the pit of their stomach when they learn they are about to become managers. Mostly they feel the excitement of being chosen, of a new challenge, but there is also a thinly veiled feeling of fear, of wondering if they can do it, if they know enough, if they have the right knowledge and connections to manage well. Usually this stage lasts just long enough for them to finish lunch because they are off on the task of learning to manage.

If they stay at this level in management they are likely to resort to threats and use of force to manage people in an attempt to cover their own fears and inadequacies. It is called management by muscling.

Hagberg's Model of Managing and Personal Power

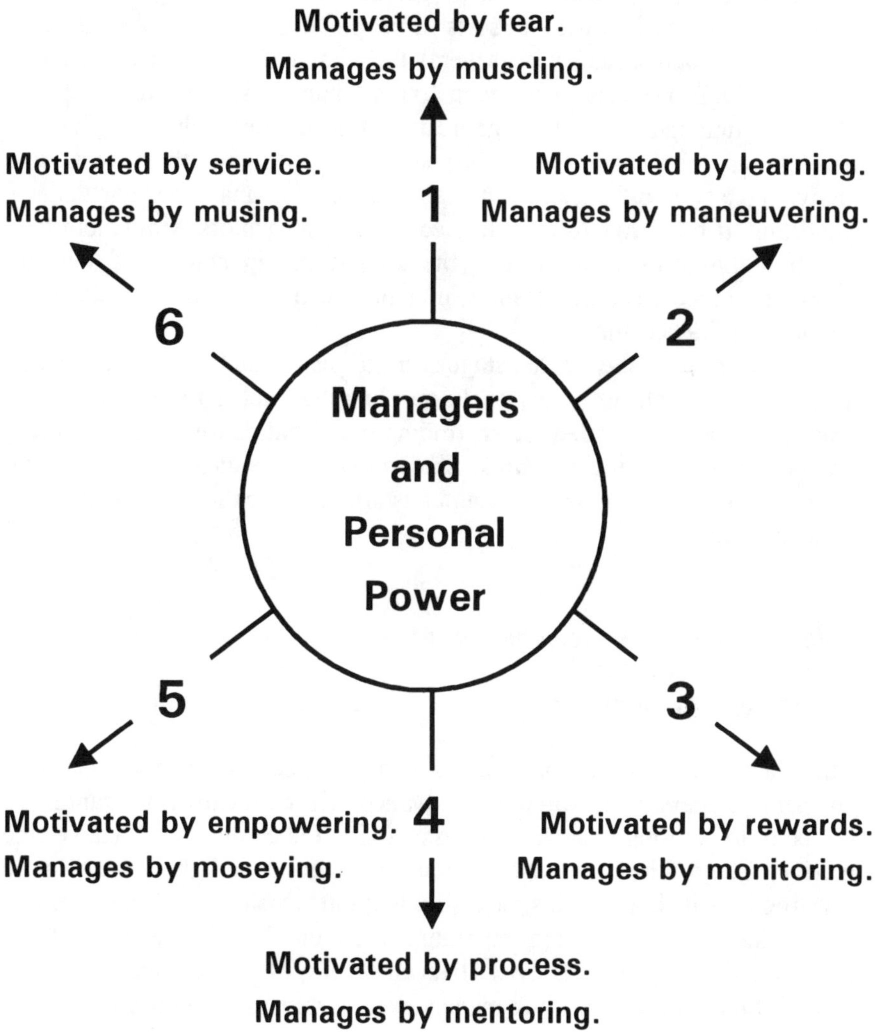
Motivated by fear.
Manages by muscling.
1
Motivated by learning.
Manages by maneuvering.
2
Motivated by rewards.
Manages by monitoring.
3
Motivated by process.
Manages by mentoring.
4
Motivated by empowering.
Manages by moseying.
5
Motivated by service.
Manages by musing.
6
Managers and Personal Power

Stage Two—Power by Association
Motivated by learning
Manages by maneuvering

At Stage Two, managers need to get as much knowledge and broad experience as possible with all sorts of people and situations. At this stage they become acquainted with several theories and practices of management through courses, observing other managers who are seen as effective, understanding the organizational norms and culture, trying out new things, observing their own behavior, observing their boss, and analyzing style differences and similarities. It may be particularly important at this stage to have trusted friends or mentors with whom they can talk things over, for this is the apprenticeship stage and they are bound to make mistakes from which they can learn. It is a stage for gaining confidence and skill.

Managers who stay at this stage seem to play "catch up management." They are never ahead of the cycle on planning, etc., so they are always balancing one thing with another, trading one deadline for another, putting things off, and putting out fires. Since power is magic, they can't quite grasp it. They end up maneuvering constantly. It is called management by maneuvering.

Stage Three—Power by Achievement
Motivated by rewards
Manages by monitoring

There are many motivations behind people's needs to be thought of as superb managers, from wanting to advance their own career, to wanting to be liked, to wanting to be known, to enjoying the challenge. Whatever the motive, Stage Three managers want to be good and they want to be rewarded for it. Usually this means finding out which style of management is practiced and rewarded in the organization and then finding a way to be particularly good at that style. It means being observant and motivated enough to learn the prevailing management system and encouraging others to do so as well.

Managers at this stage focus mostly on results and put less emphasis on process. They want the numbers to be right and the bottom line to reflect profit. They monitor themselves and their employees in order to reward results. This style is called management by monitoring.

Stage Four—Power by Reflection
Motivated by process
Manages by mentoring

At Stage Four, managers move beyond their allegiance to the prevailing management style. They develop management styles that are most suitable to them and to the people they manage. This will make them even more effective, although they may not espouse as clearly the prevailing organizational style. To make this transition, they need to learn as much about themselves as possible from various sources, looking at both their strengths and weaknesses. They should try on different styles to see which ones fit best with their personality and values and then eventually settle into a most comfortable style for a base or home style. Then they should learn to accommodate the needs of people who work for them by having at their disposal one or two other styles. They can talk with other managers who are different from them, but whom they consider competent, to find out how they manage different people.

For example, if they operate with a tight rein, they should know which employees would be stifled by that and let them have more rope than others. They should observe both their employees and their bosses to discover at which stage of personal power they are, along with other characteristics (personality, motivations, values). Then they can decide by discussion, trial and error, analysis, and intuition which type of management approach these people work most effectively with and start using those alternative styles, especially on occasions in which managers want to see particular results or in conflict situations. The longer managers practice flexible management behavior with a consistent home style, the more intuitive its use will become and the sooner it will be incorporated automatically into their own style.

At Stage Four, managers are also able to be mentors to other managers who are struggling with the conflicts of deciding which management theories and styles to study and to use. Stage Four managers look at process as opposed to content in their dealings with people. In fact, they do not feel that there is much that is more important than process. They increasingly take themselves out of the active management role and allow others to operate in their place. They are secure enough to teach others rather than doing it all themselves. They are managing by mentoring.

Stage Five—Power by Purpose
Motivated by empowering
Manages by moseying

Managers at Stage Five have an internal guide that gives them the confidence of trusting their natural sense of management. At this stage, although they have an overall operating style, each person is seen as an individual to be treated differently and to be served. Good managers seek to understand each individual, and empower him or her to develop and meet their inner potential. They mentor other managers in the art as well but by their role model, not through deliberate teaching. Managers at Stage Five seem to roam around and act more as catalysts and resource people, getting out of the way of their employees. They do not lead projects; they light the fires in others to encourage their projects. This kind of management is called management by moseying.

Stage Six—Power by Wisdom
Motivated by service
Manages by musing

Sixes get out of managing and into musing. They manage by musing.

How to Manage Employees and Bosses at All Stages of Power

The remainder of this chapter will be an outline and brief description of the ways in which people can effectively manage or be managed by others who are at different personal power stages. This discussion will be vastly oversimplified but will give impetus to a more thorough discussion within oneself and among manager colleagues as to the soundness of a more varied approach. A complicating factor will be the stage at which managers reading this identify themselves. A Stage Four manager, for instance, may manage a Stage Two person somewhat differently than a Stage Three manager would because of the Four's higher level of sensitivity, etc. These more subtle differences would have to be addressed individually since they are much more complex. For now, begin by just thinking about managing employees and bosses at each of the six different stages. Also employees who are at lower stages may have difficulty identifying higher stage managers because they do not understand their behavior. It does pose a problem for managing your boss. One suggestion would be to describe your boss's behavior to a person you think is at a higher stage and see what they think the stage of your boss is.

A simple rule of thumb in determining how to manage people at various stages may be that Stages One and Two respond more to structured or hierarchical management styles, Stages Three and Four to team approaches (Three to competitive teams, Four to participatory teams), and Fives and Sixes to laissez faire or informal management styles, if any. The real challenge, though, is to manage people at their home stage but also to encourage them to consider developing further. It means that in order to be effective, you should be moving to the highest stages too, so you can manage broader ranges of people at various stages.

Stage One: Powerlessness

Managing Employees at Stage One

They are motivated by fear.

They need support and encouragement.

1. Give encouragement and support. Build them up and encourage them to learn more skills and acquire more self-knowledge. Help them gain more information about their job.
2. Help them build a group and individual identity. Encourage a sense of identity by supporting group events and socializing informally.
3. Reward them concretely. Reward them with warranted verbal praise, salary increases, extra skill training, awards, and recognition.
4. Provide structure and limits. Give direction and structure, guidance and concrete guidelines. Provide flexibility within guidelines but not ambiguity. Set and enforce limits on behavior, rules, and policy. Help them learn to take responsibility for their behavior on basic work issues.
5. Be a strong, supportive role model, giving information about and access to new areas of learning and development. At times, this may mean almost taking on a parenting role that is appropriate as long as this role does not foster dependency or condescension.

Examples of interaction might include:

> "Please bring me all the data that I've circled on pages 3 and 5 by Friday afternoon."

"You did a very good job on the body of the manuscript. I found very few errors. I had the feeling you got tired when doing the tables in the appendix. Would you proof them and return them to me tomorrow, please?"

"I'd love to go out with the office staff for Carolyn's birthday. Thanks."

"I have some courses in mind that I want you to take this spring. They will give you much more information on how to accomplish your accounting tasks."

Managing Bosses at Stage One

1. Try never to work for a boss who is at Stage One.
2. Get another job.
3. If you are stuck with a Stage One boss, follow directions, mind your own business, and don't take anything personally.
4. Keep your fingers crossed. Your boss may retire soon.
5. Confront your boss's behavior with support from others who have as much or more power than your boss.

Stage Two: Power by Association

Managing Employees at Stage Two

They are motivated by an opportunity for learning.
They need safety and freedom to explore.

1. Give them information and experience. Let them try out as many new things, projects, and skills on their jobs as possible. The more they try the more they learn, even if they are afraid.
2. Let them learn from mistakes. Mistakes are the best opportunities for learning. Encourage risk so you can help them gain learning from both the successes and the failures. Help them learn to be competent and confident.
3. Encourage them to take responsibility for themselves on broader work issues, i.e., let them direct their own work and ask you for changes. Push them to open themselves to development, techniques, and skills, as well as personal knowledge. Be available more to Stage Twos.

4. Confront them gently. Be more straightforward but still supportive, more direct but encourage discussion. Encourage them to bat ideas around with you and talk things through. Rein them in only when necessary.
5. Encourage them to model the behavior of others. Look around for people who do things well and encourage employees to observe them and try out similar behavior. Use employees as examples of good behavior to others.

Examples of interaction:

> "This is a new project for our department and it will be a great learning experience for you. I know you can do it."
>
> "Just go ahead on it. Check with me tomorrow if you have any questions. In a week we'll get together for a briefing."
>
> "Let me give you some feedback on your behavior in the meeting this morning. You acted scared. Now, we're all afraid at times but let's talk about effective ways to deal with fear so you won't be so exposed next time."

Managing Bosses at Stage Two

1. Cooperate and be helpful. Encourage them to let you do extra work for them.
2. Ask for advice and bolster their confidence. They like you to be dependent on them. Find the area they know best and seek out their advice, encouraging their skill and expertise. Beware of becoming overly dependent on them because they may inadvertently keep you from developing further.
3. Don't threaten them. Encourage them, work hard, don't take credit, even if the work is yours, and never embarrass them in public.
4. Find someone else in the organization you can talk to who will keep your confidence. Talk to that person during stressful times. Plan your development with your boss using advice from the other person as well.
5. Hope that your boss continues to gain confidence and competence in the organization.

Stage Three: Power by Achievement

Managing Employees at Stage Three
They are motivated by symbols of success.
They need feedback, challenges, and provocative questions.

1. Channel their energy into projects that will tap their strengths. Encourage them to build confidence, expertise, and depth in areas where they've been successful.
2. Teach them about the organization's culture and norms. Give them feedback and information on pitfalls, mistakes, traps, and stumbling blocks. Let them work things out on their own. Get out of their way.
3. Give them regular and honest feedback. Let them know how they are perceived and why. Encourage and discourage particular behaviors. Discuss weaknesses with them. Ask them questions and listen carefully.
4. Reward their competence tangibly while challenging their personal assumptions about success, thus creating dissonance. Provoke their thinking and be available when they start to question their assumptions.
5. Get them outside themselves, if possible. Include them in as much of your work-related thinking as you are able to, without turning it over to them.

Examples of interaction:

> "You are so good with budgets. Why don't you put together the first draft budget for the area this year?"

> "Remember what you said to Tom this morning about the pricing? That was a real no-no. He shouldn't hear about it at all until we get the OK from Maxine. I failed to impress upon you the chain of command on pricing, I guess. Let's go over it."

> "The reason you were passed over is that you are perceived by management as moving too fast and not getting seasoned well enough. Let's think about a development plan to remedy that in the next year."

> "You have so much energy and drive. I think you would benefit from an extra project or two."

Managing Bosses at Stage Three

1. Work very hard. Don't compete with them but work hard to fulfill all the objectives of the job. Don't ask for help unless you really need it.
2. Make them look great. Focus on success. Be their shining star and cover for them if necessary. Don't ever cross them or go over their heads on anything. In other words, be good and have a winning attitude.
3. Know their unwritten rules and follow them as much as possible. Be a good member of their team. Admit mistakes and don't cover up. Know the games and rules so as not to be caught short. Talk about things in the office that show your interest in their ideas and values. Be appreciative of perks, promotions, and favors they give you.
4. Work around the politics. Try to understand where your bosses are in the political scheme of things but stay out of the middle of it so you can gather organization-wide information for them. Gain broader contacts so you can feed useful information to them in a non-threatening way.
5. If their goals and values match yours, then hold tight! They may just move along and take you with them.

Stage Four: Power by Reflection

Managing Employees at Stage Four

They are motivated by opportunities for inner exploration.
They need time and space.

1. Encourage self-direction in their work. Give them big enough projects and enough leverage to let them fly. Respect their style and self-acceptance by not forcing another style on them.
2. Expand their views and spheres of interest. Encourage them to broaden their views by involvement in the larger company, the community, and the world.
3. Encourage their ideas and exploration. Let them have time to explore, both within and without, the areas of creativity and ideas that will enhance their work. Listen to them, befriend them, and learn from them. Watch for discouragement or self-doubt because of organizational pressure.

4. Educate them in mentoring, counseling, and true leadership ideas. Let them explore new relationships within the organization to allow their influence to be used and felt. If you are secure in yourself, involve them in managing the area you are responsible for, to the point of delegating much of your responsibility to them if you can.

Examples of interaction:

> "You know what the parameters are. Just go to it and let's meet for lunch occasionally so I can keep abreast of your discoveries. We're all looking forward to the results."
>
> "A Great Books seminar would be a wonderful development for you at this juncture. Just be sure to take the time that is necessary to do it right."
>
> "Don't let George get you down. He's wondering why he can't have the same type of project you do."
>
> "I want you to serve on the company planning committee. You'd be a valuable resource and would learn a lot about the other divisions as well."

Managing Bosses at Stage Four

1. Use these bosses as mentors. Share with them, ask questions, test out ideas, and observe them.
2. Be competent and develop your own style. Observe their styles but let them help you find your own style so you don't imitate them in a phony way. Always be honest with Stage Fours.
3. Learn the nonverbal, informal styles by which they operate. Watch and ask questions of them to fully understand their role in the organization. Let yourself live with confusion and unanswered questions as well. Be patient.
4. Keep in touch. Watch their long-term effectiveness. After you've moved along, stay involved with them and help them on projects or with information. Keep them as your colleagues.
5. Help them in their projects. If you can, catch the energy they have for moving worthwhile but difficult projects along. Let your own projects be second in pursuit of a goal that is important to them. You will learn more than you can ever imagine. Watch, listen, observe, and ask questions.

Stage Five: Power by Purpose

Managing Employees at Stage Five

They are motivated to live out their calling.
They need protection.

1. Protect them. Keep them out of the reach of people who would attack them or their ideas unmercifully. They will not protect themselves and their ideas are very useful to the organization.
2. Ask them for their insights on larger issues. Be sure to consult them on the major decisions you make because their ideas, questions, and visions will be broad and will challenge your thinking.
3. Don't leash them to rules. Let them operate as freely and openly as possible. Encourage their work and keep up with their progress. You may learn a lot from them. Let them develop their capabilities in the seemingly odd ways they choose.
4. Have long personal talks with them over lunch or after working hours. Learn all you can and capitalize on their role in your organization. Ask them how they would like to be rewarded.

Examples of interaction:

"I'd really like to know what you think about this new project idea. The numbers look good but are the idea and direction sound?"

"You can work any hours you wish. Just keep me posted on progress and call with any questions."

"Would you sit in on this manager's meeting? Something's going on and I'm not sure what."

"You said something the other day that made me think long and hard. Can we chat about it over lunch?"

Managing Bosses at Stage Five

1. Thank your lucky stars. Long-term learning is near at hand with this kind of boss.
2. Don't get frustrated with their unwillingness or inability to play by the rules. Share your anxiety with them so they can teach you the art they know. Let them empower you and don't take this responsibility lightly. Try to find your own calling if you are ready.

3. Have other contacts in the organization so you can keep a realistic perspective on the way things function elsewhere.
4. Be careful not to exactly imitate them. Learn about yourself and accept yourself as separate, developing on your own path.
5. Watch and listen. Take risks. Absorb everything and ask about the things that perplex you.

Stage Six: Power by Wisdom

Managing Employees at Stage Six

They are motivated by self-sacrifice.
They need nothing.

1. Don't try to manage them at all.
2. Keep them in the organization if you can. You can learn from them and try to understand them.

Managing Bosses at Stage Six

Who are you kidding? Most people at Stage Six got out of "bossing" long ago. Become self-directed and hope for the best.

Managing Employees at Each Stage of Power

Managing employees at stage:	What motivates them?	What do they need from managers?
One	Fear	Support, direction
Two	Learning	Safety, freedom to explore
Three	Visible signs of success	Feedback, challenge, questions
Four	Inner exploration	Time, space
Five	Living their calling	Protection
Six	Self-sacrifice	Nothing

Chapter 10
Women and Power

Power is a women's issue, whether we like it or not. We are in transition and therefore confused as to what we will become. Women are the poorest of the poor in our country and, at the same time, are increasingly taking their places in the ranks of the wealthy and ruling classes. And there are thousands in between. Women have awakened and now are stretching.

Iris Sangiuliano writes insightfully about women's lives in her classic book *In Her Time*. She says that women's lives, in general, are not predictable, that they are based more on what happens in other people's lives and are awakened by crises and shocks, not by gradually evolving development. Traditionally, women often experience a new burst of energy, a second life in their forties or fifties, generally after children are launched. A forty-year-old former homemaker and community activist, now an association executive, told me that she feels like she's twenty-five in terms of her work, just launching into her second career. Full-time career women may feel that their lives are a strange concoction, including some characteristics of women's traditional patterns and some characteristics of men's patterns, as described in Levinson's classic study, *Seasons of a Man's Life*. He describes much more predictable stages in men's lives based on longitudinal studies of many men.

Marilyn Mason, in her book *Making Our Lives Our Own*, describes six challenges for women as they develop. These go to the core of who we are as women and transform us into whole people. The six challenges are leaving home, facing shame, forging an identity, integrating sexuality, claiming personal power, and tapping into the creative spirit.

My own observation has shown that for working women, age thirty-five (plus or minus two) is an important decision-making time or a turning point. At thirty-five, women feel more compelled to pursue marriage or let it go, to decide whether to have more or any children. Careers have been or can still be launched and the commitment to career becomes more conscious. What was just a job is now a career. When women decide what they want out of life, they then begin to take themselves more seriously and to invest in themselves. They realize that there is a wider variety of possibilities for them. That is the point at which the personal power model takes on the most significance. And that's where the frustration and potential excitement begin.

In relation to the power model, women who choose full-time homemaking are in a slightly different situation from those who work outside the home. If they are totally dependent on their spouses and children for their security and self-esteem, they will have a harder time becoming personally powerful. Personal power in our society is the combination of external and internal power. Unless a homemaker also reaches into the external world (the community, the neighborhood, the school) and establishes herself, she has a hard time garnering the external power that, in combination with internal power, is necessary to become personally powerful. Emily Dickenson is a wonderful role model of a woman who was confined to her home yet reached out to the world through her magnificent poetry.

The Paradox for Women

In a provocative and timeless book entitled *Reinventing Womanhood*, Carolyn Heilbrun writes that women's movements have failed to maintain momentum in their achievements because of three factors:

1. The failure of women to bond.
2. The failure of women to imagine themselves as autonomous.
3. The failure of achieving women to resist . . . entering the male mainstream, thus becoming honorary men.

I interpret Heilbrun to mean by "bonding" that women don't stick together as closely as men do. There is an analogy that may fit here, derived from an old tradition on the east coast. It seems that crab pails do not have to be covered to prevent the crabs from escaping because when one of the crabs reaches the top of the pail, the others pull it back down in their attempts to escape too. This analogy fits some women. Not that men are always supportive of each other but women have been known to be more outwardly unsupportive of their women colleagues, particularly in the last several years when women have begun to advance in organizations. A secretary will get promoted to an exempt (salaried) job and her old friends will snub her or may even try to do her in, rather than support her and hope to keep the relationship. Some would say that is due to some women not having played on teams as children and not knowing how to compete. Another reason may be that women see the resources as limited (money, jobs, manager's time) and want to get their share, like children wanting attention from mother but knowing it has to be divided among others. It may also be related to some of our messages that the only people worth bonding with are men. Men, we were told, will help us out if we are coy and seductive. Women can be closer, more intimate friends with each other than most men can be, but we were led to believe that true intimacy is sexual and that is reserved generally for men. Sexual intimacy as a bonding force has not held up very well so there is even more confusion about whom we can trust. Women at Stages One and Two need to be able to bond particularly with other women to get support and self-esteem. At Stage Three they need each other more than ever to avoid being stuck in their masculine side although it is the stage in which they think they need others the least. Women need to feel good about being women. They need to see other women as allies and partners. We need all the help we can get and we must not be divided against each other if we are to make continuing progress.

Heilbrun's second point, of women not being able to see themselves as autonomous, seems like a paradox. We cannot bond together and we cannot stand alone. We have been taught that we need to rely on, even live through, a man. If we stand alone we are either seen as so self-sufficient that we could not find anyone, or we are undesirable. It did not cross my mind, for instance, until I was involuntarily single after many years of marriage, that being single could actually be challenging, satisfying, and positive. And then it became psychologically difficult for me to remarry even though I wanted to, because I kept asking myself, "What will I have then that I don't have now?" The only answer in the end, after all other things were compared, was a husband and a commitment. Commitment is a very important thing to consider indeed, and the commitment that comes from a public ceremony is different from a private verbal one; but the thought process was very different than it had been the first time around. So I knew I could be successfully single. I knew that I had choices and that there would be joy and pain, loss and gain. Some women, though, get swallowed up in relationships or marriage and think nothing of leaving organizations or professions for the sake of them. It's as if they are living autonomously only until their prince rescues them. Ironically, these same behaviors we've been taught to nurture in ourselves—giving up our goals for theirs, being taken care of, being a helpmate and selfless mother—are those that cause some men to lose touch with and respect for us. I am not suggesting that women should always work, but that caring for themselves is just as important as caring for their husbands and children.

Women need to learn how to be autonomous, to practice the art of being alone and self-sufficient within a community of friends, family, and coworkers. This could include making financial decisions, traveling alone, having a private room of one's own, living alone, running a business, leading an organization, or having one's own name. It means keeping part of you as an individual identity, no matter what your life circumstances are, yet doing so in a context of community. Women at Stages One and Two particularly have to be able to become autonomous in order to have a healthy self-image and a life of their own. Once a woman has learned to be autonomous, both her work relationships and her intimate relationships are usually healthier.

Thirdly, Heilbrun says achieving women cannot resist becoming honorary men by entering the male mainstream. She sees these women as dependent on men professionally, not supportive of other women, seeking social status through men, being feminine but giving up womanhood. We call them Queen Bees. I see a new breed of achieving women—those who have perhaps gone one step further. They have risen in organizations to Stage Three with all the right degrees and moves, and they think that the way to get ahead is to play the games and compete just like the "boys" do. They sacrifice their feminine side and act like men, especially in language and behavior with colleagues. It may, in fact, work for a while and bring the same rewards that men seem to be getting—money, status, success, position, control. But sooner or later the word gets out. The behavior she thought would buy acceptance is now labeled aggressive. She's called a tigress, a "tough broad," and, worst of all, a bitch or a castrating female. The pendulum has swung too far and she is losing out because she is understandably out of her element and not being herself.

The catch-22 here is that she is once again dependent on men—their style, their dress, their games, their acceptance—to provide her with the self-esteem that she can get only from being herself. And the result is anger at herself, anger at others, and anger at men for deceiving her into thinking it would work. I am not suggesting that women not take on their masculine side. On the contrary: Women must take on their masculine side in order to move through Stage Three successfully. It is wonderful, even exhilarating, to be strong and to have a mature ego. It is inspiring to be considered knowledgeable and competent. We've been waiting for this for a long time. We are treated more equally than ever before. But we must not let the pendulum swing too far for too long. Women can be strong, self-sufficient, analytic, decisive, and still be women who love, care, nurture, and feel. A woman gubernatorial candidate stated that women can be loving and tough, can wield power and have a gentle touch. Women can be good wives, mothers, and sisters and still ask for positions on boards and ballots without a contradiction.

Heilbrun says it even more strongly: "If I imagine myself (woman has always asked) whole, active, a self, will I not cease, in some profound way, to be a woman? The answer must be: imagine, and the old idea of womanhood be damned." She suggests that women "while not denying to themselves the male lessons of achievement . . . recognize the importance of taking these examples to themselves as women, supporting other women, identifying with them, and imaging the achievement of women generally."

Stage Three women will have difficulty moving beyond it if they stay in the masculine too long. They need to move to the position of being themselves, at once masculine and feminine and individual. They need to ask the broader and deeper questions like "What are my real spiritual longings? What would make me whole? What do I really want out of life and work? How can I be respected and competent and still be true to myself?" It involves finding out who you are rather than who you thought you should be in order to get ahead or prove yourself. It is more authentic and successful in the long run.

Masculine-Feminine

I've been alluding to masculine-feminine dichotomies in this chapter and throughout the book. It's time to discuss more fully what I mean by this language, since it is useful as well as irritating at times. Several books about women have referred to male systems or types (alpha) and female systems and types (beta). The two are distinctly different and we all know that the male system dominates. Women (including myself) can easily slip into the male versus female debate, asking which system is better. Some suggest that if the predominant system were only female things would be better for everyone. I think that is much too simple and perhaps even naive. Organizations are less than effective whenever any one system dominates because the whole picture is not represented. Although I agree that the masculine system predominates, I have some questions to raise about separations along male-female lines.

We get into difficulty when we categorize all men like "this" and all women like "that," because all men and women are not like all other men and women. For example, I know several successful men who have the ability to show behavior that is loving, nurturing, feeling-oriented, yet they will never be female and they are not considered feminine. On the other hand, there are many men who clearly and distinctly fit all the stereotypes of the masculine—macho, emotionally tight, strong, fearless—who are not accepted in the system. I also know many women who exhibit strong masculine traits who are not successful in the system and I know as many feminine women who are very successful in their work. So masculinity or femininity alone does not determine success. And learning the male system does not mean success either in the long run. Both masculinity and femininity have negative as well as positive aspects. So how do we work this out and find ways to work together amidst all this confusion?

One answer to the confusion is for both men and women to develop the ability to use either masculine or feminine behavior depending on what is the most appropriate for the situation. This concept of behavior flexibility is described by the term "androgyny." Androgyny is the harmonious coexistence of masculinity and femininity within the same individual (June Singer, Jungian analyst). Men and women always have been and always will be different. I applaud that. What I will call flexibility means that men can be masculine and at appropriate times can draw upon their feminine behavior; it also means women can be feminine, and at appropriate times draw upon their masculine behavior. This is obviously ideal behavior I am suggesting, for none of us would ever be totally balanced. But it gives greater ranges of behavior for those who want that. The following analogy explains this well: Each of us is born with our very own watercolor paint set containing all the colors of the rainbow. The warm colors (yellows, reds, oranges) are our feminine colors, and the cool colors (blues, greens, purples) are our masculine colors. Some people have limited themselves to using only one side of their paint set, only cool (masculine) or only warm (feminine) colors. Others use only bold colors or only muted colors. Androgynous or flexible people use all the colors in their paint set and even mix the colors as needed. This means that if the picture they are painting has in it a bold red building, they can paint that accurately. They can also paint the muted shades of gray-green in the building next to it. They may *prefer* one or the other, but they can still paint a full, representative picture. In organizations and families, flexible (androgynous) people use all their emotions; they can nurture others, make tough decisions, use their intuition, disagree openly, do kind things for others, and be strong. The key is that they know what the appropriate behavior is for the given situation and they use it. Then if they have shifted from their most comfortable "color" in order to respond, they can move back to paint where they are comfortable once again. It means men can cry and women can shout. And it means crying may not necessarily be seen as reflecting weakness but as evincing feeling and wisdom. And shouting may not be seen as evidence of aggressiveness but as rising to the occasion. As I said, this is the ideal direction in which we must continue to move to develop together and work successfully in organizations.

I am concerned that the management and leadership potential in women will be stifled if they are not able to achieve this balance and if men do not appreciate it in themselves. Effective management theory can support a flexible way of relating without sacrificing the bottom line. Some people feel that women in organizations have a greater capacity for interdependence than men do. It is threatening for men to exchange dependencies because it goes against the culture, threatens sex role differences, is seen as a sexual come-on or an invitation to take care of women. Women's most important contribution may be to role model the forms of interdependence that some men need to learn. Research shows that having people of color and women in organizations makes for better-managed companies.

I firmly believe that women will be a key factor in helping to move organizational leadership from Stages Three and Four to Stage Five (Power by Purpose). But in order to do that, women will have to stay in the system and work through Stages Three and Four without becoming honorary men and they will need support from men to do that. Men will have to be willing to learn from, as well as teach, women. They will both have to help the management and organizational norms change slowly from within to bring about flexibility, a use of both masculine and feminine, without losing either. In the future I see organizations that have been predominantly alpha (masculine) in the past now seeing the usefulness of incorporating some beta (feminine) styles, as a result of competent, strong, and feminine women who have not become alpha along the way.

Betty Friedan summed up our challenge forcefully in an excerpt from her classic book *Second Stage*. It holds true equally well today as it did over two decades ago. "We have to break through our own feminist mystique now and move into the second stage—no longer against, but with men. . . . We have to free ourselves from male power traps, understand the limits of women's power as a separate interest group and grasp the possibility of generating a new kind of power, which was the real promise for the women's movement."

Emerging Women

To talk about women as a category these days is difficult because there are so many more categories of women. We are not largely homemakers, nor all married, nor all in nearly the same income brackets as we used to be. Sangiuliano writes mostly about women who raised children and then launched another career, whereas now many more women launch careers and then decide about children. Three groups of women are rapidly emerging in our society, who I think will be very involved in different ways in the leadership and power issues of the next decade.

Ambitious Career Women: Dropping Out

The first group consists of those ambitious career women who were born in the period from the mid-thirties to the mid-sixties, who are between the old and the new worlds of women in organizations and who are not living the traditional homemaker lifestyle. A friend of mine described them as being "on the seam" between the old and the new. They have had more options than their mothers in education and opportunity and they grew up as the forerunners of today's opportunities. They were the "front line" in a lot of ways. They were super achievers and are quite successful in their careers—sometimes even more successful (position, salary) than their husbands. They are strong, independent, educated, goal-directed, determined, self-confident and career-oriented. Many of these women are single or married with no children. They simply do not have strong domestic ties. Now many of these women are once again forging new territory as senior activists.

Another part of this group has decided to work and raise children—and achieve superwoman status all the way around. This puts enormous pressures on them both at home and work, and they feel they can opt out of neither. If this were ten years hence, they might hire live-in help, but being on the seam means they want the old and new at once and at the same level. They don't want to give up their career success and they don't want to change their view of what a good wife and mother should be—so they have more guilt to deal with. None of us has the energy or stamina to carry both roles at a super level and surely not the amount these women need in order to once again lead the way by creating options that will relieve the pressure on them. This may be the time for men to do more than ponder their role as parent, to take action in a more concrete way (as many have), to really share the childrearing and homemaking. Lack of action on the part of men may lead to burned out women.

A somewhat alarming option for many professional women who have had children in their mid or late thirties is to leave their organizations altogether. I understand why this occurs because several women have told me that some organizations will not bend an inch to accommodate family responsibilities and neither will some spouses. It is sad that these women feel this is their only option at this point and it would not be their choice. Thousands of other professional women are voluntarily dropping out or dropping back for reasons unrelated to children. And it is not totally related to the glass ceiling either, at least not for the women to whom I have spoken. It has more to do with an inner gnawing that comes at odd times asking the question "Is this all there is?" These are highly successful women who leave or somehow even sabotage themselves so they can get time to sort out their lives, find more balance, and live out their deeper values. Their lives have been chronicled in a recent book by Elizabeth Perle McKenna called *When Work Doesn't Work Anymore: Women, Work, and Identity.*

It's yet unclear exactly when or where they will reemerge—but believe me, they will. Many of them are taking an inward journey into Stage Four and the Wall. They are taking the descending journey into their own shadows and finding their strength at the bottom of the well. They are developing themselves as more profound leaders. They are connecting with women in poverty and women on the fringe to forge new communities. They are developing courage. And as a result, they will transform glass ceilings into blue sky, releasing themselves and their leadership from the constraints they knew.

These women will be the leaders who emerge at Stage Five and Six and become the wisdom figures of our era. They will claim, in their late 40s, 50s, 60s, 70s, and 80s, the third stage of womanhood, the wisdom figure or the Crone. They will help us rethink what success is and how to live it out. They will revive our hope for the future. They will lead us in this new millennium in a peaceful and healing way.

Young Pacesetters

The second group of women emerging these days consists of the young pacesetters in their twenties and thirties, who have all the qualities of the older pacesetters except that they are not on the seam. They have not had to fight for what they want (yet), nor do they feel much discrimination. They simply do not have the history of their older female colleagues. All education and graduate programs are open to them, and their male peers are more like brothers than potential spouses. They make a better starting salary than many women who have been working ten years. They have almost no conception of what it's like to be poor or displaced or dependent or rebuffed by society. They are young "whippersnappers," as the saying goes. They are starting out, in fact, more even with men for the first time in history—capable, intelligent, educated, determined, motivated, and knowing no bounds.

But do they identify with other women? And what will happen to them in the next decade as they watch their older female colleagues achieve, have children later, and drop out? Will they become more balanced, more flexible, and more feminine? Or will they take the male world on and become honorary men? I think the saving grace for these women will be that which is inherent in most, if not all, women: the need for balance and for loving, caring relationships. Many of these women will face, sooner or later, the idea that life is too short to be successful if it means being lonely. Another saving grace is this: these women are motivated more by self-actualization and income than by traditional forms of power. So people at higher stages should be able to influence them by modeling androgynous behavior.

Women in Poverty

The third group consists of the growing number of women in our society who are in poverty. In fact, some writers now call poverty a female issue. These women in poverty are usually single heads of households, uneducated and unskilled. They are discontent and lack self-esteem, feeling trapped by the system in which they once believed. They are in a vicious circle, not knowing how to break out. At the same time, they shrink back from responsibility even when given it, perhaps because they don't believe anything will change. The chapter on powerlessness describes them quite well. The concern I have is that the first two groups are moving far out of touch with the third group. In the past more women could identify with "women's issues." Now it seems there are distinctly different issues for different groups of women; there is some danger that women leaders may increasingly become the enemy.

Unless high-achieving women stay connected to women on the fringes (see leadership development chapter) they will lose the essence of what it means to be women and leaders. They will lose touch with the poverty within themselves and grow calloused. We as women need to experience a new idea of community for women—a community without walls—in which women on the fringes are our mentors. Only then can we say no to poverty and victimization, in ourselves and in the culture.

Critical Issues

In summary, the critical issues I see for women in this new era are:

1. Staying true to their inner selves, no matter what their age.
2. Finding the courage to face their inner secrets and demons.
3. Finding and claiming the strengths of female community across artificial boundaries.
4. Developing leadership at Stages Four, Five, and Six.
5. Saying no to victimization and poverty, in themselves and in the culture.

Women and the Power Model in Organizations

In the introduction to this book, I pointed out which stages were feminine, which were masculine, and which stages organizations reward most. Let's refresh our memories.

Stage Two appears to be more feminine.

Stage Three appears to be more masculine.

Stages Four, Five, and Six are androgynous.

Stages Two, Three, and Four are most rewarded in organizations.

It appears from this information that women's most comfortable stage is generally the least personally powerful and the least rewarded in the organization. But the easiest move for women on the power model is the move from Stage Three to Stage Four. I affectionately call Stage Five the light at the end of the tunnel for women. My reasoning is that those qualities of Stage Five (having purpose, giving power away, using intuition, empowering and developing others, being stable, seeing visions beyond oneself) are the qualities that are androgynous, using both feminine and masculine. In fact, men have to take on their feminine side in order to move from Stage Three to Stage Four and then learn to balance both at Stage Five. So, if women in organizations can prove themselves capable of working and competing with men at Stage Three without renouncing their femininity and, if they can become better acquainted with their own style and competence through Stage Four, they can come into their own and be rewarded for their most comfortable way of being (while still using all the colors in their paint sets) at Stage Five. And they can then be the role models for men in the organization who want to move beyond their tightly prescribed masculine roles. Women and men leaders at Stage Four and Five will lead us more effectively through our new century.

Hagberg's Model of Personal Power

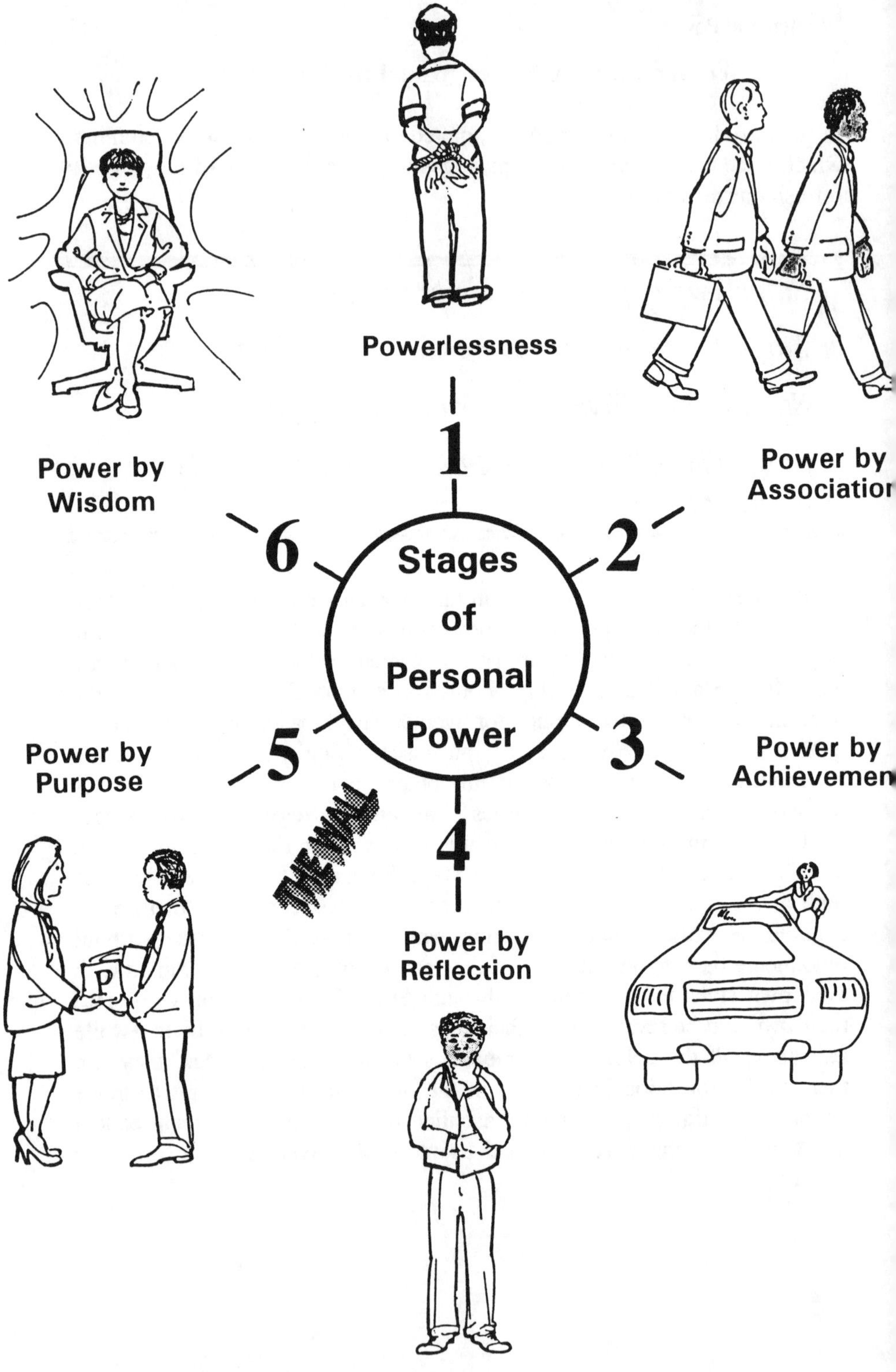

In an over-simplified summary, the power model operates in the following manner for women:

Stage One—Powerlessness

Women at this stage are powerless and dependent on others (some women, but mostly men) for almost everything, even though many of them live alone or with children. Men are our bosses, our teachers, our partners, even our knights in shining armor. We can feel secure as a result but we can also feel like children. Some of us, in fact, don't like ourselves and may even allow ourselves to be used, physically, emotionally, or intellectually, in order to obtain love or attention. To move to the next stage, we need to learn who we are, what we can do, what our worth is, and get support for ourselves, preferably from other women. This may be the hardest stage for women to break out of because of the cultural pressures on us to depend on and wait for others.

Stage Two—Power by Association

We learn that we are individuals and that we have skills and abilities. We look to role models or mentors (bosses or others) whom we can work for or emulate. We get to know the culture of the organization that sometimes frightens us and at other times gives us energy and exhilaration. We are striving for the credentials that will make us acceptable to others. We make mistakes. But we need to learn, especially from our mistakes. Deborah Tanen has written lucidly about the differences that men and women have in conversations. These differences are particularly strong when women are in Stages One or Two and men are in Stage Three. It is helpful to understand these dynamics in order to work better together.

To move to the next stage, we need to take more responsibility for ourselves, volunteer for assignments, go out on a limb, push ourselves, get degrees or credentials, set goals, take risks. At the end of this stage, we need to take on the masculine side of ourselves, those behaviors that may not come naturally and that may make us uncomfortable. This is a major turning point for women and difficult to do. To keep from getting overwhelmed women could ask themselves "What's the worst thing that can possibly happen?" If we can prepare for that and then see ourselves surviving it, we can continue to move toward our goals. Movement out of Stage Two doesn't have to entail a promotion in the organization. Much development can occur inside of us as a result of our involvement in the community or in professional associations.

Stage Three—Power by Achievement

This is our most uncomfortable stage but it can be highly rewarding. Our egos are developing and we can stand on our own, make good and tough decisions, and be independent. We enter the masculine side of ourselves requiring us to be more responsible, competitive, and energetic. The rewards are alluring—money, success, prestige, and moving up. If we buy in totally, we lose our womanhood. If we don't buy in at all, we're not accepted or respected. We can become bitter and discouraged and drop out, or we can recognize and understand Stage Three as potentially fun but certainly temporary and ultimately a necessary experience in order to move to the future stages. We need to be in Stage Three but not of Stage Three. We can get support from others who understand, avoid getting trapped in games, ask a lot of good questions, take our bumps in stride, not resort to tantrums, and be straight and clear about our feelings. To move we need to become more reflective about who we are and what it is we truly want. Can we be more our real selves now within the organization?

Second, we can try our leadership skills outside the organization, like professional organizations or community boards, thus giving us practice if and when we take on more inside the organization. We need to learn more about the scope of the organization and be clear about our strengths and limitations, fitting into that scope, not trying to do everything and burning ourselves out in our prime. Third, we need to stay closely connected to supportive women and men at all levels, those who are below us in the organization, those who are our peers, and those who are our role models and mentors. It is important to maintain contact with other women because at this stage we can too easily believe we can do it alone or that we do not need the feminine. We need to gain visibility but within our own areas of strength. One way to do this is to get involved more widely in the organization on committees or projects, always doing a very competent job.

Stage Four—Power by Reflection

At this stage we can increasingly take on our own personal style because we have proven that we understand but do not necessarily always play the game. We can take more risks and broaden our activities in the organization and in the community because we have a base of support. We're trusted, perhaps because we trust ourselves. And we trust others, delegating much to them or sharing with them. We are finding our sense of integrity, what we truly stand for as opposed to what others want us to be. We should avoid becoming haughty, self-sufficient people who think we've made it. This could be a hollow victory if abrupt changes occur in the management of the organization. Collaboration is even more important to develop now so we don't get caught in tricky Stage Three games. Our confidence should be much broader in the organization now as well because we have wider spheres of influence. Most important, we need to remember that our energy no longer goes toward our own personal gain, but toward helping others to gain what they need. Our focus must shift, or we will get stuck in reflection at Stage Four.

To move we need to reaffirm the feminine in us, our true nature as women, no matter where we are in the organization—manager, secretary, supervisor, director, clerk, engineer, president, or chair of the board. We are beginning to take on the other form of power, power for others. We need to be reflective, to assess our deepest values, to look at larger visions, to take a deep breath, to experience the Wall, and possibly observe a whole new world for ourselves. We need to let go. . . .

The Wall

The Wall is a profound place for women. They must go deep inside and let the pain and healing occur in order for the Wall experience to be a growing experience for them. Sometimes the Wall is triggered by deep disappointment at work, but more often it is triggered by a loss of relationship, by a loss of connection, or the loss of a dream. It feels like a rupture in one's soul. Women do well to get a mentor, counselor, or spiritual guide while struggling in the Wall, since the true nature of who women are in the world is forged in this dark place.

In the Wall we find out what we are really afraid of, what we ignore, and what we regret. It is not an easy path but one that is necessary to our future vitality and our compassion for others. And courage is often the result of a Wall experience that connects women not only with their pain but with their deepest heart's desire.

I am reminded again of quotes from two of my favorite writers, who write so cogently about the darkness. The first is from Frederick Beuchner's book *Now and Then*.

> Listen to your life. See it for the fathomless mystery that it is. In the boredom and pain of it no less than in the excitement and gladness: touch, taste, smell your way to the holy and hidden heart of it because in the last analysis all moments are key moments and life itself is grace.

And the other quote is from Parker Palmer, in his booklet, *Leading from Within: Reflections on Spirituality and Leadership.*

> Great leadership comes from people who have made that downward journey through violence and terror, who have touched that deep place where we are in community with each other, and who can help take other people to that place. *That* is what great leadership is all about.

Great leadership is forged in the Wall.

Stage Five—Power by Purpose

Stage Five women are in the most comfortable stage of all for them, although it is decidedly less secure than Stage One. We are able to channel energy to others in the organization, give things away, delegate more, be role models for men, but only as we fully accept ourselves and the struggles we face in organizations that reward Twos, Threes, and Fours. We will feel at home and free ourselves but out of sync with many other people. They may misread our motivations. We know our life calling, our inner aims and goals. And these things go beyond us, our egos, our reputations, and the organization. But particularly, our thinking goes beyond our egos. We draw our strength from a source beyond ourselves. Stage Five women do not calculate where a decision will get them but how it will affect others and whether it is the best for all in the long run. In fact, they involve a lot of others in their decisions, teaching and learning as they go. We trust our judgment and we are not aroused by promises of money, titles, or power plays; or threats of losing these things. We are part of a much larger life plan in which our work efforts now take their proper part. We involve ourselves in the larger world, in visions for the organization or professional groups. We mentor men, we nurture others, without knowing where it will lead, and without having to. We may have gotten pretty far in the organizational sense, or we may not have, but we like ourselves and accept ourselves. And we enjoy respect from others for our competence and integrity. To move we need to relax.

Stage Six—Power by Wisdom

Stage Six is a wonder to behold in women. We are personally purposeful but in a quiet sort of way, integrated and calm because life is best when we try the least. We have internal calm and external respect based on the painful and joyous experiences of life that have formed us. We see paradox and we love it because we know too much to believe otherwise. We have nothing to prove, no one to impress, and our community is the world. We care not for titles or even for glory. We're victorious because we're human and can fully admit it. Our behavior is truly our own and the masculine/feminine dichotomies seem to have slipped away somewhere a long way back. We say what we think and it is usually wise because we are not trying to be wise anymore. We are at peace with ourselves. We may believe strongly in causes or questions or ideas and work valiantly for them but our identity is not tied up in the ends, only the means. No one fights us for control because we have voluntarily given up control to others and our need for self-control long ago. Now we just are. To move, we need to enter into another level of reality.

Women and Leadership

Many women are natural leaders. We just don't think we are because we don't tend to lead in the traditional Stage Three ways that are so accepted. So we lack confidence in our ability to guide others, particularly men. I would strongly encourage women to read carefully the chapters on leadership and power and take note of the behaviors and styles of leadership at each stage and the development process for leaders. Women can learn much from men about leadership at Stage Three but, to go beyond it to true leadership, they must learn from each other, from themselves, and from the few role models, both male and female, who are at those higher stages. The worst thing women could do is to accept a lesser model of leadership that is evident in many people today. Women, being less constricted by role and expectations at this point in time, have the potential to go beyond the familiar territory, to be models for others of the way true leaders (Stage Four and beyond) behave. It will be challenging but also frustrating. For example, one woman manager told me that she likes to motivate her employees by mostly praising them and fueling their energy, then asking them to critique themselves. She feels this style is successful in the long run but takes longer and requires more patience. She gives them responsibility and then has to teach them how to use it day after day. Her male boss tells her she's not tough enough, that she should critique and criticize her people because only then will they really learn to toe the line. She has tried that but she comes across as a phony, and her people resent the feedback. She is trying to get people to be more self-reflective and responsible but her boss wants short-term results.

Women in organizations are beginning to come together to discuss among themselves what power and leadership mean in their organizations. This is a wonderful first step in breaking down the barriers that separate women from each other and encourage competition. Here are some questions to use to stimulate discussion of the power stages and leadership:

1. Which stage of personal power do you identify with most in your work?
2. What are the predominant values in your organization? In other words, what is the organizational culture? What power stage is valued the most?
3. How can you keep from becoming an honorary man in the most masculine sense of the concept?
4. Have you ever embarked on an inner journey to find out what else is emerging in you? What did you find?
5. Are you spiritually connected to a Higher Power? What difference does it make in your life, your leadership?
6. Have you ever considered consciously developing Stage Four or Five leadership qualities? Would you ever consider doing this with other women? Why? Why not? What stands in your way?
7. What examples of courage can you identify with in yourself? How did it feel to be courageous?
8. Are you consciously mentoring other women? What is the experience like?
9. Have you experienced a vocational calling? A passion in your work, volunteer life, or personal life? What is it?
10. How does a true leader act in your organization?
11. How can you develop your own leadership qualities?

I strongly encourage women to meet together, preferably with some higher stage women present, to discuss their own feelings about leadership honestly and sincerely and to discourage women from getting stuck as honorary men in organizations. The future leadership of America is being formed through the values and behaviors that are being learned right now; if women are the hope for a different kind of leadership, they must begin to develop further now.

Chapter 11
Men and Power

Men and power have been, in most cultures, synonymous from the beginning of recorded history. As children, wherever we turned the power of the family, neighborhood, community, state, and country was in the hands of men. Or if they didn't possess it, they certainly desired it, and they moved with great speed and deliberateness to gain it. I do not mean to say there were not women of such mind; but we have witnessed mostly men pursue power throughout history and they continue to do so today. What do they work so hard to obtain and retain? Why do they want it so much? Why are they so afraid if someone else gets more? What dilemmas does it bring them? What are the stages of power that tend to represent men more than others?

Men in our culture—particularly white men—are in the middle of a deep dilemma. They are the most externally powerful group of people in the world; they know the formula for success; they are privy to the old boys' club; they have all the advantages of strength and skill; they still make a lot more money than women; they have visibility. At the same time many of them feel trapped in their role with very few other options in life, having to compete forever to get to the glorified top, and they are very unhappy. The dilemma is that they can't figure out why they're unhappy. They have or are headed for all the things that society has promised men who do well. Yet something is wrong and they're unclear about what it is. No one feels sorry for them because, after all, they're on top and they should be happy. So characteristically they twist and turn and about the time of mid-life reveal their deep-seated dilemma by leaving their wives, losing their jobs, moving away, becoming twenty-five again, getting ill, being miserable, or dying.

The problem is that the dream they thought they had bought into freely is a myth. They are in much more tightly prescribed boxes than most women are and they don't know how to get out. The prescription for men is to get education or skills to land a job at twenty, work with few breaks until age sixty-five, and then die within five years. They look at the dream, the right position with all the responsibility and authority and power, the right salary, the right home in the right place, the right spouse, and the right kids. And somewhere along the way they discover (or more accurately try to hide the fact) that they either do not really want or cannot really achieve the dream that the family, their peers, the community, and they themselves had fostered for them. So they feel like failures because they are not perfect. And that is the first big part of the myth that says that perfection is desirable and that men surely can attain it because of all their opportunities. The second and equally big part of the myth says that being perfect means being all the "successful" things in our culture and that ultimately these successes bring satisfaction or happiness or something good.

So most men who face this dilemma just take a peek at it and find it too awesome to investigate. They close off the part of themselves that is beginning to ask questions, the part that is getting suffocated in the narrow box, and they plod along complaining of something wrong in the organization or of their inability to change because they're too invested already. To look at the unknown and to sort out and unravel the long-term myths with which they have learned to operate is just too frightening and confusing. Also the culture prescribes men's behavior and emotions. They are to be characteristically strong and not to show emotion. Looking at the dilemma and the myths would force them to look at their real selves, their inner lives, perhaps even to feel some new emotions, and that is very new and frightening.

It is one thing for me to explain to men that external power is not enough and that men in our culture may have to move beyond the traditional expectations they have of themselves; it is quite another thing to be a man wondering whether he will lose all he has gained, or lose what it means, in his mind, to be a male. For most men, to be male is to be powerful, to have the success and symbols of external power. And that power is synonymous with men; it seems that power was and is, in fact, a way to describe men and to consider taking it away from them is, in fact, to ask them to give up their primary identity. As we all know, any change is difficult. It implies giving up something, a difficult task even for the strongest. Let's examine how the quest for external power in men became so entrenched and what power means to men.

The pursuit of power, and therefore control, is something men are all taught from their earliest days as boys. This gets played out in competition with siblings, fights on the block, in sports, and in school. The message is clearly that if they are the best at whatever they do, they will be respected and, in turn, will be successful. They hear this message throughout their youth and adult lives and it continues to haunt them until they die. The irony of it all is that the things they have managed to master, control, or accumulate do little to give them the satisfaction that they were told to expect. We all know of people who are the best at what they do but still find themselves unsatisfied with life. These people have been accumulating things that they were told would bring them much satisfaction and peace. And they found that these things did, in fact, bring them satisfaction but not all that they had hoped for. More important, the attainment of these goals tended to bring satisfaction for only short periods of time. Therefore, it became necessary to continue to reach for more in hopes they would get back the feelings of accomplishment, satisfaction, and, in turn, success. The cycle resembles addiction to drugs, alcohol, relationships, etc. And we all know the result of such addiction.

By acquiring external success men seek the assurance that they are in control of their lives and the lives of their loved ones. They want assurances that they will be able to determine their fate and most important, that they will avoid pain from outside forces. They understand intellectually that this is impossible because they see people of all socioeconomic levels experiencing pain and anguish regardless of their station in life. And yet they still work hard to be more successful so everything will be all right. At the base of this is their feeling of powerlessness, the fundamental fear of not being important, cared for, and loved by others. These emotional needs far outweigh their intellectual understanding of their folly. *So the pursuit of success is, in fact, the pursuit of themselves as worthwhile human beings.* They, in fact, feel it is their responsibility to prove to the world that they are worthwhile human beings. This can also turn them against those who are not able to "pull themselves up by their boot straps" and cause them to treat others as less worthy, the basis of prejudice of all sorts. They believe that the more they can own, the higher they can climb, the more money they can make, the more powerful they are. They want this external success badly because without it they think they will not be accepted and respected and, therefore, they will be nothing. Again, the focus is obviously on the externals without any reference to internal factors.

The origin of man's quest for power and success is found in the identification of the family as the most important organizational group in any society. Traditionally, man is described as the head of the family with primary responsibility for providing and protecting it from outside forces. All other members of the family group are given areas of responsibility only if they, as members, are in support of the family growth and protection and, more importantly, if they are in support of the man who is charged with being the leader and the person ultimately in control. If a man is in this role or aspires to it then he must begin early to prepare himself for it: get good job training, or get a degree, get a good job, work hard to move up the organization to a higher position, get a bigger office, a higher title. All of this puts him in a better position to be the leader of the family unit. Sadly, even if he does get to this high level and salary, he will not be guaranteed health, happiness, or peace of mind, but he will have a big house, office, and fat checkbook.

The point in all of this is that the culture calls men to find and accumulate power so they can accomplish their role with the family. But in the meantime, the family has changed. Only seven percent of American households are rated as the traditional form, with father the working head and mother and children at home. More than fifteen percent of households are headed by women. Forty-five percent of women between ages twenty-five and fifty-five are now single. And the economic situation in our country in the last twenty years has left the real income of middle-class and lower-class people flat when adjusted for inflation, which means that couples are under tremendous pressure to have a dual income just to stay in the middle class. This economic reality puts more pressure on men to stay at Stage Three—or get stuck there—and diminishes the chances that men will explore something beyond Stage Three.

If men were to focus more on finding their own sense of inner peace and balance, they would ultimately be contributing more to the strength of the family. To move from Stage Three, men must learn to think of power and success without control and of empowering others as a superior way of collectively gaining more for everyone concerned.

Sam Keen has aptly described the journey of men in his classic book *Fire in the Belly*. He describes a new kind of heroism with different virtues than tradition prescribed, but every bit as powerful. His virtues include wonder, empathy, moral outrage, right livelihood, friendship, enjoyment, communion, husbanding, wildness, and a heartful mind.

Emerging Groups of Men

While the opening scenario of this chapter applies to white men in our culture in general, it does not take into account some important groups of men who are not experiencing the myths and the dilemmas in the same ways. These three groups have either not bought into the myth of success and power, have tried to avoid it, are struggling with a different form of it, or have overcome it.

Gentle Men

The first of these groups is the one that was mentioned in Chapter Two, those men we will call gentle men, those who are, as a book title suggests, "too gentle to live among wolves." They do not express and adhere to the values of the predominant culture of males, and they do not fit into the prevailing organizational structure or display its symbols. They feel out of the mainstream and more than a little lonely at times. They do not accept the macho image of themselves as males. On the other hand, they are quite aware of and sensitive to the feminine side of themselves. It's as if they developed the feminine side before or in place of the masculine because macho looked like the only male alternative, and they didn't want that. It appears they are in Stage Two because they see no way to be Stage Three in our society and not be competitive or macho—almost the reverse problem of the men in Three who can't imagine moving to Four and looking at themselves reflectively.

The poet Robert Bly describes the problem for these gentle men in his classic book, *Iron John*, saying that while they are more thoughtful than most men, they are not more free. He says they are unhappy even though they're ecologically superior to their fathers and sympathetic to the harmony of the universe. This is because they have little energy in them. They are life-preserving but not life-giving. Bly uses a Grimm's fairy tale to illustrate the process these men need to go through to once again regain their balance. It speaks of making contact with Iron John, a wild man, who lives in the bottom of a water hole. He is not the macho man but the "deep masculine," the primitive, instinctive male, who is under water. The key to understanding and releasing the Iron John within all men lies with their mothers, or more succinctly, it consists of letting go of their mothers. This is a slow, painful task, done with other men, Bly insists, and results in "an energy of forceful action undertaken, not without compassion, but with resolve."

These men have been disserved, in a sense, because they are unaware of a third option—of going beyond the traditional masculine and their own feminine to a more seasoned, strong but sensitive masculine side. The women in their lives have reinforced their gentle side by rewarding them for it. These women have generally been strong, energetic women, mother-figures, in whose presence these men have not allowed themselves to develop. "Getting in touch with the wild man means religious life for a man in the broadest sense of the phrase," says Bly. And their energy needs to be revitalized. They need to "make a connection in their psyches to their kala energy—which is just another way to describe the wild man at the bottom of the pond. If they don't, they won't survive."

My sense of this process in terms of the power model is that this group of men needs to define Stage Three for themselves in their own masculine terms, not in the terms of the macho male under which we still operate. They need to define the characteristics of themselves and their wildness and then behave in their new masculinity—as true men. Only then will they be able to go on to see the integration of their newly found masculine with their feminine and respect them both, a task not unlike that for women who are moving into Stage Four. The role models for this growth in men are just beginning to emerge.

Here are a few ideas that gentle men might try in order to define their own masculine terms.

- Find a mentor or a group of men who you respect and who exemplifies your idea of a mature man. Spend time with them and ask them how they developed.
- Have a long talk with your friend, boss, spouse, and mentor about your skill areas, strengths, values, personality traits, blocks to effective work, and possible directions in life or in work.
- Decide to do at least two new things that you have never done before and that constitute some kind of a risk for you. Record how you felt in preparation for them, during the event, and after. What were the results? What did you learn about yourself, about taking risks?

Men of Color Who Are Professionals

Men of color, especially African Americans and Hispanics, are emerging as a vibrant force in our culture, but until recently they have not been sufficiently recognized or given credit for their accomplishments in our culture. They are slowly finding their way among the conflicting values and cultural pressures of organizations and grappling with the issues of not only what it means to be a man in our culture but, more important, what it means to be a person of color. Some interesting issues come to the fore when one thinks about men of color and personal power in our culture. I am referring to professionals, men who have achieved some respect through education, skill, and organizational experience and who have acquired positions of some responsibility as a result. I am focusing comments on this group because in achieving a status in the academic, organizational, or political world, they have a sense of the kinds of success to which most men aspire.

Their issue, in a word, is confusion. They are caught between the male-dominated values of the organization (and the frustration of trying to be like white men to be accepted) on the one hand and, on the other hand, their own values, norms, and culture, many of which they are proud and want to maintain. The question is, how much do they buy into the dominant culture in order to be accepted, powerful, and successful? Once black became beautiful, for instance, it was not as necessary to be white to be taken seriously, and with that increase in self-confidence came the possibility of becoming more equal. Becoming more equal unfortunately usually means becoming more like the majority, the powerful, thereby possibly losing what it means to be different. Being assimilated, we sometimes call it. So do they learn to play the game the same way or do they develop their own rules? Will they be any happier, more satisfied when they become part of the system and take on the responsibility for it? Aren't they too still defining themselves according to white men's definitions by relating their success to white male standards? Many are asking the question at this time, "Who are we, anyway? And what do we want to be?"

These are challenging questions and challenging times. This group of men has more potential perhaps than most other groups to help men change the way they do things. History reveals that those who have been governed by others and have gained power do not necessarily act in a more humane way, nor more democratically than the way in which they were governed, *unless the emerging leaders are thoughtful and wise.* Professional men of color have the opportunity to be different types of leaders, just as women have that potential. It depends on the kind of people they develop into and whether they become just like the system from which they are emerging. They can be personally powerful by incorporating Stage Three without getting caught up in it. They are men in our culture who have had a different way of viewing the world. They understand not being on top but still having self-worth and valuing things other than wealth and fame. Martin Luther King, Jr. would be an example, as would Colin Powell, who chose not to run for the presidency and was, in my opinion, one of the sanest voices to emerge in the early days of the tragedy of September 11.

They can be an example of men in organizations who do not all want external power, whereas women can't do that for men in the same way. Men of color can show white men that differences between men are widespread and that there are other ways to be and still be masculine. They can be one form of a new model for the future. At the same time white men must get over their deep-seated fear and insecurity, which cause them to behave paternalistically or hatefully towards men of color.

By describing professional men of color as a hopeful emerging group I do not mean to overlook the doleful situation confronting many of them (and women) in our culture. On the whole, they still have the highest rate of just about everything: unemployment, discrimination, health problems, crime, and educational failure. The situation for most is still appalling, yet the emerging professional leaders who do not forget their own roots and their identity are a hope for the future.

Integrated Males

A small but growing number of men have done battle with the crises of integrity and ego (the major struggles on the way to inner power) and are emerging, not as new men but as whole men. They do not have to measure themselves by the traditional symbols of power because their worth comes from the inside. It doesn't matter what positions they hold because they know their life purpose goes beyond their work. They do not feel they are weak because they are sensitive and alive to their feelings, yet they do not hide behind their feelings either. They have a full range of behaviors at their disposal, firmness and resolve as well as compassion and caring. They use the behavior that is appropriate for the time. They have passed perhaps the biggest hurdle in their lives: finding out and being who they are rather than who they thought they had to be.

They have grappled with the myths of men's lives and accepted themselves with all their shadows instead of attempting to be perfect. They are real. They are thoughtful. They are becoming wise.

The lingering dilemma for them is to become comfortable with another way to be in our culture. Giving up the glory and would-be success for an uncharted alternative is frightening and unpredictable as well as exciting. They ask, "If our leaders, our 'big men,' are not just those in positions of power, then how will I emerge as a leader in the new model? What does it mean to not be the head of a group and to still lead? What if I am in a leadership position but see it as enabling others rather than myself? Or what if I just want to be, to read and talk and touch people and ask questions and love and not take on any more responsibility? What role is there for this "whole" me? I'm not sure what the road is to this place I'm on my way to. Perhaps I'm carving my own road!" The most important step is stepping out before they know what the future holds. That is the risky adventure for each one of them.

Whole men know many of the questions, but they do not have to have the answers. They are confused at times but find that not having to know is part of the delight too. Many of these men credit women at some point along the way for being instrumental or even critical to their continued growth. Many women who trust their intuition and deep wisdom can encourage men to explore more deeply the new ways to be beyond Stage Three. A few other men who crossed the threshold into Stage Four can also be very instrumental in showing men that there is life after attaining the visible symbols of success. But in the end, the process of movement is a solitary one. Whole men will tell you that it is a lonely, long, continuous struggle to uncover the long-capped feelings, let go of the myths, believe in another way even though it's not always apparent, and give up power and control for peace of mind. Ironically, another kind of power—inner power, which is so much stronger—is the result, but it is definitely not clear to Stage Three men that anything is beyond where they are. To think so would be heresy to the male club. The new male community includes friendships and vulnerability with each other beyond the sports or work buddy model. Men hunger for friendship.

The integrated males can risk more than ever because they have principles that cannot fail. They can make surprising moves in their lives because they are not afraid of losing. There is very little to lose anyway. Life is an adventure, a peaceful, empowering walk on one's own real path. As Thoreau says, "Dwell as near as possible to the channel in which your life flows."

I recently met a man who is a great example of a whole man. I'll call him Joe. His story begins with a major crisis in his life twenty years ago. He was ousted from his job as a minister when he told his conservative congregation he was getting a divorce. It was a very painful time. He was wondering what he would do next with his life when a man he knew invited Joe to help him run his business. He leaped at the chance and started right in. But only a few months into the job the friend got deathly ill, so Joe stepped into the leadership role, without much experience, and ran the business—successfully. The friend miraculously healed and came back to work in six months. As a reward for Joe's work in saving his business, his friend found a way to fund a franchise of the same business for Joe to run himself. It was fun for a few years but something else gnawed at Joe; something deep inside that he wanted to work on.

Over time Joe remarried and found out his wife was interested in the business and great at running it. This gave him a chance to pursue what his heart really wanted. Now he is working on a doctorate and has found and adapted a conflict resolution process that helps troubled churches approach conflict in a healing and healthy way. This is his passion and his calling in the world. He is happier than he's ever been and he is not only healing his own past but helping the larger church with the nagging issue of unresolved conflict.

Critical Issues

If men are to go beyond the stage at which the myth is complete (Stage Three) and emerge into something else, they must face or reconcile several critical issues. For each man it may be a different issue or the struggle may be different, but nevertheless there will be no movement if there is no integrity crisis. For many men there will be no crisis because there is no desire or need to move. Some men have bought so strongly into the myth of male as powerful and in control that they are hardened. Others are stuck at Stage Three because it has replaced their own sense of self-worth. Others have closed off their feelings thoroughly because of the fear of facing painful memories or the fear of getting hurt.

We need men and women in families, organizations, and governments who lead out of personal power not position power. To do that, the crisis of integrity that is encountered between Stages Three and Four must be faced; to do that, some of the following issues must be addressed.

Self-Worth/Security

Unfortunately, many men view themselves as worth something only to the extent that they make a continuous and rising wage and get promoted to new positions along the way. They know they are good people because they do well at work. And the better they do the more secure they feel. The more secure they feel, the greater the price they pay because they depend on the ongoing security and benefits resulting from their work. The term "golden handcuffs" is descriptive of the reason men and women can't leave or even consider changing what they're doing on the job.

Until self-worth and security can be generated from within, no matter what job, health status, or position one holds, there is no true self-worth and security. Self-worth disappears the minute any of the safety elements are taken away. The sad thing about men and retirement is that many men identify so strongly with their work that they die within a few years after they cease to work. As the adage goes, "If you are what you do, then when you don't you aren't." If there is no interest or identity within oneself or outside of work, the gap that retirement brings is too wide to bridge.

So the issue here is getting self-worth from inside. But this is not an easy task. It involves soul searching, self-knowledge, and self-acceptance. It is a daily practice of accepting the bad with the good and believing in the worth of who one is, not the worth of one's work or place in society. It is a practice in humility but also one of forgiveness of self and thankfulness for self. It is spiritual work. It is a slow and constant task, often brought on by unexpected loss of one of the security props one was holding on to. Finding self-worth requires admitting what their high achievement covers up, and feeling the pain that is lurking at their center. It involves exploring the myths about masculinity from the culture as well as uncovering the pain in their family when they were kids. That work is best done with a professional counselor. It is difficult but it heals the soul.

However or whenever it happens, the lasting effects are known. The basic question for testing self-worth is this: If all I have was to be taken away and all I had left was my core (my personhood, my psyche, my spiritual self without any of the trappings of family, work, or home) would I still be a worthwhile person? If the answer is yes, in behavior and in feelings, then one's self-worth is indeed emanating from the inside. If the answer is no, then those things that one does, has, or controls are the means to self-worth. Changing that is a long, slow spiritual process, which only begins when one admits that self-worth is important and that one is willing to risk uncovering all the layers that separate the real worthwhile person from the current facade.

Vulnerability

This is a word that most men do not even like to hear, for all its connotations seem negative. To them, being vulnerable means to not be in control, to be weak, to let someone else have the advantage. In fact those things are true about vulnerability. But that's precisely the advantage. Men learn how to relinquish control by letting go of having to know and be in charge and by allowing themselves to be known emotionally, which is the finest kind of vulnerability. Yet I've never seen men squirm and struggle more than when they are emotionally vulnerable. It's easier to lose on the gridiron or the battlefield than to break down and admit to emotional needs and fears.

Yet men do have deep and strong emotional needs and fears. The more aware they are of them, the sooner they can understand the role these underlying feelings have in their behavior and in their lives. Two elements seem to be necessary in order to be vulnerable. Both are difficult to accept. One is that one cannot be vulnerable alone. Being vulnerable means to be in danger of being wounded or open to attack. The fear in being deliberately vulnerable with other persons is that they will get you when you are down. They will attack your weak spot and hurt you. Although this is indeed possible, in every case I've known exactly the opposite occurs. People respond to honest vulnerability with sympathy, love, or with their own vulnerability in return. And the relationship usually becomes closer or stronger as a result. To be vulnerable with another is to be intimate with another.

The second element in vulnerability for men is even more difficult to achieve. They must give up the myths and the constricting boxes they have been living in. To do that requires discussing and understanding what it means to be in the boxes and what it means to accept the myths and to leave them. It means fear, anger, disappointment, loss of meaning, loss of love, loss of prestige, loss of pride, or abandonment. Whatever the constraints are, they have to be put out on the table, to be exposed for what they are and what they mean. That is vulnerability.

The Meaning of Strength

To be strong in the culture of men is to be the one who is always responsible and can be counted on. The strong one never flinches, never cries or buckles, one who shows appropriate kindness but never compassion. The strong one is impregnable and indestructible. Those descriptions sound like a stone fortress, certainly not a human being. But then, some would say, men are not raised to be human beings; they're raised to be strong. Men, in fact, get robbed of half of the experience of life if they accept this as the only way to be. Being vulnerable and in need of love and care is a comforting experience, that of going back to childhood with the memory of a parent who indeed knew how to care for and nurture the "helpless part" of each of us. Before we could grow up we all needed to learn to be small and some of us cannot accept the fact that a small child is still in all of us that wants to be loved. Some of us did not get that nurturing as a child and have never been able to admit or accept it. Yet we need it desperately. So the cover-up continues.

To always be strong means to lose sight of the humanness of us all, the part that needs someone else's arm, loves someone else's warmth and touch, that secretly craves the times when we don't have to be in charge. To be human means to be in charge sometimes, to not be so strong at other times, and to be weak once in a while too. There is nothing honorable in people who pride themselves in not shedding a tear over a close friend's or family member's death. It is a denial of perfectly understandable and acceptable feelings. To deny them is to stash them away and be haunted by them in the future.

Men need to redefine male strength as the ability to be human and responsible but also to feel and to be able to accept love, care, and nurturing from others. True strength comes from deep within, tempered by experience and fueled by a wide range of emotions. The pathway that will bring men to this new strength is fatherhood. This means coming to terms with how they were not adequately fathered and how they, in turn, father. Men need mentors in order to find their own fathers again and to find the nurturing fathers within. It is a path to liberation.

Leadership

Men need to seriously rethink the form of leadership they have been practicing in the family, the community, the organization, and the world. It has not been of sufficient integrity to enable us to live together peacefully and it threatens to destroy us. People in this country do not trust power because they say it is always self-serving. That is why people always want a balance in power, even if they dislike one side or the other. The American people increasingly mistrust the organizations that are dominated by personalities or can be led by a single person. That describes the shadow side of Stage Three leadership precisely and, until self-service is not a major motivator of power, we will not have integrity in our political and organizational leadership.

So the whole or integrated men, the professional men of color, and the women beyond Stage Three may be our major hope in redefining what leadership is and how it behaves in practice. They may begin soon to be the models for the transforming, empowering leadership we will require for being successful in this new century. The chapter on leadership describes how people at each stage lead and it stresses the concept of integrity as the key factor necessary for the emergence of true leadership.

Since most men in our culture are still scrambling for Stage Three, it leaves a lot of work undone. But since men have hold of the reins in our culture, I suspect the leadership revolution will go on among them, with those whole men and professional men of color moving themselves surreptitiously around in organizations, acting differently than the Threes, but remaining strong and competent in the organization. Slowly they will move to Stage Five behavior, not by any mandate but by the process of their own development, until the norms eventually begin to change. It will take men working with men, often aided and abetted by women who have moved beyond Stage Three, to make any changes in the future. There are no tricks, no techniques, no magic clues to making organizational leadership change. It takes individuals changing themselves and then acting differently wherever they are, treating people differently, asking different questions, questioning policies, working unceasingly on issues, seeing a vision, and acting in everyone's best interest. It means becoming a Stage Four or Five individual and living accordingly. It means being alive, being lovingly detached, being sensitive to self yet putting more energy into empowering others, working to serve, not living to work. It is a transformed individual who transforms others, and together they transform organizations and countries. Nothing happens that is not thought of by someone and agreed upon by others. And the most profound way of changing others is by personal contact.

Men Moving Beyond Stage Three

There are various ways for men to become unsettled at Stage Three. Sometimes an outside event catapults them into thinking things over. At other times, the satisfaction they thought they'd feel when success arrived as a result of being a provider, of having a good position, or of acquiring the necessary possessions just wasn't enough. Somehow they were still disappointed, in themselves or in the things they'd accumulated. The material things didn't continue to bring the kind of acceptance that they'd been seeking. The next step for them is to try by some means to understand what is blocking them from the peace and satisfaction they want in life. Many possibilities are available but it is important they understand the process. I have described one such process in the chapter on Leading from Your Soul (Chapter 12). Whatever process they use to confront the move beyond Stage Three, whether counseling, reading, listening, or writing, the real process begins in earnest when they stand face-to-face with themselves. That usually requires a personal guide with much patience and wisdom. Some men choose to make changes by going to a personal counselor, a trained person who can talk out the situation and help them gain insights. Let's explore this path that many men take.

Counseling is a logical path because it is difficult to be objective or insightful enough to see oneself as others can. One of the first things many Stage Three men discover in counseling is that they are insensitive to the needs or feelings of an individual, of a group, or of an organization. So they work first on becoming more sensitive, more aware of their behavior, more in touch with their feelings. They must understand more about themselves and slowly let their feminine side emerge as a legitimate part of themselves.

Many men leave counseling at this point, assuring themselves that if they are just nicer and more aware of others they will be accepted and loved and satisfied. But frequently they discover that this, too, falls short of the satisfaction they now so desperately want. They return to counseling, thoroughly discouraged, only to find that the real search now, at the next deeper layer, is the search for themselves—for the self that goes beyond masculine or feminine to the core of one's being. In this search they find out that they are multifaceted and that real satisfaction comes from standing face-to-face with their shadows, their fears, and their unhealed wounds. Then, and only then, can they really heal and accept themselves. Then they are able to go outside themselves to meet the needs of others from a deeper base.

Males and the Stages of Personal Power

There is one stage of personal power that men identify with more than women do. This is Stage Three. Men move quickly through Stage One and usually stop off only temporarily at Stage Two on the way to Stage Three. And the most difficult transition for men to make is the move from Stage Three to Stage Four. Here is a brief description of the ways men behave at each stage of power.

Stage One

Most men quickly move out of Stage One due to their position in society and in organizations. However, there are still large groups of men in our culture and in the world who are powerless compared to other groups of men. Men of color who are poor or uneducated, the disabled, prison inmates, the aged, and the chemically dependent are some of the less powerful groups. Men who are seen as powerless are those men who are emasculated, who are not in control of their lives or the lives of others, or who are barely able to be in control due to poverty, lack of education, discrimination, or illness. They are not able to perform the functions they have expected of themselves and are dependent on someone or something else for their survival. Of course, anyone who has not embraced their own particular disability or addiction is also powerless.

Stage Two

Men at Stage Two are usually just passing through the stage on their way to the next. They are finding their way, learning the ropes in the world, and getting ready to take it on. They often see this time as their warm-up period, preparation time during school, or their apprenticeship. Once they've paid their dues, they can go on to where the real action is.

Apprentices in the trades are one example of Stage Two, and medical residents are another.

Another type of Stage Two male is the one described in the section on gentle men. They are stuck at Two because they are pseudo-innocent and passive. They think lofty thoughts and care about the right things but they bring no energy to the world. They have ceased to grow, to develop, and to confront their masculine side, and now it's too scary to do so.

Stage Three

This is the spot on the model where most men think they ought to be or wish they were—their dream-come-true stage. They are competent, respected, and show they can make a difference. They achieve recognition and rewards. They are finding their American Dream. To be at Stage Three is to be successful and in control, to be the ultimate that men in our culture wish to be. It is satisfying and allows men to achieve what they have worked so long to attain.

Stage Four

For many men, moving into Stage Four is definitely the most difficult of all transitions, even though they increasingly desire this stage. Stage Four requires an inner journey, a deeper questioning, while at the same time maintaining the outward competent facade. It means being reflective and honest, willing to let go of some of the symbols that have for so long dominated men's lives. It is scary and new. The crisis is one of integrity: each man must find out who he is instead of who others want him to be. Men must explore their feminine side before they can proceed through Stage Four. The qualities of self-reflection, of finding one's own style as different from the organization, of learning to use one's intuition make many men feel as if they're losing whatever had made them strong in the first place. It is a deep and often frustrating dilemma but it always alters the way in which men live henceforth.

The Wall

The Wall puts men face to face with their shadows. If they deal with them, they will emerge as transformed, whole men. Usually their shadows have to do with their identity in the work world, but there is frequently something underneath wanting to be healed, like a childhood pain, an addiction, or a family pattern.

In the example of Joe, the minister, he was very successful in his ministry until his marriage dissolved. He was judged by his congregation as not fit to lead them if he could not keep his own marriage together. The divorce started an inward and outward journey of identity loss, shame, and unemployment. This long dark time eventually led to his new life and in that life he found his deepest heart's desire, healing the church in conflict. The work he does now came directly out of his own story.

Stage Five

The crisis to overcome in moving to Stage Five is one of ego. This is a different type of task altogether, because no one warned men that after searching to build up their egos and self-esteem they would then be asked to give them up. How can anyone justify being a king of the culture and not have all the ego gratification that goes along with it? It's hard to voluntarily give up something that has provided so much security for so long. And letting go of ego goes hand in hand with finding one's life calling, that for which one lives. For men to give up control of their lives to a purpose in life larger than themselves is a monumental task, especially when they may not have had such experiences before.

Most of us can understand Stage Five if we think about how love works, about how it multiplies only when we give it away freely. To have love is to give it away. Men who truly understand what all of this means and live it usually find it necessary to have a guide because it is so easy to slip back into controlling themselves and others. They feel so out of the mainstream of men that to be comfortable with the inner peace and vision of Stage Five almost requires them to look weak, weird, not strongly motivated, not on the cutting edge. It takes real courage to be a Stage Five male in our culture but it also signifies potential wisdom as well as leadership. Men in this stage make other men uncomfortable. Stage Five men have tapped deeply into their personal spirituality and have emerged fearless and at the same time peace filled. They call us to non-violence as a lifestyle—an eerie call in a turbulent world. They are servant leaders in the most profound sense.

Stage Six

Men at Stage Six are sages. They are so at home with the universe that they have no need to be in anyone's way with a right answer or even a right question. At Stage Six, they just are. There is a wonderful peace about them that permeates those around them. Their calling reaches out of the organization and into the world. They are wise and they have a glint in their eye.

Chapter 12
Leading from Your Soul

> Ultimately we have just one moral duty: to reclaim large areas of peace in ourselves, more and more peace, and to reflect it towards others. And the more peace there is in us, the more peace there will also be in our troubled world.
>
> Etty Hillesum, holocaust victim, *An Interrupted Life*

Leadership is a journey. It is not a trip with an identifiable destination and road maps to keep you on the right road. A journey unfolds gradually. It meanders. You stop and start, take side roads, get bogged down. You meet travel companions and sometimes stay with friends for a while. A journey is not predictable, even though there may be an end goal. On a journey, the process of getting there is part of the overall goal.

So it is with leadership. The end point of leadership is not just the position or stage of power we reach, but the continual change and deepening we experience that makes a difference in our lives, our work, our world. Our leadership journeys are only at *midpoint* when we have achieved a position of power.

The second half of the leadership journey comes once we admit our first feelings of dissatisfaction with our leadership, for it is then that we have the opportunity to lead from our souls. We find increasingly more role models and also more written on this type of leadership. Soul leadership begins to emerge when we find our existing leadership style less rewarding, less satisfying than it was; when we must either shift to the inner leadership journey or recycle to an earlier leadership style that is more comfortable and predictable.

The leadership journey is a matter of the soul and that is where the energy and the focus have to be. As Etty Hillesum writes in the introductory quote, this is more about inner courage and peace than it is about strategic planning. It is not about skill development, it is about facing fear, letting go of control, gaining self-worth and inner strength, finding inner freedom and moral passion—the things you learn only after you think you know it all. This journey takes you to your core, including your dark core (shame, fear of abandonment, rage), wherein lies the raw power of transformation. It is not an easy journey, and the goal is not to be successful in the traditional sense; it is to be faithful to the journey itself. The only requirement is courage.

I am describing a different kind of leadership than we are accustomed to. Leading from your soul involves things like meaning, passion, calling, courage, wholeness, vulnerability, spirituality, and community. It does not represent the traditional forms of leadership and it goes beyond the newer feminist forms, intriguing as they are. This leadership, which I call soul leadership, transcends both masculine and feminine forms, reaching to another level, in which we connect with our souls, our cores, our essence. Why is it necessary to have leaders who lead from their souls, people who can operate from a place of inner power? Because the future requires leaders who do not operate out of fear or ego gratification, who do not revert to traditional authoritarian styles when things get tough, who do not have to prove their worth by supplying the answers. To repeat the quote from Rob Harvey of Herman Miller, Inc., from the introduction to this book,

> Leadership always comes back to the issue of character, of deep foundational values. In the current reformation this country is experiencing, and the instability we are feeling, you cannot lead by forcing compliance. It simply doesn't work. The rate of change is too high to be managed from the top down. In order to lead, one must engage followers. You will not find followers without caring, connecting and creating. Would you follow someone who did not care about you, connect with you, or did not wish to create a new reality? Mere compliance today is a recipe for disaster. As leaders, or would-be leaders, we must be vulnerable. None of us has arrived. We must recognize our own voyage. We can only lead effectively by enabling others to maximize their contribution. We are all on the journey together, accomplishing things that none of us could accomplish alone.

David Whyte, in his wonderful book, *The Heart Aroused,* describes in sacred terms what the preservation of the soul in the workplace means:

> Preservation of the soul means the preservation at work of humanity and sanity (with all the well-loved insanities that human sanity requires.) Preservation of the soul means the palpable presence of some sacred otherness in our labors, whatever language we may use for that otherness: God, the universe, destiny, life or love. Preservation of the soul means allowing for fiery initiations that our surface personalities, calculating for a brilliant career, would rather do without.

People you and I know who lead from their souls have some of these characteristics in common:

- They know intimately what it means to be part of or create community.
- They do not depend on themselves for the vision of the organization.
- They can give power away without feeling a loss of self.
- They are peace-filled in crises as well as in calm times. And during crises, they do not revert to authoritarian or avoidance behaviors.
- They are connected intimately to a Higher Power.
- They do not project their pain or addiction on others.
- They do not burn out or succumb to stress.
- They practice integrity, reflection, and collaboration.
- They have a strong sense of humor and creativity.
- They are courageous.
- Above all, they are life giving.

We all have the potential for leading from our souls. We were made to do it that way in the first place. When we begin to lead from our souls, we feel as if we are coming home, coming to the place in which we were meant to be, even though it usually means living counter to the culture. But inside, it is a wonderful and relieving feeling.

Getting to that place in which we lead from our souls requires a giant leap of faith. The whole world tells us to lead in another way, the way the books tell us to lead, the way the people in positions of power do it. It tells us to be in charge. It defines leadership as vision, mission, engaging others to meet goals, confidence, career climbing, strong ego, program planning, and long-range strategies. And for the first half of our leadership journey this style of leadership works, and works well.

But in the second half of our leadership journey, for many of us after we reach the age of thirty-five, being in charge doesn't work anymore. It helps us prosper but it will never transform organizations. To transform organizations we need to transform ourselves. We have to become whole. And that is a profoundly spiritual journey requiring courage.

It requires a leap of faith to lead from our souls. It requires courage: a conscious reflective decision to act on life-giving principles, despite the consequences, even if they threaten our priorities or existence. Think about this. Courage is not spontaneous or instinctive like heroism, or a learned skill like bravery. How do we get courage and where does it lead us? Courage is what we develop on this journey to soul leadership. It takes us into new territory. It allows us to go beyond what we were capable of saying and doing before. We go to our depths and find our heights and in our lives we emerge as wise leaders. The journey of leadership I have been discussing is depicted in this rather convoluted-looking model.

In this model, the first half of the leadership journey is represented by a horizontal and then vertical line. Moving out in early leadership ventures requires risk. Then you build on those experiences, develop skills and move up in leadership. This part of the journey parallels power Stages One and Two. The peak of the journey, at the top of the model, coincides with Stage Three.

The second half, the phase of soul leadership, is more of an inward, downward, and then onward journey, depicted by the second half of the chart and described in Stages Four, Five, and Six. The moving in phase, the downward and inward journey, requires courage and the transformation happens in the swirl of lines that looks like a collapsed web. That's what it feels like when we are in the thick of change. Next we experience the inevitable, onward journey that rekindles our spark in a totally new way and results in a sense of calling. Moving beyond requires grace, which is unconditional love from a sacred source inside and outside yourself.

Unfortunately, no seminar or workshop program can move you quickly to this next place on your journey. It can only introduce you to the concepts and let you try on a few. The journey takes a long time, generally several years, and requires immense soul searching. The work of this inner development requires that your foundations shake, jarring you into a new way of thinking. It is not easy work and cannot be done quickly. Remember, courage is a decision.

Developing Soul Leadership

What follows is a long-term process for developing people who lead from their souls. It is based on the behaviors and practices of people in all walks of life who live and work from their souls. As you read it, you may agree with the principles and think you are well on your way. I applaud you. Keep going. My experience tells me that you must genuinely engage in two-thirds of these activities before they make a life-changing difference, and that a few, like embracing shadows and taking spirituality seriously, are absolutely necessary.

Leadership Development Model

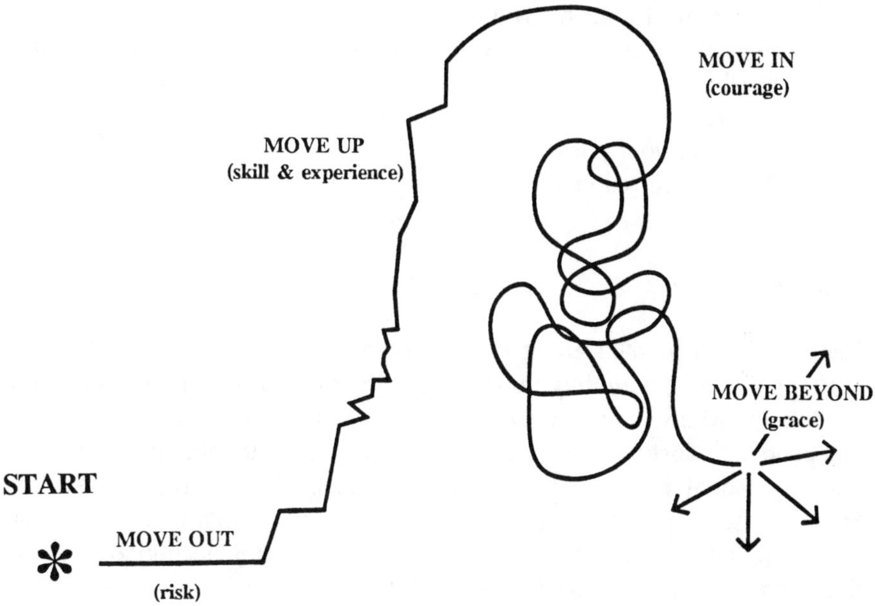

This soul leadership process allows you to enter into transformation gradually in your own way, either in the order listed or randomly. Some aspects of your life—your work life, your community life, or your home life—may lend themselves more to this process than others. Since we operate differently in different parts of our lives, it may be wise to pick one part in which to begin this journey. Then, as you continue to develop on the journey, you can integrate additional parts of your life gradually into the transformation.

The first seven suggestions are intended to get you started, since they are less difficult than the second set. These are:

1. Be accountable.
2. Assess your leadership journey.
3. Practice vulnerability.
4. Play without feeding your addictions.
5. Experience solitude regularly.
6. Try one new artistic endeavor.
7. Travel as far from home as possible.

The next six are more difficult. They ask you to enter into a covenant for inner healing and life transformation. Enter into them seriously and reverently. These are:

8. Take your spirituality seriously.
9. Find a mentor at the fringe.
10. Find peace and intimacy in your relationships without avoiding conflict.
11. Embrace your shadows and childhood wounds.
12. Discover your passion.
13. Accept your calling.

1. Be Accountable

The first myth to shed about soul leadership is that you can do it alone. Perhaps the most humbling thing you will learn on this journey is that you need help. Many power leaders are loners, very much in control and independent. Most people—leaders and otherwise—are not used to talking about personal issues with people and can easily deceive themselves. However, soul leaders never isolate themselves or operate in a vacuum. A critical foundation for all the other soul experiences is accountability. So this is an appropriate place to begin the inward journey.

The second myth to shed is that you are in charge. The soul leadership process is not about taking charge. It is about letting go. Part of letting go is letting others into the process with you, to keep you honest and to support you. You need to be regularly accountable to another person or to a group in order to do this soul work. I recommend meeting every three to four weeks with a counselor or mentor who is beyond you on the journey, or with a small group with wise people in it. If you don't have these people, the process will eventually be aborted, because ego will be leading ego.

Meet regularly and start keeping a personal journal on your experiences and their effects on you. A journal is simply a notebook you write in, a safe, private place to record your thoughts, feelings, reactions, and questions. This reinforces your experiences and helps you reflect more deeply on them. This leadership development process is profound, not programmatic. It has whole life consequences, not merely quarterly or annual results.

You may also choose to engage in specific group experiences over a shorter period of time to take on burning topics. One group of people from several different cultures started an "isms" group, simply to look at all the ways in which they live out their prejudices. They learned that they had more isms than they thought, and they became more aware of them in everyday life. They also learned that each of them had a characteristic that was on someone else's list of isms in some form. It was an enlightening insight. Each of them committed to making specific changes and reporting on her progress to the group.

A group of men call themselves Talking Heads. They meet for breakfast every month to talk over what is going on in their lives and how that affects their families and the community. They ask for feedback from the other members and bring in articles and ideas that they want to discuss or question.

Vaclav Havel, playwright, dissident, and former president of Czechoslovakia, described the process of accountability for soul leaders well when he spoke before the U.S. Congress.

> We still don't know how to put morality ahead of politics, science and economics. We are still incapable of understanding that the only genuine backbone of all our actions—if they are to be moral—is responsibility. Responsibility to something higher than my family, my country, my firm, my success. Responsibility to the order of Being, where all our actions are indelibly recorded and where, and only where, they will be properly judged.
>
> Consciousness precedes being, and not the other way around. For this reason, the salvation of this human world lies nowhere else than in the human heart, in the human power to reflect, in human meekness and in human responsibility. Without a global revolution in the sphere of human consciousness, nothing will change for the better in the sphere of our being as humans, and the catastrophe toward which this world is headed—be it ecological, social, demographic or a general breakdown of civilization—will be unavoidable.

Another great thinker and wisdom figure, Eleanor Roosevelt, summed up the process and results of moving to true leadership when she said,

> Somewhere along the line of development, we discover what we really are and then we make our real decision for which we are responsible. Make that decision primarily for yourself, because you can never really have anyone else's life, not even your child's. The influence you have is through your own life and what you become yourself.

2. Assess Your Leadership Journey

Create a leadership journey chronicle by looking back over your life to the events, experiences, behaviors, and people who were integral to your leadership development to date. Write these events, experiences, and people on a sheet of paper in any way that makes sense to you, by influence, event, or chronology. Take a while to reflect on this, because more experiences will emerge as you allow them into your consciousness. Ask yourself these questions:

1. How did you develop as a leader before the age of twenty?
2. What have been your leadership turning points, both negative and positive?
3. How do you describe yourself as a leader now?

After establishing where you are and how you got there, ask yourself the following questions and answer as honestly as possible in your journal.

1. What was the most important question you asked yourself about leadership and about life ten years ago? What is the most important question you are asking yourself today?
2. What do you consider success?
3. What gives you your identity as a person? As a leader?
4. What are you most proud of? Most sorry about?
5. What is the energy or passion that drives your life?
6. When were you most vulnerable? What happened?
7. When do you experience powerlessness in your life? How does it feel?
8. When have you practiced soul leadership? What was it like for you? For others?
9. What's become clear to you?
10. What beliefs about power do your current leadership behaviors reflect?

Share your answers with your accountability group or person. If you really want a dose of reality, summarize your leadership self-portrait and give copies to one or two people with whom you've had adversarial relationships, asking for their feedback. Explain to them that you are assessing your leadership and that their ideas would be helpful to you. Their views won't reflect all of reality, any more than yours do, but you might use their feedback later on in the process when you get to the section on embracing your shadow.

At this point you need to read about leaders who operated at a soul level. Biographies are best. Read about Anwar Sadat, Mother Theresa, Ghandi, Nelson Mandela, Rosa Parks, Bishop Tutu, and Martin Luther King, Jr. for starters. Read leadership books if you like, but choose carefully. In *Leadership*, James McGregor Burns describes transformational leaders well. The ethics and morality chapters of John Gardner's *On Leadership* are inspiring. The chapter titled "Inside-Out" from Stephen Covey's *Seven Habits of Highly Effective People* cites the character principles that have been missing from the leadership ethic since World War II. And in *Managing as a Performing Art*, Peter Vaill writes well about whole people working collectively, reflectively, and spiritually smarter. And in *The Heart Aroused,* David Whyte writes about preserving soul in corporate America.

The best writing I have seen on the topic of soul leadership is a book by Parker Palmer titled *Let Your Life Speak,* in the chapter called "Leading from Within" in which he describes the responsibility leaders have to be in touch with their own inner monsters so they know clearly how they can damage people if they are not in touch.

More important than reading, though, is interviewing several people you think are soul leaders. Ask how they got there, how they think about themselves, what they do to stay grounded in times of stress, what they consider worth doing. Ask them some of the questions you asked yourself in your leadership journey assessment.

After you have read books and interviewed these people, ask yourself what success is for a soul leader and what might it be for you.

It is important to take this assessment process to its next inevitable incarnation. It must be manifested by your behavior in the real world. Try one new behavior at work or at home to push you into a new place as a leader. Here's an example from an executive who has worked on soul leadership.

Diversity was a goal of Helen's organization. She could have hired a diversity manager to develop or fix things, but she decided to try a new approach. She chose two of her best, most open and alive managers to join this project with her. Together they made it their goal to learn as much about ethnic differences as possible. The three got together regularly, read and talked candidly, and attended seminars. They found out about their overt and hidden racism. They also found out that they had all been discriminated against in some way and could therefore identify with other people's pain to some extent. They asked each other to hold them accountable for their behavior and review it regularly.

The result was that they constructed their department as a community, not as a group of individuals. They began talking and acting as a community, using each other to learn, grow, and help solve issues, not just to satisfy diversity goals. They began hiring more people of color and people with various disabilities, making the environment conducive to differences and talking about different ways of approaching issues and ways of life.

What evolved was a new culture that valued differences as ways to attain community and to be more effective. Fears, problems, and conflicts were addressed without retribution. The community has slowly coalesced and, even during hard times, they work better together than ever before. Turnover is at an all-time low and other managers want to know how they did it.

If you are an especially high achiever, here is a sure way to challenge yourself and your leadership journey. Find two or three young people in your organization whose skills, style, or personalities attract you. Work with them as a mentor until they are better than you at the same work. I did not say as good or competent as you, but better. This will bring you into uncharted territory. Record your observations of and feelings about this experience in your journal and talk with your accountability people about your reactions.

3. Practice Vulnerability

In order to be a soul leader, you need to develop vulnerability. Vulnerability means knowing yourself first and then being willing to disclose who you are to others. It requires you to be self-aware and willing to admit your fears, joys, and sadness to yourself and others, even if it puts you at risk. Vulnerability is refreshing and generates trust in others. This is because you have to be secure and self-trusting in order to be vulnerable. Max De Pree, retired chairman of Herman Miller, Inc., said the two top qualities he looks for in leaders are integrity and vulnerability.

Let's start with a simple experiment to see how readily you take to being vulnerable. For the next few weeks, observe and record honestly what you laugh at each day. At the end of that time, ask yourself why you thought each incident or joke was funny. Who got hurt or diminished as a result of the humor? Why? Do you feel defensive when asked to look at your humor? How did you feel when you acknowledged what is funny for you?

Even a cursory examination of humor shows that we laugh mostly at things that embarrass others or treat them like objects. The topics are wide ranging: sex, mothers-in-law, politics, current events, ethnic groups, women, senior citizens, abuse, personality quirks. I am sobered when I look at what makes me laugh. The more one laughs at others in demeaning ways, the more it points out one's own insecurities. We frequently cover our fear, anger, or hurt with diversionary humor.

Try instead to learn to laugh at yourself, not in a put-down way, but by looking at the funny, ironic, eccentric things in your own behavior and seeing the humor in them. It helps the process of not taking yourself so seriously. Somewhere I read a great philosophy of life and adopted it as my own. It is, "If you don't learn how to laugh at yourself, sooner or later, someone else will." If you can laugh at yourself—and not in a demeaning way—it helps your vulnerability.

When I was a child, a small plane crashed into my elementary school playground. No one was hurt but the incident is marked indelibly in my mind. I have told the story so many times that my family can fill in the sentences for me. Now when I say, "Did I ever tell you about the plane that crashed in my school playground?" they all smile and say, "No, Janet. Why don't you tell us about it." I say, "Well, just one more time."

Reflect on how it feels to be gentle with yourself and others by laughing at shared foibles. Write about this in your journal. Observe how other people react to self-observant humor.

Another way to be aware of vulnerability is to accept your body with all of its idiosyncrasies and weaknesses. We are part of a culture that values physical perfection. Yet none of us measures up, really. Try seeing your body not as an adversary or a training machine, but as a message center that is trying to talk to you, alert you to what is healthy or dangerous, and teach you to slow down or let go.

For one year, listen to your body instead of talking to it, swearing at it, or cramming it into uncomfortable things. Listen to aches and pains as messages. What is your body asking, saying, or shouting? Eat when you are hungry, and eat what your body asks for. Listen to what your body tells you about your sexuality, your interests, desires, and attitudes.

Draw an outline of a body on a sheet of paper and mark with a heart the places you like and with an X the places you don't like. Ask yourself why you like or dislike each part. When did you stop liking the unliked parts? If you want to go deeper, write to the parts you like and dislike, allowing them to answer you back.

If you want to work more on vulnerability, skip to the section on embracing your shadows and childhood wounds.

4. Play without Feeding Your Addictions

Most high achieving leaders think they know how to play because they engage in competitive, adventurous, or physically strenuous exercise. Our culture encourages these activities as a way to balance a stressful work schedule. I would suggest that these activities be called stress reduction techniques but not be confused with the concept of play. Most of them inadvertently feed people's addictions, especially the work addiction, and do not relieve long-term stress, which leaves deep scars on the psyche.

Before I discuss play, list on paper the activities you have done in the last six months for recreation, exercise, or play. (Do not list things you would like to do but never get around to.)

Play is a concept many of us left behind as children, but playing without feeding your work or other addictions helps you understand soul leadership behavior. Consider these as the primary characteristics of play and see what activities come to mind for you. Which of your regular activities have these characteristics? Which don't? Why?

- Activities that leave your body, mind, and spirit rested and refreshed, even though you may get physically tired.
- Activities in which you do not have to win or be an expert to feel good about yourself.
- Activities that stimulate your creativity.
- Activities that take your mind completely off your work and problems.
- Activities that increase your appreciation of others, of nature, of relationships.
- Activities in which you laugh freely and do not feel angry, tight, or ashamed afterward.
- Activities that do not require you to travel long distances.
- Activities in which you do not have to prove yourself or be in charge.
- Activities that do not require a large investment of money or exhaustive maintenance.
- Activities that bring you closer to who you were as a child.
- Activities that feed your soul.

Ask yourself if the activities you listed meet at least half of these criteria. Some probably do and some won't. Try substituting one new play idea for one of your current ones. You may have to expand your concept of play to include things you previously would have rejected. Or you may consider doing your current recreation in a different way. Don't expect people to applaud you when you change. Most people are moving too fast to notice. You can applaud yourself. My list of play activities includes doing jigsaw puzzles, playing golf according to Hagberg's Rules (I'll explain that later), riding roller coasters, reading in my favorite chair, walking, driving on curvy roads, watching murder mysteries on TV, drawing, reading mail order catalogues, browsing in card shops, parasailing, and watching college basketball and pro baseball.

In my family golf was an important activity. My father-in-law was the son of the head groundskeeper of a large metropolitan golf course. He plays exceptionally well. His handicap has been eight for most of his adult life. My husband and two stepsons also played well. So naturally I played too. It was our family sport, and it was competitive. Tempers flared when things did not go well. I finally figured out that although I love golf and can hold my own with these men around the greens, it was not fun or relaxing to always be competing, betting, or asking for scores.

I decided to play my own golf game. First I read the book *Inner Golf* and practiced the principles until I was playing a relaxed inner game. I forgave the golf god who gives only three good shots a round and rewards each shot with either direction or distance, never with both. Then I decided to enjoy the weather and nature, since they are major reasons I like golf. Lastly I decided to scrap the official rules and make my own rules, called Hagberg's Rules. If I don't like the lie of my ball, I improve it. If I don't like the length of the hole, I shorten it. When I am tired and we come to a long par five, I use what I affectionately call the 250-yard mark rule. I drop my ball at the 250-yard mark and play from there.

Then I have the ball redemption rule. If I hit a ball into the woods and I can't find it, but I find another ball instead, I have redeemed a ball from oblivion and I move it to the edge of the fairway without counting a stroke. If I find two balls, I subtract a stroke. I began enjoying golf so much that I made a decision that almost started a riot. I quit keeping score. It was like I had committed a mortal sin. I told my family I wasn't playing against them but for me. I now keep letter scores: W for wonderful holes, S for scenic holes, and G for one great shot. There are now two sets of rules, the official rules and Hagberg's rules. My philosophy of golf is, "It doesn't matter." Not only do I enjoy it immensely, my game is more relaxed and consistent.

5. Experience Solitude Regularly

The world is afraid of being alone lest it face itself. Yet no amount of frenetic activity, or even strategic planning, can bring you to the inner journey of your soul. You must set aside time and space to be alone and let the pace, noise, and activity of your external life quiet down. At first this may be frightening. What will you do with your time? What if you are bored? The point is not to find things to fill the space but to ask how being busy got to be your identity, how what you do, not who you are, came to determine your worth.

One place to start being by yourself is to go on a retreat or weekend workshop in which there are activities and quiet time, so you can get used to being alone. Some people find, as I did, that when they first take time to be alone all they can do is sleep, even in the middle of the day. They are experiencing soul fatigue, a result of being on the merry-go-round of work too long without stopping.

A good solitary activity is walking by yourself in your neighborhood without thinking about work or problems. Listen to the birds. Observe the flowers, grass, and trees. Smell the fragrances. Watch the seasons change as you travel that same path every week for a year. Stop running and start walking. It is a great metaphor for life, even though it may frighten you to think you are slowing down. It will stimulate all kinds of internal dialogue. Listen for your wise inner voice, that little voice that tugs at you, gives you courage to ask for what you want, tells you to stop, or turn around, or call someone on a particular day.

Find a place for solitude in your home as well as away from home. It can be a den, kitchen, office, bed, or even bathroom as long as it is a place where you can go to be alone, to be with your inner thoughts, feelings, voices. Let others know that when you ask to be alone there, you are not to be interrupted. It is a haven. It is your place to get grounded. My quiet place is a bedroom reading chair that faces out over the skyline of the city.

After practicing ways to be alone, try setting aside at least three hours every week to be alone. Even extroverts need time to themselves, especially after age thirty-five. One woman who works and has small children schedules childcare regularly on Wednesday nights and does relaxing things for a few hours that evening. Her only rule is she can't work at the office or do household tasks that evening.

When you are alone, observe how your body reacts, how you feel, what comes up in your mind, and what you read. Observe which books, ideas, or people emerge in your life. Listen to your inner wisdom, even if it flies in the face of reason. Follow its direction and be thankful you have not drowned out the inner voice. If you have, wait and be quiet. It will come.

You may want to try this sobering exercise after you have practiced solitude for a while: Have an inner dialogue with your own death. Think and write about what it will be like. Where will it be and with whom?

What do you want to say to family and friends before you die? And what would you want to be said about you at your funeral? Write down how you would sum up your life. What would you want to do before you die that you haven't already done?

You may get in touch with some of your core feelings, fears, dreads, joys, and memories. Many people are afraid of solitude for that very reason. And solitude reminds us of the quieting of our bodies and souls, which feels like the beginning of death. The truth is that if we can't begin to approach our death, emotionally or physically, we will be afraid of living our lives in the fullest way possible.

6. Try One New Artistic Endeavor

A whole new world speaks to you when you tap into your creative side and listen to it. It operates on a different wavelength and takes you to places you have never been before. Creativity is latent within all of us. Creativity is wide ranging, not limited to painting or writing. Expand your views of creativity to cooking, conversation, letter writing, gardening, music, dancing, designing, or wit. Add your own ideas.

It is valid to cultivate creative activities you already engage in, but the chances are you do them with a vengeance or at a high level of competence already, as most achievers are prone to do. To really experience this process of soul leadership, start fresh on a new artistic endeavor as a fledgling, a newcomer. Take a class in something you have never tried before but which interests you. You will get in touch with your fear of making mistakes, your need for approval, your drive to be the best or quickest. Stay with those experiences and let yourself learn naturally, asking the questions your child inside would ask, not just the ones about getting it right.

Creativity does not call you to achieve. It calls you to go deeper, to plumb your depths, to find your voice, to express your truth. It will exasperate you, but it will bring you closer to who you really are. I promise you that. Before you begin any artistic activity, stop and ask of it what it would like you to experience today. Ask the wood where you should begin, ask the paper what it wants from you, and ask the garden where it wants assistance. It may sound strange, but it needs to be strange to get your attention away from racing to the place you think you need to begin. After a while it becomes second nature to be more in relationship with your art rather than be in charge of your art.

Art can feed you, touch you, and inform you at times of distress in ways nothing else can. It can get through the defenses and fears by going in the back door when the front door is heavily guarded. I experienced this vividly when I was in a deep personal abyss. I went to my drawing teacher to tell her I couldn't draw any more. I was too distraught. She asked why. I told her about how dark and dank the abyss was and how alone I felt. She said gently, "Draw what you see on the walls of the abyss." "Right." I said sarcastically, "I can't even see the walls."

She said, "Just wait. You will."

So I waited. In a few weeks an image came to me from a book I happened to be reading. It was of a powerful ancient woman figure, full of wrathful energy and resolve. It was a scary image but I began drawing it. Over the months of drawing it, I felt power and energy returning to me. But it was a different kind of power than I had felt before. It was the calm power that comes from facing the darkness. The darkness was becoming the light. And slowly I began to emerge from the abyss.

7. Travel as Far from Home as Possible

Get away from what is familiar and safe for you. You may want to start by moving into a different place in your organization, a different board in the community, or another person's culture. But put yourself in a place where you are the oddball, the token, or the stranger. Women and people of color have known what this is like all their lives, so this is most important for white males who are rarely in the minority or disenfranchised. If you are uncomfortable in the new arena, you have found the potential for learning. If you are still comfortable or people are treating you deferentially, you are not far enough away from home.

When you feel uncomfortable, try not to write off the experience by projecting blame, stupidity, or lack of sophistication on those around you. We usually do this to cover our fear and insecurity and to reject what the experience has to teach us. It keeps us arrogant. Instead, feel your ignorance, inadequacy, fear, anticipation, and floundering. Ask for assistance.

Then up the ante on yourself and go to another ethnic culture outside the comfort of your work place, or outside your own country. Don't go primarily as a spectator, teacher, vacationer, consultant, or anthropologist. Go as a student, even if you use one of those previous roles as a way to get to the culture. Think about what it would be like if you had grown up in this culture. Get inside the culture. Taste it, smell it, touch it, ask for help, speak the language as best you can. Take down your own strong defenses. Be a child again. Cast aside prior assumptions. Leave your take-charge attitudes at home. How would you be without your title, salary, or privilege? Who would you be?

Take these experiences back home with you and apply the attitudes and learning you gained from outside your culture to inside your culture. You will find yourself a more receptive and wiser person. Observe the differences. Write about these experiences in your journal and share them with your accountability person.

Here is an example of a professional who traveled to Central America to interview people as part of an academic project and instead experienced a transformation. He writes:

> Doing the interviews made me aware of how much my power depended on my title, position, and capability to communicate, none of which "fit" for three months. I felt frustrated, angry, powerless, and dependent on my oldest son, who is fluent in Spanish and in the culture. He was the one who was respected. And out of our travels and travails grew an entirely new relationship, a friendship. Even now, four years later, tears come as I write about it.
>
> On that same trip I gained a whole new appreciation for my father, who at the age of twelve came to a strange land and strange language, with no return ticket to a home of comfort and security. Others in Europe were dependent on him to make a living and send for them: a mother, sister, and brother. I am sad because Dad is gone and I can't tell him how much I respect him now that I have a better understanding of who he was and what he had been through and what he had accomplished. I still wish I could ask his forgiveness for judging him so harshly because he wasn't a "modern" American.

Soul Leadership Process: Phase Two

These next six suggestions will engage you even more deeply in the process of soul leadership. They are not to be taken lightly or to be engaged in frivolously. They ask a commitment, a covenant for inner healing, leading to transformed leadership. Stop and ask yourself how you have changed by engaging in the previous activities. Are you ready and do you have the support around you to take further steps?

8. Take Your Spirituality Seriously

It is risky to talk about spirituality in a secular world, but the simple truth is you cannot be a soul leader without it. To be a soul leader, you must change your focus from leading to being led. And this cannot happen without an ever-deepening spiritual base. Many powerful leaders write off spirituality or denigrate it, calling it soft, weak, or inappropriate. Nothing could be farther from the truth. Their attitude is a sign that they are deeply afraid of the power it actually has.

Unless the spiritual undergirding of your life is closely attended to after the age of thirty-five, your leadership may become rigid, in danger of atrophy. If you nurture your spiritual life and allow yourself to be led by a power beyond yourself, new levels of intuitive, inspired, creative, and courageous leadership will emerge, unique to your life calling.

Most leaders who have had a profound effect on the conscience of our world have a deep spiritual base, because they know that one cannot do such courageous things on their own. As a result of their spirituality and courage, soul leaders call us to think differently about the things we worship, take for granted, or even deny. Consider how these leaders made us rethink things: Dag Hammarskjold, Mother Theresa, Vaclav Havel, Elie Wiesel, Martin Luther King, Jr., Anwar Sadat, Rosa Parks, Bishop Tutu, and Gandhi. But you do not need to be famous to have a profound effect on someone. What is essential is that you let your spirituality guide your life, your response to deep crises, and the way you live out your calling. Leaders become aware through their life crises what their spiritual calling really is about.

In *Managing as a Performing Art*, Peter Vaill says:

> To work spiritually smarter is to pay more attention to one's own spiritual qualities, feelings, insights, and yearnings. It is to reach more deeply into oneself for that which is unquestionably authentic. It is to attune oneself to those truths one considers timeless and unassailable, the deepest principles one knows.

I will go even farther than that and say that spirituality is our response to the Holy, whoever or however we name it, and the life changes that result from our response. Faith is a dynamic process of gaining intimacy with the Holy or our Higher Power. Belief systems and religious dogma are not central to gaining intimacy with the Holy, although they can be part of the process. In other words, you can be spiritual without being religious, or you can be religious without being spiritual, or you can be both.

The central struggle in becoming intimate with the Holy is to understand what gets in the way of that intimacy, what separates you from closeness. And that struggle takes you to your core issues: what you worship, where your pain is, and where the healing will take place.

Henri Nouwen, a prolific writer and a priest, says it well when he describes the dilemma religious leaders have with power in his book, *In the Name of Jesus*. His words have a very familiar ring in the corporate world as well.

> Maybe power offers an easy substitute for the hard task of love. It seems easier to be God than to love God, easier to control people than to love people, easier to own life than to love life.

How do you gain more intimacy with the Holy? What kinds of things deepen your spiritual base? A simple answer is you get intimate with your Higher Power in much the same ways that you get intimate with friends: you spend time together, talk and listen, work through conflict, share crises, make yourself vulnerable, give and receive love, laugh and play.

Moving spirituality from a nice concept to a reality in your life requires involvement in personal spiritual disciplines. There is no substitute, no short cut. These spiritual disciplines vary depending on a person's background and form of spirituality. It also presupposes a relationship with a higher power as part of spirituality. Disciplines include being in nature, meditating, writing, doing dream work, listening, reading, studying, praying, journaling, enjoying music, visualizing, and discerning.

In *Principle Centered Leadership*, Stephen Covey offers an approach that is used in many spiritual traditions. He suggests that daily reflective study of Scripture is "the single most important and powerful discipline in life because it points our lives, like a compass, to 'true north'—our divine destiny."

Some people encourage their spirituality in a professional relationship called spiritual direction. This is a relationship in which a trained person walks with another on his or her spiritual journey, listening to his or her inner voice, making observations, and asking questions. It is not dogmatic or rigid, and the experience can move a person to a deeper level of intimacy with the Holy, adding an element of accountability that is healthy as you go through transitions. If you enter into such a relationship, be sure you are comfortable with the person, that they are qualified, and that they honor your form of spirituality.

Several issues emerge for people as they seek out intimacy with their Higher Power. Images of the Holy are one and childhood religious experiences, good and bad, are another. Exploring these issues can lead to astonishing insights and healing of childhood hurts. Use these questions as starters to begin your spiritual deepening:

What do you want your spirituality to give you?
What is your image of the Holy and how has it changed, if at all, since you were a child?
Where do you experience deep awe and joy in your life?
What are the truths you believe in most deeply?
How has your parents' spirituality affected your own?
How did your early religious experiences, or lack thereof, affect your life? How have you avoided spiritual intimacy?
What does your heart want?
For what in life do you have the most passion?
Why do good people suffer?
How can you tell the difference between your voice and that of your Higher Power?
How is the Holy involved in your pain?
What are you called to do with your life? Why you?

What happens when you take your spiritual life seriously and do inner spiritual work? You will feel unconditionally loved by your Higher Power, perhaps for the first time. You will slowly gain feelings of deep self-worth. You will begin to see the truth about your life. You will face your fears. Your character will begin to be changed, refined, and rekindled. You will find yourself feeling less anxious, more courageous, more willing to live out principles that are life-giving. Inner peace will allow you to tolerate pain without chaos. Gifts of the spirit of life will emerge.

Anwar Sadat learned about intimacy with God when he spent eighteen months in solitary confinement in Cell 54 of a Cairo prison, awaiting trail for assassinating a traitor. He says in his autobiography that he learned the most important things in his life there. He found self-knowledge in a deep sense, going to his very center. He found out what he could and could not accept in life. He found a relationship with a "God who created us and cannot be evil in any sense." He goes on to say,

> My relations with the entire universe began to be reshaped, and love became the fountainhead of all my actions and feelings. Armed with faith and perfect peace of mind, I have never been shaken by the turbulent events, both private and public, through which I have lived.

Sadat was acquitted and resumed public life, a changed man. Later in his life, he shocked the entire Middle East by going to Jerusalem to make a peace gesture toward Israel.

If you want your life to be transformed, to experience profound levels of leadership, begin by spending your best fifteen to thirty minutes of the day alone with your Higher Power, and then write about it and talk to someone else about it. Do this in whatever way is best for you, by being quiet, reading, writing, listening, or walking. The activity needs to be solitary, and it needs to be done for the rest of your life. Gandhi set aside one day each week for this. You will deepen, your soul leadership will slowly emerge, and you will be awed by what intimacy with the Source can do.

9. Find a Mentor at the Fringe

In our culture there are lots of people in the mainstream. These are the people most of us interact with every day. On weekends we see more of them, only in different activities. If we live in suburbs, we see almost exclusively mainstream people.

But there are also people on the fringes of our society. Our society is increasingly set up so there is no physical meeting of the mainstream and the fringe, and especially no contact between the wealthy and the poor. Guarded communities are deliberately designed to keep out anyone who does not have permission to be there. We isolate ourselves to feel more secure, when in fact it makes us more frightened.

Let me make a suggestion. Get to know someone on the fringe. Who are the people on the fringe? They are the people who you think are as different from you as you can imagine. They may be the homeless, the retarded, people over ninety, battered women, people in prison, gang members, children, people of other ethnic groups, drug dealers, or prostitutes. They may be corporate executives, ministers, teachers, politicians, social workers, or Caucasians. Remember, we are all on someone else's list of fringe people. Now let me suggest something outlandish. Let this fringe person be your mentor for at least a year. Let him or her teach you more about yourself than you ever knew before.

How do you let one of them become your mentor? Find a way to engage personally and regularly with one fringe person or a group of fringe people you are not related to. You may have to be clever to find a way. You may find you can work through an already established organization or activity. Ask your network to help you. You may have to begin this relationship by trying to help or be helped by the person, alleviate some problem, or give him or her something. That's the way a lot of people start and fringe people are used to it. They can see it coming. You may lose some money, or get conned, or get angry that the person doesn't appreciate your efforts. If this happens, it's an opportunity to learn, but only if you stay with it and don't leave.

Eventually you will get to the point of admitting failure. This is where the real learning and mentoring begins. Just be with the person in his or her real life; listen, and get to know him or her. Get on his or her bus and ride it for a long time without having to help or save the person. Be with your mentor in his or her pain. It is holy to just stand with a brother or sister in pain. You will eventually tap into something inside yourself that totally resonates with that person's pain, feels compassion, feels familiarity, and finally feels love, because love is what it is all about.

Then you can look at your own homelessness, your own inner prisons, your own retardation, your own battering in a new and more compassionate way. Your mentor will bring you to your fringe issues and you will live differently in the world. You have been found out and you are still okay. You are on your way to a new wisdom. Stay with your mentor long enough and you may even be led to making a dent in the world's pain.

Some good examples of this concept have come out of Hollywood, of all places. The movie *The Fisher King* chronicles the story of the homeless man, Perry, played by Robin Williams, as he struggles with his inner demons, portrayed graphically by a flaming horse and rider. His friend Jack, played by Jeff Bridges, thinks he can change Perry's life by giving him money and finding him a new girlfriend. Paradoxically Jack finds out instead about his own brand of homelessness. Perry teaches him, in a very strange and roundabout way, what friendship and love are all about.

Other superb Hollywood examples of the fringe mentor concept are *Nell, Rainman*, *Dances with Wolves*, *Forrest Gump, What's Eating Gilbert Grape,* and *Children of a Lesser God.*

10. Find Peace and Intimacy in Your Relationships without Avoiding Conflict

This step in the soul leadership process is about intimacy. Many people go through their entire lives without intimacy, even though they may have good friends, live with other people, or marry. Intimacy is based on vulnerability and trust with another person. In an intimate relationship, caring, conflict, and differences can be dealt with openly and without retribution. In primary relationships, intimacy also includes sexuality. The ability to be appropriately intimate with other people is a primary quality of soul leaders in organizations.

Single people sometimes think it is more difficult to work on intimacy or to expect it because of the lack of everyday continuity in their relationships. Yet it is just as important for singles to develop intimate, committed relationships and to work through the process of commitment and conflict as it is for married people. We all need intimacy in order to survive and thrive.

The process of developing intimacy is similar in all relationships. It involves knowing who you are and what baggage you bring to the relationship, being vulnerable and open, having appropriate boundaries, knowing how to nurture both yourself and the other person, knowing what baggage the other person brings, working through conflict, and respecting your differences. It sounds simple until you try it.

I want to focus on committed relationships because they are riddled with myths and unreal expectations. Most people find that, contrary to what they thought, they have to work at their committed relationships in order to get their basic needs met. It doesn't just work automatically. And for that reason, marriage and committed relationships have been, for most people, both their heaven and hell. Instead of focusing on our marriages, we focus on work or children because we get more recognition and gratification there. We cover well and achieve a lot as a result. If we are succeeding externally, then we have something to be proud of. The greater our insecurity is, the higher our need to achieve.

If we ignore our relationships, however, they will rise up eventually to remind us, just as our bodies do. Committed relationships are the most obvious but also the hardest place to admit and take care of our real needs because in these relationships we have the most potential to be loved and to be rejected. Wherever there is a potential for emotional and physical intimacy, there is also a potential for rejection. So our committed relationships store within themselves all our unspoken fears and insecurities.

If there is love in a relationship, even a little bit of love, and if there is resolve, then working on your issues is possible. Doing this calls forth an inner courage that you may never have tapped, even in years of a conflict-ridden career. It is the inner courage that comes from facing fear, conflict, shame, and abandonment head on and finding that not only do you survive, you are stronger, individually and as a couple. You address who you are in this relationship and what you want. This can be done best with good therapy and it may take years to accomplish. Sometimes during the process, your relationship has to sustain your love because your love would not sustain the relationship. But finding peace without avoiding conflict revolutionizes relationships.

Courage in facing couple and individual issues allows each person eventually to come as a whole self to the relationship and to allow the other to be a whole person too. This is called differentiation. Courage means not avoiding the conflict that is inevitable, but it also means dealing honestly with the conflict without projecting the anger inward (seeing one-self as victim or getting depressed) or outwardly (as abusing or blaming others.) Courage also means finding ways to take care of yourself instead of asking the other to do that for you. Then joy, freedom, and fun can also emerge more freely in the relationship.

If you take the time and garner the courage to find peace in your relationship, you will have taken a big step toward finding peace in your career, your community, and the world.

An organizational leader told me he was having an affair and was thinking seriously about a divorce. A friend challenged him, telling him an affair was a symptom of not facing the issues, of lack of courage. That got to him. He decided to face the issues. It shook up his marriage of twenty years. The inner work was difficult for both him and his wife. They nearly separated and lived in different parts of the house at times. But, with help, they resolved their trust issues and started over again. The most interesting result was he respected both himself and his wife more. He saw the effects of his new behavior in his organization too. He wasn't afraid to face conflict in the workplace any more. He could hear the truth and deal with it. The ripple effects among his staff are still going on.

11. Embrace Your Shadows and Childhood Wounds

Parker Palmer describes leaders as people who have the most potential for affecting other people's lives, either positively or negatively. Leading is an awesome responsibility. Most leadership programs have lots of skill building and self-assessment components. Rarely do they take us beyond the self-descriptive stage, however. Soul leadership requires us to be keenly aware of our shadow behavior, the negative effects we have on people because of our own denial.

For instance, we may subconsciously diminish others because we are afraid or have been diminished ourselves; we may overwork to cover our insecurity; we will dislike other people because they remind us of hidden things we dislike in ourselves. Nouwen says boldly, "The temptation to power is greatest when intimacy is a threat. . . . Many empire builders are people unable to give and receive love."

To embrace these shadows, we have to go down into them and face our demons. It is like riding monsters down into our own depths. The only way out of the depths is through them.

Parker Palmer, in an earlier edition of his powerful chapter on shadows of leaders, *Leading from Within*, says this about great leadership.

> Great leadership comes from people who've not only made the downward journey through violence and terror, who have touched

> the deep place where we are in community with each other, but who can help take other people to that place. That is what great leadership is all about.

Why would anyone want to go there? No one would. It is a call we receive, an inner yearning to touch our core, and to connect with community, compassion, and our ground of being.

Palmer goes on to say that leaders' shadows are usually composed of the following five issues.

1. Insecurity about their own identity and worth that is so deep they try to deprive other people of their worth. They reduce people to numbers, employees, or patients. Who they are depends on what they do.
2. The belief that the universe is hostile and life is fundamentally a battleground. It is based on competition, which has at its base fear.
3. The belief that ultimate responsibility for everything rests with me. This leads to workaholic behavior, stress, and burnout.
4. Fear of the natural chaos of life. This leads to overordering and control. It destroys creativity.
5. The denial of death, which leads to fear of failure and hanging on to things that need to die.

Palmer maintains the key to working on these issues is to affirm our spirituality, which allows us to move through darkness to great leadership. Because of our strong egos, successful track records, and confidence, it is difficult, almost impossible, for us to see our shadows, our negative projections. That's why they're called shadows, because they are behind us when we face the sun. How can we find out what our shadows are?

One simple but excruciating method which I referred to previously, is suggested by William Miller in his book *Making Friends with Your Shadow*. Try it with great care, because it may awaken your monsters. Think of the two or three people in your life or in the world who you really do not like or get along with. Get them firmly in mind. Then on the left-hand side of a sheet of paper, list all of their qualities that you do not like. You may need more than one sheet. Look over the list and choose those qualities that you find absolutely despicable. Write those in capital letters in a list on the right-hand side of your paper. The qualities written in capital letters are your shadow, the parts of yourself that you would rather not see. Compare them with the feedback you got on your leadership assessment from the one or two people you've had trouble with. Are there any similarities?

Another way to understand your shadows is to observe your children's behavior. They frequently live out the behavior that is hidden inside you. That's a sobering thought.

To make matters even worse, you are not to try to eliminate all those qualities from your life but to embrace them and see what they want to teach you. By embracing them, I mean knowing them so intimately that you know what they mean in your life. You do not need to act them out but to listen to them and let them teach you.

If this sounds difficult, it is because you are facing the place where your ego must be relinquished. Soul leaders must reach that place to become great leaders. The inner journey is the key to interior freedom. Your shadows will lead you to your addictions and to your monsters and they, in turn, will inevitably lead you to your childhood wounds, the wounds that were inflicted on you early and were incorporated into your self-image. They need to be discovered, grieved, understood, and healed for you to gain interior freedom.

I will use myself as an example here. I have to admit to being intellectually arrogant. I despise arrogance in others, so, of course, it is my shadow. Because I teach, I am especially arrogant in situations where I am the learner. I slowly came to realize that the flip side of arrogance is insecurity. Ouch. When I am arrogant, I am really insecure. That is what my arrogance is trying to teach me. So now when I feel my arrogance rising, I ask myself what I am afraid to learn. When I can answer that question, I embrace my shadow.

A more complex example involves abuse. A friend of mine abhors people who abuse others, physically or emotionally. How could she possibly be doing that herself? It took a life crisis and therapy for her to uncover the immense amount of self-abuse to which she was subjecting herself. She was abandoned by her mother and left with her father when she was ten years old. As an adult, she never understood her fear of abandonment. She went to counseling because she was in a dating rut and she was sick of it. She dated men serially and always left the relationship when it was just starting to go well, or she chose men who would be emotionally unavailable so there was no risk of love. Her friends saw the pattern long before she was ready to.

Once she did face the monster of her fear, she slowly began to feel the powerful energy that comes from facing the truth. Out of her pain, sadness, and anger came a rebirth. Light shined in the darkness. Now she can more fully understand the abandoned orphan part of her and therefore give herself choices in every situation. She has a freedom she has never experienced before—an awesome inner power.

Now she can also ask herself what she really wants in a relationship. And she can see herself as worthy of being loved and not abandoned. It was a transforming experience. She stopped changing jobs every three years and asked herself whether she wanted to be such a driven, high-flying professional. She had been abandoning her work before it could abandon her. Now she is on her way to finding out what her calling in work is and how she can live it out both in the community and in her paid work.

Retrospectively, she sees that the darkness became a gift—a painful gift, as any reawakening experience is. Suffering or pain does not happen so that you can learn. It just happens. And it is excruciating. But if you stay with it for a while, live one day at a time, take care of yourself, let your spirituality be your guide, and reinforce your strength with good outside professional support, you will emerge as a whole person.

What you learn down among the monsters is how to befriend pain without shedding responsibility for self-care. You can confront your basic fear, which always stands in the way of courage. You can look death in the face and not cringe. Miller writes that behind the dark shadow is your golden shadow—those qualities you admire and envy in others—just waiting to be embraced as well. By embracing your dark shadow, you free your golden shadow to emerge. By entering your own inner darkness you will find the light.

When you embrace your shadow, your leadership will also be transformed. You will not be able to work the same way. Your rationalizations will be gone. Your projections will fade. Your self-incriminations will not stick. You will emerge as a whole person, embracing shadows and helping others to face their shadows as part of your work, whatever you are called to do.

12. Discover Your Passion

In my twenty years of career counseling, I learned a few nearly universal truths. One is this: Most people want to have meaning in their lives. They want to know that something they have done has made a difference, has touched someone else. They want to get up in the morning and look forward to something. They want to care about something and see how they can affect it positively.

Most people, even hard-working people, even leaders in positions of power, struggle with meaning. Going to work isn't enough; making money isn't enough; getting promoted isn't enough. Where and in what ways do people find meaning?

I think people find the deepest meaning when they find their passion. Oh, they are challenged and kept busy for years by other things but once they know they can achieve, the old longing for meaning comes back again. And the higher people go in organizations, gaining success but no meaning, the lonelier and more alienated they become.

Passion is the relentless pursuit of those life-enhancing activities or experiences that give our souls meaning. Passion comes when we connect with the things, people, causes, or issues that touch us at our deepest place.

We may not even be sure what it is about, we just know that we are inextricably drawn to these things. At other times we know why we are drawn and we are grateful.

Passion can occur on the job, as the focus of our work, or it can be part of our personal or volunteer lives. Whichever it is, it fuels our energy and gives the rest of our lives added meaning as well. Once we have found our passion, we feel a strange contradiction: On one hand, we could die today and life would have been worth it and, at the same time, we want to live forever to continue our connection to our passion. Passionate work is not easy work, nor is it always rewarding. That is not the point. Passion is the engagement of our soul with something beyond us; something that helps us put up with or fights against insurmountable odds, even at high risks, because it is all worth it.

People with passion are incredibly inventive and tenacious individuals. They go way beyond the call of duty and frequently either work on their passion without pay or give more of themselves than their pay warrants. And I do not equate passion with workaholism, in which people say they love their work so much they do it all the time. Workaholics are working to fill a vacuum or to escape, not to connect with their souls.

When we hear examples of passion, we are usually inspired because it taps into the part of us that longs for meaning. Passion can emerge from events that forged us early in our lives, or from a scene we view which taps into our own soul. If we were victims of racism or abuse, we may end up working on those issues; if we viewed the death of a child, we might work with sick children; if someone we love commits a crime, we may be drawn to crime prevention.

Passion can come from that same profound place in which our deepest pain or wounding lives. The energy for working on both is the same. Many people who engage with their childhood or adult wounds are surprised to feel passion arising out of those ashes. They find energy they never knew they had, coming from a different, and not frenetic, force.

The following are examples of people working on passion. You can name many of your own.

- Mary lost her eight-year-old son to leukemia. During her grieving process, she felt led to work with families of leukemia patients as a volunteer. She felt a strong sense of connection with the families and she gave tirelessly of her time and energy to journey with other families.

- A businessman became aware of the loss of hope and spirit in recent emigrant communities due to the loss of manufacturing jobs. It tapped a fear he felt for his own future. He set about the task of working with the city and the business community to create training programs for skilled jobs and new futures.

- A minister responding to the African famine initially visited Africa with gifts of food and money to build wells. He was so deeply touched by the spirit of the people that he went back with teams of people every year and dedicated his life to furthering this work.

- A business manager felt so strongly about community in the workplace that she kept it as a goal in everything she managed. Her emotional abandonment in childhood made her especially sensitive to the issue. People asked to work in her department and they learned her philosophy, spreading it throughout the company as a result of her support.

- A mother grieved her daughter's death at the hands of a drunk driver. She turned her anger into action and created an organization to monitor, convict, and treat drunk drivers. It is called Mothers Against Drunk Driving, MADD. They successfully reduced teen-age drunk driving fatalities sixty-four percent in twelve years.

- My own passion is speaking out against domestic violence with art, writing, and community awareness. This interest comes out of my own family journey and it fuels my energy. The main forms it has taken are these: helping to create an art exhibit, the Silent Witness Exhibit, honoring the twenty-seven women who were murdered in Minnesota in one year; leading a national march to call for a healing of domestic violence in this country; promoting several projects that have proven to be successful in eliminating domestic violence; and a web site and international grassroots initiative linking people in thirty-three countries with the successful work of others. I wrote about this in the chapters about the Wall and Stage Five.

Passion is important, yet it can be driven by ego. If you want the credit and limelight for the work you do on your passion, if it is only your project, it is driven by ego. If you want your passion to be truly from your soul, you need to undergird it with spirituality that is rooted in humility and calling. That is why both spirituality and calling are included in this section of soul leadership.

13. Accept Your Calling

Once you have engaged your shadow, you are more able to see and accept your life's spiritual and vocational call. You have interior freedom. You have courage. You are more willing to let your Higher Power and your inner power entrust you with a life's work, no matter how small the task. And you are willing to use skills or abilities that are not your strong suit, because only then are you dependent on a Supreme Being as your mainstay. Remember the call from a Higher Power is to be faithful, not to be successful. Success appears in a different form than the one with which you are familiar.

Understanding your call, whether it emerges out of your experience of darkness or out of your passion, is a life-long venture. It may or may not involve a change in your career, but it always involves a change in who you are and how you relate to others through touch, love, sacrificial living, or service. Calling involves more of you than your passion does, and feels more all-encompassing. It can be equated with your life's purpose. There is no workaholism or burnout when you live out your calling because you are in intimate touch with the Holy and therefore can honor your limits. And your ego will be relieved not to have to prove itself any more.

Calling is different for each person and it is designed especially for each person. It frequently goes against the grain of who you were. High achievers frequently find their calling in things that are not instantly successful, or they take a different pathway from the typical success-oriented ones. There may be little external reward to show for their effort. This is as it should be. The internal reward is enough. But our calling always relates to what our hearts really want. Our hearts remind us of who we are and whose we are, and they remind us why life is worth living.

The chairwoman of a corporation told me that her calling is to encourage honesty and true collaboration in the workplace. It has gone beyond passion. It is her work, her raison d'etre. In turn, she counts on honesty and collaboration on the hard issues, even during tough times. This is the way in which the workplace is transformed. She said,

> I didn't think it would work at first because I thought everyone would give up easily on all our work when business took a downturn. One year during a long recession, the department heads came through with several ideas generated by their task teams working overtime. They actually sustained *me*. And we came through with flying colors.

I know a man whose life calling is to live peacefully, inside and out. He has to be diligent in his internal spiritual practices to do this and his life stance is noticeably different from that of others. In his consulting practice, he is strong, creative, respected, and sought out for his wisdom. My own life purpose is so simple yet perplexing to me that I think I will never live into it. To appreciate it you have to know me, my passion for angels, both figurative and literal, my love of winter, and my spiritual and vocational calling. My purpose is "Make angels in the snow and elsewhere." I use the words "life calling" and "vocation" interchangeably, since the root meaning of vocation is "to call." In *Wishful Thinking*, Frederich Buechner says vocation is "where my deep gladness and the world's deep hunger meet." Because vocation is so individual and internal, it is difficult to cite examples. It can be complicated, like ending violence or reducing poverty, or simple, like being available, connecting with strangers, or empowering others. It doesn't matter what it is. What matters is that it is yours and that you are not doing it from the strength of your ego. Your calling will emerge as you continue on the journey to soul leadership. Remember this is a long-term process.

Soul Journey Results

It is impossible to predict how each person will experience the journey to soul leadership. That is why it is a journey, a process. The process is as important as the destination. In fact, the process may be the destination. Etty Hillesum, who went voluntarily to a concentration camp to be with her friends and family, writes about her inner process in an intimate way in her journal, *An Interrupted Life*. I started this piece with her words and I want to end with them as a reminder to us all of what soul leadership is about.

> Ultimately we have just one moral duty: to reclaim large areas of peace in ourselves, more and more peace, and to reflect it towards others. And the more peace there is in us, the more peace there will also be in our troubled world.

I can attest to a few characteristics that emerge universally in people who have taken the inner journey I have described. They have peace even in chaos, they are clear and undiluted, they are compassionate, they are courageous, and they listen to their calling. Henri Nouwen describes them well in an uncommon view of maturity when he writes that maturity is "the ability and willingness to be led where you would rather not go."

Soul leaders will change the world.

SUMMARY OF THE SOUL LEADERSHIP DEVELOPMENT PROCESS

Discipline	Behavior It Develops	Effects
Be accountable	Responsibility	Reduction of ego
Assess your leadership journey	Self-reflection	Insight
Practice vulnerability	Self-awareness	Honesty
Play without feeding addictions	Relaxation	Calmness
Experience solitude regularly	Intimacy with self	Clarity
Try one new artistic endeavor	Trust in self and in the Process	Creativity
Travel as far from home as possible	Accepting differences and uniqueness	Appreciation of others
Take your spirituality seriously	Surrendering, letting Go	Peace of mind
Find a mentor at the fringe	Humility	Healing
Find peace and intimacy in relationships without avoiding conflict	Courage	Intimacy
Embrace your shadows and childhood wounds	Facing fear	Interior freedom
Discover your passion	Self-connection	Going beyond self
Accept your calling	Faith	Wisdom

Appendix

Janet O. Hagberg
20 Second Street N.E., Suite 1101
Minneapolis, Minnesota 55413

If you would like to read *The Critical Journey: Stages in the Life of Faith* or other books by Janet, go to her web site or the Personal Power Products web site mentioned below for a more detailed description and ordering information. She also has published self-scoring profiles measuring your stage of personal power, your learning style, and your stage of spiritual development. If you would like more information on Rose Mary Boerboom's Self Mastery Model please email her at rose_mary_boerboom@hotmail.com or call her at (612) 936-0973.

Write: Personal Power Products
1735 Evergreen Lane North
Plymouth, Minnesota 55441-4102
(612) 551-1708
www.personalpowerproducts.com

If you would like to have Janet Hagberg speak to an organization or at a conference, retreat or convention on the topic of Soul Leadership or Stages of Power in Organizations, go to her web site at www.janethagberg.com.

SPECIAL NOTE ON COPYRIGHTED PAGES: If you are teaching with these materials there are many additional resources for you to use on Janet's web site, free of charge. All she asks is that if you copy pages from this book or use the free materials available here or on the web site, that you consider giving a tax-deductible contribution to her passion, the Silent Witness National Initiative. Contributions can be made at their web site, www.silentwitness.net or directly to her personal address above. Please make checks payable to Silent Witness. Thanks and more power to you as you teach with these materials.

Bibliography

Ambrose, Delorese. *Leadership: The Journey Inward.* Dubuque, IA: Kendall/Hunt Publishers, 1991.

Becker, Ernest. *The Denial of Death*. New York: The Free Press, 1973.

Bly, Robert. Interview with Keith Thompson, *New Age* magazine. May 1982.

______. *Iron John*. Reading, MA: Addison-Wesley, 1990.

Bridges, William. *Transitions: Making Sense of Life's Changes*. Reading, MA: Addison-Wesley, 1980.

Buechner, Frederick. *Listening to Your Life: Daily Meditations with Frederick Buechner.* Editor, George Conner. San Francisco: HarperCollins, 1992.

Burns, James McGregor. *Leadership*. New York: HarperCollins, 1982.

Capra, Fritjof. *The Turning Point*. New York: Simon & Schuster, 1982.

Cleveland, Harlan. *The Future Executive*. New York: Harper & Row, 1972.

Covey, Stephen. *Seven Habits of Highly Effective People*. New York: Simon & Schuster, 1989.

de Chardin, Pierre Teilhard. *Toward the Future*. New York: Harcourt, Brace, Jovanovich, 1973.

DePree, Max. *Leadership Is an Art*. New York: Doubleday, 1989.

Dluhy, Milan. *Changing the System: Political Advocacy for Disadvantaged Groups*. London: Sage Human Services Guide, No. 24, 1981.

Dyckman, Katherine, and L. Patrick Carroll. *Inviting the Mystic, Supporting the Prophet*. New York: Paulist Press, 1981.

Ferguson, Marilyn. *The Aquarian Conspiracy*. Los Angeles: Tarcher, Inc., 1980.

Fiedler, Fred, Martin Cheners, and Linda Mahar. *Improving Leadership Effectiveness*. New York: John Wiley and Sons, 1977.

Franki, Viktor. *Man's Search for Meaning*. New York: Washington Square Press, 1963.

Friedan, Betty. *Second Stage*. New York: Summit Books, 1981.

Fuller, Buckminster. *Critical Path*. New York: St. Martin's Press, 1981.

Gandhi, Mohandas K. *Gandhi: An Autobiography*. Boston: Beacon Press, 1951.

Gardner, John W. *Self-Renewal*. New York: Harper & Row, 1964.

______. *On Leadership*. New York: Macmillan, 1990.

Gilligan, Carol. *In a Different Voice*. Cambridge, MA: Harvard University Press, 1982.

Goodman, Ellen. *Turning Points*. Garden City, NY: Doubleday, 1979.

Gould, Roger. *Transformations*. New York: Simon & Schuster, 1978.

Gray, Elizabeth. *Sacred Dimensions of Women's Experience*. Wellesley: Roundtable Press, 1988.

Greenleaf, Robert. *The Servant Is Leader*. Peterborough, NH: Windy Row Press, 1973.

______. *Servant Retrospect and Prospect*. Peterborough, NH: Windy Row Press, 1980.

Hagberg, Janet and Richard Leider. *The Inventurers*, rev. ed. New York: Perseus Books, 1988.

Hagberg, Janet, and Robert Guelich. *The Critical Journey: Stages in the Life of Faith*. Salem, WI: Sheffield Publishing Co., 1989.

Hay, Louise. *You Can Heal Your Life.* Carson, CA: Hay House, 1987.

Heilbrun, Carolyn. *Toward a Recognition of Androgyny*. New York: Harper & Row, 1973.

______. *Reinventing Womanhood.* New York: W. W. Norton Co., 1979.

Helliwell, Tanis. *Take Your Soul to Work.* New York: Random House, 1999.

Janeway, Elizabeth. *Powers of the Weak*. New York: Morrow Quill, 1980.

Josefowitz, Natasha. *Paths to Power*. Reading, MA: Addison-Wesley, 1980.

Jung, C. G. *Modern Man in Search of a Soul*. New York: Harcourt, Brace and Co., 1933.

Jung, Emma. *Animus and Anima*. Zurich, Switzerland: Spring Publications, 1957, 1972.

Kantor, Rosabeth Moss. *Men and Women of the Corporation*. New York: Basic Books, 1976.

______. *The Change Masters*. New York: Simon and Schuster, 1983.

Kavanaugh, James. *There Are Men Too Gentle to Live among Wolves*. Los Angeles: Nash Publishing, 1970.

Keen, Sam. *Fire in the Belly*. New York: Bantam, 1991.

Leonard, Linda. *Wounded Woman*. Boston: Shambhala Press, 1982.

Lerner, Harriet. *The Dance of Anger*. New York: HarperCollins, 1985.

______. *The Dance of Intimacy*. New York: HarperCollins, 1989.

Levinson, Daniel, et al. *Seasons of a Man's Life*. New York: Ballantine, 1979.

Lindberg, Anne Morrow. *A Gift from the Sea.* New York: Pantheon Books, 1955, 1975.

Lips, Hilary. *Women, Men and the Psychology of Power*. Englewood Cliffs, NJ: Prentice-Hall, 1981.

Maccoby, Michael. *The Leader*. New York: Simon & Schuster, 1981.

Maitland, David. *Against the Grain*. New York: Pilgrim Press, 1981.

Maslow, Abraham. *Religions, Values, and Peak Experiences*. New York: Viking Press, 1964, 1970.

Mason, Marilyn. *Making Our Lives Our Own*. San Francisco: HarperCollins, 1991.

May, Rollo. *Power and Innocence*. New York: Dell Publishing Co., 1972.

McCall, Morgan, and Michael Lombardo, eds. *Leadership: Where Else Can We Go?* Durham, NC: Duke University Press, 1978.

McClelland, David C. *Power: The Inner Experience*. New York: Wiley, 1975.

McConnell, Patty. *A Workbook for Healing: Adult Children of Alcoholics*. New York: HarperCollins, 1986.

McKenna, Elizabeth Peck. *When Work Doesn't Work Anymore.* New York: Bantam Books, 1998.

Miller, William. *Your Golden Shadow*. San Francisco: HarperCollins, 1989.

Muller, Wayne. *Legacy of the Heart: Spiritual Advantages of a Painful Childhood.* New York: Simon and Schuster, 1993.

______. *How Then Shall We Live: Four Simple Questions that Reveal the Beauty and Meaning of Our Lives.* New York: Bantam Books, 1996.

Myss, Caroline. *Anatomy of the Spirit: The Seven Stages of Power and Healing.* New York: Random House, 1997.

______. *Why People Don't Heal and How They Can.* New York: Random House, 1998.

______. *Sacred Contracts: Awakening Your Diving Potential.* New York: Harmony Books, 2002.

Nakken, Craig. *The Addictive Personality*. Minneapolis, MN: Hazelden Foundation, 1988.

Nickles, Elizabeth. *The Coming Matriarchy*. New York: Seaview Books, 1981.

Nixon, Richard. *Leaders*. New York: Warner Books, 1982.

Northrup, Christiana. *Women's Bodies, Women's Wisdom.* New York: Bantam Books, 1998.

______. *The Wisdom of Menopause*. New York: Bantam Books, 2001.

Nouwen, Henri. *In the Name of Jesus*. New York: The Crossroad Publishing Co., 1989.

Palmer, Parker. *The Active Life: A Spirituality of Work, Creativity and Caring*. San Francisco: HarperCollins, 1990.

______. *Leading from Within: Reflections on Leadership and Spirituality*. Indiana University Campus Ministries, 1992.

______. *Let Your Life Speak: Listening for the Voice of Vocation*. San Francisco: Jossey-Bass, 1999.

Pascale, Richard and Anthony Althos. *The Art of Japanese Management*. New York: Simon & Schuster, 1981.

Paulus, Trina. *Hope for the Flowers*. New York: Paulist Press, 1972.

Perera, Sylvia. *Descent to the Goddess*. Toronto: Inner City Books, 1991.

Peters, Thomas and Robert Waterman, Jr. *In Search of Excellence: Lessons from America's Best Run Companies*. New York: Harper & Row, 1982.

Progoff, Ira. *Jung, Synchronicity, and Human Destiny*. New York: Julian Press, 1973.

Richardson, Jan L. *Sacred Journeys: A Woman's Book of Daily Prayer*. Nashville: Upper Room, 1996.

Rilke, Ranier Maria. *Letters to a Young Poet*. New York: Norton, 1994.

Rubin, Lillian. *Intimate Strangers*. New York: Harper & Row, 1983.

Russell, Bertrand. *Power*. New York: Norton & Co., 1938.

______. *In Praise of Idleness*. New York: Simon & Schuster, 1972.

Sangiuliano, Iris. *In Her Time*. New York: Morrow Quill, 1980.

Schaef, Anne Wilson. *Women's Reality*. Minneapolis, MN: Winston Press, 1981.

Sheehy, Gail. *Passages*. New York: E. P. Dutton, 1976.

______. *Pathfinders*. New York: William Morrow & Co., 1981.

Silf, Margaret. *Inner Compass: An Invitation to Ignatian Spirituality*. Chicago: Loyola Press, 1999.

Sinetar, Marsha. *Ordinary People as Monks and Mystics*. New York: Paulist Press, 1986.

Singer, June. *Androgyny*. Garden City, NY: Anchor Books, 1977.

Steiner, Claude. *The Other Side of Power*. New York: Grove Press, 1982.

Thompson, Helen. *Journey toward Wholeness*. New York: Paulist Press, 1982.

Underhill, Evelyn. *Practical Mysticism*. London/New York: J. M. Dent & Co./E. P. Dutton & Co., 1915.

______. *The Life of the Spirit and the Life of Today*. San Francisco: HarperCollins, 1986 (originally published 1922).

Vaill, Peter. *Managing as a Performing Art*. San Francisco: Jossey-Bass, 1991.

Wheatley Margaret, and Myron Kellner-Rogers. *A Simpler Way.* San Francisco: Berrett-Koehler Publishers, 1996.

Whyte, David. *The Heart Aroused: Poetry and the Preservation of the Soul in Corporate America.* New York: Doubleday, 1994.

Whitfield, Charles. *Healing the Child Within.* Pompano Beach, FL: Health Communication Inc., 1987.

Woodman, Marion. *Addiction to Perfection.* Toronto: Inner City Books, 1982.

______. *The Pregnant Virgin.* Toronto: Inner City Books, 1985.

Yankelovich, Daniel. *New Rules.* New York: Random House, 1981.